Athens 415

KEY DATES IN THE ANCIENT WORLD

Key Dates in the Ancient World focuses on the important periods and dates in the history and culture of ancient Greece and Rome. Even the casual explorer of the ancient world will know that not all years, not all periods, are equal: the year 44 BCE, when Julius Caesar was murdered; the year 404 BCE, when Athens finally lost its empire—these and other dates offer unique opportunities to examine people and cultures under pressure.

Original sources are presented in contemporary translation, together with analysis of the documents, creating a narrative students can easily follow. Volumes are sized and priced for classroom use, and no Greek or Latin is required. Students in Classics, Ancient History, Comparative History, Political Science, or Archaeology may use volumes in the series as stand-alone texts, or in conjunction with others.

Titles in the Series

Athens 415: The City in Crisis
  Clara Shaw Hardy, with translations by Robert B. Hardy

Athens 415

The City in Crisis

Clara Shaw Hardy

With translations by Robert B. Hardy

University of Michigan Press
Ann Arbor

Published in the United States of America by
the University of Michigan Press
Manufactured in the United States of America
Printed on acid-free paper

First published May 2020

A CIP catalog record for this book is available from the British Library.

ISBN 978-0-472-07446-4 (hardcover : alk. paper)

ISBN 978-0-472-05446-6 (paper : alk. paper)

Contents

Acknowledgments

This book has been an embarrassingly long time in the making, and I am in debt to many for its completion. I was able to test the core idea, a focus on a limited moment in the life of ancient Athens, through many iterations of a course I had the privilege and pleasure of team-teaching with my colleague Chico Zimmerman. His creativity, support, and friendship were instrumental in this endeavor, as were the hundreds of enthusiastic students who worked through the material with us and made it fresh and exciting again each year. Carleton College has supported the work in multiple ways, including two sabbatical leaves and our Humanities Center's funding for two extremely helpful undergraduate research assistants, Elliot Schwartz and Madison Chambers. I did the preliminary research for the project at the University of Warwick as a visiting scholar, and I am grateful for the use of their library as well as the excuse it provided for many walks on the blackberry-lined footpath between Kenilworth and the University. I inflicted early drafts of the book on my mentor, colleague, and friend Tom Van Nortwick, my sister Mary Houlgate, my friend Mary Dunnewold, and of course my husband Rob; the book would be much the worse without all of their keen eyes and generous encouragement. The anonymous readers for University of Michigan Press were also very helpful, as was my editor Ellen Bauerle.

I didn't start work on this book until after the death of my father John Shaw, but his example as a dedicated teacher and scholar, as well as wonderful parent, was before me through the whole of the process. I have shared my frustrations and excitements with him in spirit every day, and I like to imagine that he has enjoyed spending this time with Alcibiades and the rest as much as I have.

Figure 1. Herm. Greek, archaic period. Terracotta, 25.5 cm (10 1/16 in.). Museum of Fine Arts, Boston. Gift of Edward Perry Warren. 13.108. Photograph © 2019 Museum of Fine Arts, Boston.

Introduction

In the year 415 BCE, Athens erupted into months of turmoil sparked by the discovery of crimes against the city's gods. The Athenians were just then preparing to launch a major military expedition against a distant and little-understood target, so the threat the crimes presented seemed especially frightening. In addition to the risks of divine anger, the crimes hinted at conspiracy against the democracy itself. For years afterward, the city would feel the repercussions of the ensuing investigations, accusations, trials, and convictions.

The dramatic story of these religious scandals, along with the events that precipitated and resulted from them, is not well known outside the field of classics. Yet it offers an exceptional opportunity for a multifaceted view of life in late fifth-century Athens. A deep dive into this particular moment allows examination of how the radical democracy worked, both for those it empowered and those it excluded. We can hear traces of voices usually less audible to us: of women, noncitizen residents, slaves. We can see how still-famous works of tragedy and philosophy were embedded in the communal, political, and religious life of the city, and speculate about what it was like to experience them for the first time. Debates seethed in the public assembly, private households, the theater, the marketplace, and the law courts. Reconstructing them opens a window on a society that is both familiar and strange, attractive and repellant.

This book does not offer a comprehensive history of Athens. Rather it uses the mysterious crisis as an entry point for a first encounter with this famous and influential society at a particularly important moment. Before we get to what happened, though, we need to fill in our setting a little.

Attica: Population and Demography

Attica is a triangular wedge of the Greek mainland that juts toward the southeast into the Aegean. On the north side, Mount Cithaeron and the river Asopus separate it from the Boeotian plain. On the west, a narrow isthmus provides a bridge to the much larger area of mainland known as the Peloponnesus. The rest of Attica is rocky, mountainous terrain surrounded by sea. Legend had it that the hero Theseus had united under the city of Athens the many small demes, or villages, that dotted this peninsula. These were scattered from Sunium, forty miles south of the city on the very tip of the promontory, to Rhamnous, thirty miles northeast of the city on the Euboean gulf.

This relatively tiny area (not much bigger than the state of Rhode Island) exercised a remarkable dominance over the northeastern Mediterranean throughout the fifth century. Its geographic sphere of influence would be dwarfed by the empire of Alexander the Great to come in the following century, not to mention the vast Roman Empire that would rise by the end of the millennium. Yet its contributions to politics, philosophy, architecture, art, historiography, drama, and rhetoric make it the subject of enduring fascination. In the last third of the fifth century, Athens was at the peak of its political and cultural power. An astonishing number of men still remembered today rubbed shoulders in the marketplace and at the assembly meetings: men like Socrates, Euripides, Thucydides, Plato, Xenophon. Each of these will have their voice in the story of the year. But that story will be easier to follow if we understand the city they lived in and the people who lived there along with them.

Ancient population figures are notoriously speculative, so what follows should be taken as nothing more than a reasonable guess based on what little data we have. Attica seems to have had a population of somewhere around forty thousand voting citizens (men over the age of twenty) at the outset of the war with Sparta in 431, but that figure will have been eroded by warfare and plague in the years after. If we count women and children, the entire citizen population was probably somewhere between eighty and a hundred thousand. To this number must be added the resident aliens known as metics, mainly Greeks from other city-states, who had chosen to live and work in Attica but lacked citizen status. Estimates for these vary widely. A later census finds ten thousand (likely only men; the total number including their wives and children would presumably double or triple this figure), but for the fifth century some posit as many as fifty thousand. And finally, at least a hundred thousand slaves, who worked in the households, farms, factories, and silver mines. This gives a total population between two hundred and two hundred and fifty thousand. The majority lived outside the city in the villages around Attica. The rest were squeezed within the walls of Athens and its nearby port, Piraeus.

We customarily think of the citizen population in the broad economic categories of rich and poor, mass and elite. A small minority of the citizens was very wealthy; something like 5 percent of the citizen population qualified for the special obligations of the wealthy to the city. Among the remaining 95 percent, there was a smaller variation in wealth than what we are accustomed to. In the sixth century, the Athenians had been divided into four categories depending on their level of wealth. The majority seems to have been in the second lowest of these; there were fewer in the poorest category. The bulk of the citizen population, then, would have been poor but not destitute. Their small holdings of land would have provided their own food and a small surplus to sell. If they had no property, they would have earned a daily wage (as stonecutter, carpenter, potter, shoemaker, etc.) sufficient to support themselves and their families.

It is a peculiarity of the Athenian democracy that some thirty thousand men, a fraction of the full population of two to three hundred thousand, had a legal status and sets of rights not shared by women, metics, or slaves. Citizen status allowed a man to speak and vote in the assembly, to fill offices or magistracies in the democracy, to collect pay for sitting on a jury, to inherit property. Citizen rights could be lost, or, much more rarely, won, based on behavior, or contested based on parentage. But it was impossible to tell a man's legal status by looking at him, learning his name, or hearing him speak. And while citizen and noncitizen were completely distinct in law, people also lived, worked, or socialized in groups (based on gender, for example, or wealth) that cut across these lines of legal status. The intelligentsia included wealthy metics along with citizens. Records of construction workers on the Acropolis show citizen, metic, and slave working side by side. It is more difficult to reach conclusions about relations among women, but it seems at least possible that women, whose lives were spent largely segregated from men, would have formed friendships based on proximity rather than legal status. Why should a citizen wife feel closer to her much older and often absent citizen husband than to the metic wife who lived next door, or even her slave girl?

This mixed population of distinct status categories could cause mutual suspicion and general unease. During periods of crisis like the one in question, the boundaries between the groups were felt to be under dangerous pressure. In fact, the year 415 shows with exceptional clarity the fragility of relations among the many groups in the city, both within the citizenry and outside it. The decision voted on by an assembly of some six thousand citizen men would have a profound effect on the hundreds of thousands who made Attica their home. Popular as this decision may have been among some male citizens, it clearly unnerved others. In the chapters ahead we will investigate whether there may have been pockets of dissent, and with what consequences.

The City of Athens

While the city of Athens was in no way segregated, the city's public and private spaces constrained and facilitated the interaction of its people in important ways. As we focus on different groupings and subgroupings within the city we will also be looking at specific places within its walls, so a quick tour will be helpful. In 415 the city would have been a warren of narrow streets, lined with blocks of mainly smallish contiguous houses and apartments. Rising above them, then as now, were the sheer high walls of the Acropolis.

Still called simply "the city" by residents of Athens in the fifth century (rather than the "high city" that the full Greek word means), the Acropolis had provided an irresistible building site since Neolithic times: its dominant height combined with a spring to provide water made it ideal for fortification. In the Bronze Age (c. 1200 BCE) it was the site of a Mycenaean palace, and the natural defenses of the hill were at that time enhanced with a giant circuit wall. But by the beginning of the fifth century, the hill had shifted from being the political to the religious center of the city, and was covered with cult sites, temples, and offerings. When the Persians invaded Greece in 480, they burned the temples on the Acropolis, along with the sacred olive tree that had been a gift to the city from the goddess Athena. The historian of that invasion, Herodotus, tells us that the following day the tree sent forth a shoot one cubit in height— emblematic of the speed and energy with which the Athenians responded to the sack. After the defeat of the Persians in 479, the Greeks swore an oath not to rebuild the temples destroyed by the Persians, but to leave their ruins as memorials of barbarian impiety.

Yet by the middle of the century, Pericles, the most influential politician of the day, persuaded the people of Athens to approve a massive building program on the Acropolis. The iconic ruins we see today on the Acropolis are the result of Pericles' vision: the winged gateway of the Propylaia, with the elegant Ionic temple to Athena Nike to the right; the Erechtheum; and above all, the Parthenon, visible from almost any point in the city. All these were almost entirely completed within a forty-year period from the middle to the end of the century. Remarkably, Athens was engaged in an expensive war during half of this period; this slowed, but did not halt, the ambitious project. The Roman-era biographer Plutarch, writing some five hundred years later, remarks that they were "created in a short time for all time" (*Pericles* 13).

Although the major components of Pericles' building program still stand in their places after two and a half millennia, it requires an effort of the imagination to re-create what the Acropolis would have looked like in 415. The Parthenon and the temple to Athena Nike were complete, but work had been halted on the Propylaia, the monumental gateway to the temple complex. The Erechtheum, a curious temple famous for its caryatid columns, was still under construction. Buildings would have been obscured with scaffolding, and the site would have been swarming with masons, carpenters, metalworkers, sculptors, and painters. For parts of the temples were painted: the pristine white marble sculptural decorations so familiar to us today would have been bright, even gaudy, with deep reds and blues. And the expanse of the hilltop that now fills with tourists taking selfies with the temple remains was instead crowded with statues and dedications. Upon entering the space through the gateway of the Propylaia, you would have been immediately confronted by the monumental bronze statue of Athena Promachus ("Athena who fights in the front line"), thirty feet high. Against her shoulder leaned a spear, whose tip was visible from Cape Sunium at the tip of Attica, forty miles away.

The statues weren't all that took up the space on the flattened top of the Acropolis. Pericles' advice to build the new temples had been controversial because of an oath the Athenians took in 479 to leave them in ruins. It seems, however, that his coordinated program compromised on this issue: he both rebuilt and left ruins standing. Between the Parthenon and the Erechtheum stood the ruins of the old temple to Athena, its middle section destroyed, its walls blackened by the Persians' fire. The new temples may in fact have been very consciously planned around this preserved ruin, just as the cathedral in Coventry was planned around and designed to focus attention upon the standing ruins of the original structure, destroyed during World War II, or the 9/11 monument in New York calls attention to the absent World Trade Center. Ruins make an impressive and emotionally evocative memorial to past trials and heroics, and the dazzling new buildings on the Acropolis must have gained much of their significance from their orientation around these remains. The incorporation of ruins into new construction is manifest in the Acropolis' north wall, where column drums from the temple to Athena destroyed by the Persians have been carefully set into the wall in positions corresponding to where the temple had been. These are still visible today, and would have been a prominent memorial to the sack, particularly as one approached the Acropolis up the road from the Agora, which was commonly used for sacred processions.

Thus the Acropolis was much more than a constant reminder of Athenian wealth and artistic supremacy, although it was certainly that as well. In its complex of new and ruined temples, it was a memorial to Persian daring and impiety, and to Athenian courage and devotion to the gods. Everyone living in the city, and everyone who visited the city, had this powerful symbol of the Athenian character ever before their eyes. Athenian foreign policy throughout the century fed on and justified this sense of national identity. It would certainly have repercussions in the fateful decisions of the year in question.

Visible from this high and central space were all the areas of the city that will concern us in the chapters that follow: the Pnyx hill to the west, where the assembly met some forty times a year; the Agora to the northwest, where crowds gathered to buy and sell goods and trade news and gossip; the *dikastēria*, or law-courts, surrounding the Agora along with other civic buildings; and the theater of Dionysus nestled into the slope to the southeast. Everywhere were the tiled rooftops of private houses, some cut directly into the rocky hills, others constructed to fill any available space. Within them the city's inhabitants slept and woke, ate and drank, celebrated births and mourned deaths, just as they had for centuries previous and would for centuries to come. For a few, this year would alter their lives forever.

Primary Sources

The ancient sources from 415 itself, along with accounts in later texts and material evidence from the time, allow us to reconstruct a relatively full picture of life in the city during these eventful episodes in its history. Yet substantial gaps remain. We know much more about the citizen men of Athens than we do about the women, more about the wealthy elite than about the poorer wage laborers and craftsmen, more about the Athenian citizens than about the metics or the slaves. Many aspects of daily life remain opaque to us, and we must extrapolate from our knowledge of other times and places to fill gaps. Even at this relatively richly documented moment, many questions remain about the central events.

In the following chapters I have endeavored to pull together a coherent and plausible narrative from the ancient sources that remain. I have mostly smoothed over the scholarly debates surrounding the material; the knottiest problems I sketch along with suggestions for further reading at the end of the book. While I try to be clear about areas where we really cannot be sure of the facts, it is in the nature of this material that much of what I will present is to some degree speculative. Thus the reader will have to keep inserting "probably" or "as far as we know" into most of the sentences of the story. I have, for the most part, left these words out not because I claim certain knowledge of the events I'm recording, but simply for ease of reading.

The most important ancient sources for the vexed events of 415 are texts by Thucydides and Andocides. Thucydides chronicled the conflict between Athens and Sparta which we call the Peloponnesian War, and we refer to his work by that title as well. We know little of him other than what he himself tells us in his great work. An Athenian, he was "of an age to understand what was happening" (5.26) when the war began in 431. He was elected general in 424, for which the minimum age was thirty. He might, then, have been as young as his early twenties at the outset of the war, but could plausibly have been older: an Athenian's notion of "an age to understand what was happening" might be quite a bit different from our own. His term as general was not successful, and he was exiled from his city that year. After 424 he continued his research on the war from his property in Thrace and other areas outside of the city. He likely returned to Athens at the end of the war in 404, but he died before finishing his work; it breaks off abruptly in the middle of his account of the year 411.

The work itself is extraordinary. The prose is dense and difficult, and the objective voice masks an unparalleled artistry in the author's arrangement and analysis of events. He clearly had strongly held views on the dynamics of power and the tendencies of human nature, among other things, but his shaping of the war has been so monumentally influential that it is now impossible to avoid his perspective when reconstructing the events. While inscriptions and other material evidence tend to support the accuracy of his narrative, his text still presents challenges of interpretation. Most notoriously, he includes in direct quotation the speeches of political and military leaders throughout the work. He offers a cryptic and much discussed note on these. After admitting that it was difficult both for himself and his informants to remember precisely what was said on these occasions, he goes on to say that his accounts of the speeches have been written "as I thought each would say what was most necessary concerning the situation at the time, while keeping as close as possible to the overall substance of what was truly said" (1.22). Thus (to take one example) Thucydides' account of the debate before the Sicilian Expedition, from which I have drawn extensively in my narrative in the second chapter, is doubly problematic: Thucydides would not have been in Athens to hear it in 415, and he himself admits that the speeches reflect "what was most necessary" more than what was actually said. Yet Thucydides very likely knew both speakers personally, and his account of their speeches is an excellent match for what we know from other sources of their personalities and their concerns. While I have noted places where Thucydides' account is open to question, then, or conflicts with what we know from other sources, I have in general relied on him as an intellectually masterful, if not photographically reliable, source.

The second major contemporary account of the events of the year presents altogether different challenges. While Thucydides was not in Athens in 415, Andocides was, and was by his own account personally acquainted with many of the principal actors. His narrative of the events occurs within a speech he gave some fifteen years later, called *On the Mysteries*. In 399, Andocides faced trial on a capital charge of impiety related to the events of 415; *On the Mysteries* is his defense speech and thus is written to be as favorable as possible to himself. Many of the men in his audience would have remembered the events that he recounts, and thus he would be unsafe giving a flagrantly false narrative. Yet the distance in time and the circumstances of the speech together make many of his details suspect. His narrative must be used, then, with great care and a critical attitude.

In addition to these two essentially contemporary witnesses to the year we have two authors important for other reasons. Euripides' tragedy *The Trojan Women* was first performed in the spring of 415. The play takes place in the aftermath of the Trojan War, while the captured women of Troy wait to be awarded as slaves to the Greek heroes who conquered their city. While the play does not, of course, offer any sort of narrative of the year's events, it formed part of the experience of the year itself. Many thousands of people will have seen Euripides' play and wept for the fate of those victims of war in the thick of the debate about whether to invade Sicily. Finally, Plutarch, a Greek from the area north of Attica called Boeotia, wrote biographies of two of the men most dominant in the year's events, Nicias and Alcibiades. Plutarch lived some five hundred years later than our year, and his interests are more about human virtue and behavior than historical narrative. But he had access to sources now lost to us, and his vivid sketches of personality, as well as the anecdotes he preserves, make him an entertaining window on the year.

A great number of other ancient authors, as well as the material evidence of inscriptions and other remains, have been valuable in constructing this account; as they become important in the narrative I include information on each of these. A translation of a relevant source (or, in the case of chapter 4, sources) follows each chapter. This will both give the reader a sense of where the material comes from and a glimpse of the challenges involved in assessing these texts. Finally, a note on the spellings of Greek names and words. For all names, I have used the Latinized versions (e.g. "Thucydides" rather than "Thoukudidēs"); but for Greek words I have directly transliterated the Greek (e.g., *dikastēria*).

Account of the Crisis in 415

Because I hope this book will be of interest to a wide range of readers, I have proceeded on the assumption that the audience is without specialized knowledge of Athens. Thus interspersed with my narrative, I have included enough background material to make the events intelligible. In the course of my account of the debates on Sicily in the first two chapters, for example, I offer some background on history (particularly earlier Athenian involvement with Sicily), on politics (how the democracy and empire worked), and on society (class divisions and tensions, and important notions of honor and shame). Thus the narrow focus on some months in 415 serves both as the context for a more expansive look at life in Athens in the late fifth century, and a case study on the interdisciplinary nature of the field of classics. Building this portrait requires examining many different genres of text, as well as the material evidence that remains.

Each chapter takes as title and starting point one space within the walled city of Athens, as a window on the activities likely to happen there and the people involved with them. The book unfolds in roughly chronological order, but the focus alternates between public and private settings. The three large sections each contain two chapters. The first section focuses on the citizen men who ran the city, and their consequential decision to launch the Sicilian Expedition: the initial chapter examines the public, open-air forum that was the Athenian assembly, where poorer men dominated; the second turns from the masses to the elite, and from the public assembly to the private houses of the wealthy. Here drinking parties behind closed doors offered elite men opportunities to discuss love and philosophy, or plot political maneuvers, away from the eyes and ears of the demos.

In part 2 we consider whether the desire for conquest in Sicily, so intense among the men we met in part 1, was shared among other groups in the city. Chapter 3 explores the annual festival to Dionysus which was the occasion in 415 for the first performance of Euripides' *Trojan Women*, a tragedy commonly perceived as antiwar in modern times. How would the audience in the theater, so much larger and more diverse than the assembly of citizen men who had voted on the Pnyx, have responded to his three tragedies on the Trojan conflict? As in part 1, we move in the fourth chapter from the full sun of the theater of Dionysus into the household, to construct a picture of the lives of the women usually invisible to us from male-authored texts focused on political affairs. In the summer of 415, a celebration of a women's-only ritual on the rooftops of private houses was particularly unruly and disruptive. Is it plausible that the women were making their opposition to the looming expedition heard?

In the last section, we come to the religious scandals that dominated the city for the rest of the year, and would have such far-reaching consequences. Chapters 5 and 6 recount the mutilation of the herms, the desecration of the Eleusinian Mysteries, and the investigations and trials that followed. Here the nominal division between public and private that structured the first two sections breaks down in alarming ways, as the informants and trials brought into the public spaces of the Agora and law court the speech and actions that had occurred in the private dining rooms of the elite.

Two interrelated themes emerge from the year's narrative. First is the issue of power and control in the democratic city. We see this in several areas. There is, for example, ongoing tension between powerful individuals and the larger community of citizens, or between the egalitarian ideals of the democracy and the realities of running the city and its empire. Examined at close range, the events of 415 show a complex mix of fantasies and anxieties about powerful individuals and their effects on those around them. Related to this urgent question of how much power any one individual should wield is the larger issue of the relations between groups within the city. Within the citizen population the mutual suspicion between the elite and the masses, and the jockeying between them for power and influence, would have drastic political consequences. Beyond that limited group of citizen men, the slaves, metics, and women who were barred from the assembly on the Pnyx found other means to make their voices heard. Finally, there is the pervasive power of the divine: the city's relationship with its gods is central to the decisions and crises that played out that summer and beyond.

Second is the notion of boundaries, both physical and social, and the problems of maintaining or rupturing them. The struggles over political power just mentioned are closely related to boundaries of status and class. The potential for blurring or transgressing these limits produced inordinate anxiety in 415, evident from individual and group responses to events as well as in the literature of the year. The mutilated statues that caused so much turmoil were themselves physical boundary markers, often positioned to guard the doors of private homes and thus emphasize the border between public and private space. But this very line between public and private is tested repeatedly during the year. Politicians' private lives dominate perceptions of their public ambitions. Women's private celebrations on their own rooftops interrupt the public business of the assembly meeting. The intimate activities of the private dinner party erupt into public scandal.

If we can learn most readily about the structure of an object when it is under stress, perhaps society as well can be best understood during moments of tension. The story of 415 offers an intriguing case study of the social fabric of an extraordinary city, the factors that precipitated a serious crisis, and the qualities that ultimately would allow it to recover from the dangers it had faced.

PART 1

Desire

In the middle of a summer night in the year 415 BCE, anyone who happened to be awake in Athens would have heard the repeated clink of metal on stone. Had they dared to investigate, to put a head out a door, they might have heard furtive voices as well. Nobody found the noises odd or threatening enough to warrant tracing them to their source. Or if they did, they were too frightened by what they found to come forward and speak of it later.

The next morning it was discovered that all over the city statues known as herms had been systematically vandalized in a bizarre and terrifying attack. The city was thrown into a state of confusion and turmoil that lasted for months. Athenians saw the mutilation of the herms as a frightening omen for the massive military expedition against Sicily then in preparation, and potentially even a threat to the Athenian democracy itself.

The first two chapters of this look at the year's events, with the primary documents that follow each, begin to lay the groundwork for understanding this episode and the reaction to it. The decision to launch the Sicilian Expedition, made early in the spring of 415, is an essential part of the background to the mutilations, as well as the reaction they engendered and its consequences. What kindled this desire for conquest in the Athenian demos, or citizen body? To make some sense of their decision and the responses it provoked, we need a closer look at the context that gave rise to it: the maritime empire that Athens had led for much of the century, the radical democracy that had developed over the same period, the tensions between and within classes both democracy and empire provoked, and the driving impulses of the specific men involved.

We start our explorations in the open air of the Pnyx (chapter 1), where the Athenian assembly met. What sorts of men attended these meetings, and what impulses drove their decisions? How were they influenced by politics within the city and foreign policy beyond it? What were their beliefs about the dynamics of power and how best to preserve it? This chapter is followed by Thucydides' exploration of imperial expansion in the Melian Dialogue.

In chapter 2 we move from the daylight, public debate of the demos to the nocturnal, private, aristocratic symposion, or drinking party. Here we look for insight into the acute personal rivalry between the two generals in charge of the Sicilian Expedition: Nicias and Alcibiades. We explore the cultural context for this kind of elite competition and in particular the volatile economy of honor and shame that circulated within the Athenian leisure class. The tension between the two very different leaders has important consequences for the events to come, and is evident in Thucydides' account of the second debate on Sicily following the chapter.

CHAPTER 1

Pnyx

Democracy, Empire, and Sicily

Pnyx was the name of the hilltop area where the Athenian citizen assembly met, and by extension it was used to designate the hill itself, which rose just west of the higher Acropolis hill. In Greek, the word *pnyx* sounded much like two others: *pyknos*, meaning "compact" or "tightly packed," and *pnix*, meaning "suffocation." In the late fifth century, the natural amphitheater on the Pnyx hill occupied about twenty-four hundred square meters, or slightly less than half of a football field. Certain important procedures in the assembly required six thousand citizens to vote, which would mean about two and a half men sitting in each square meter of the available space: certainly tightly packed, if not suffocating.

A character in a late fifth-century comedy complains that everyone is late for the assembly, that he arrives early on the Pnyx but then has to sit alone and "groan, yawn, stretch, fart, doodle, and pluck out his stray hairs" while everyone else gossips down in the market; the officials in charge of the meeting don't even show up until noon (Aristophanes' *Acharnians* 20–31). In fact the meetings started early in the day, although it must have taken some time for thousands of men to file in and find a bit of ground to sit down on. Imagine a low roar of greetings, anticipatory discussions or quarrels, the general smell of garlic and sweat and worse in the warming air as the sun climbed over the Acropolis, and then the call of the herald for silence. A small pig was sacrificed and carried around to purify the area; libations were poured; prayers were spoken for divine favor; curses against any who threatened the democracy invoked. Then the business at hand could begin.

The agenda for the assembly was posted in the Agora four days before a meeting, so the men arriving at the Pnyx on a spring morning in 415 knew what topic they would debate. An ally had requested military aid. The vote that day would determine whether Athenian forces would be called up and sent off to assist in this distant campaign.

Who were these men squeezed onto the hilltop that morning for the assembly? Passing comments in contemporary comedy give us a glimpse of figures "covered with dust and having eaten only pickled garlic, looking sour and sharp" (Aristophanes, *Assemblywomen* 291–94). Xenophon's Socrates speaks of "fullers, cobblers, carpenters, blacksmiths, farmers, merchants, or barterers in the marketplace" (*Memorabilia* 3.7.6). Toward the end of the following century we get a character sketch of a wealthy, haughty type who finds it dishonorable when someone "skinny or squalid sits down next to him in the assembly." We might even be sympathetic to his distaste for this kind of forced proximity, when in a different sketch we find a country bumpkin who "sits down with his cloak thrown up, so that his naked bits show" (Theophrastus, *Characters* 26 and 4)!

Rich men and poor, urban craftsmen and country farmers converged on the Pnyx for meetings of the assembly. This was the *dēmos* part of the word "democracy"—the people that wielded power in the *polis*, or city-state, of Athens. Votes taken on the Pnyx were recorded in inscriptions starting with the formula "the demos decided . . ." Every male Athenian citizen over the age of twenty, no matter how poor or rich, could attend the assembly and vote on issues of domestic or foreign policy proposed there. He could even address the gathered throng with his own thoughts and arguments. After the herald stated the business at hand, he would invite forward anyone who wanted to make their opinions known. Later orators proudly emphasize this right to speak: "the lawgiver does not drive anyone away from the speaker's platform if their ancestors didn't serve as generals, nor if they work some trade or other to supply their daily needs; but especially welcomes these, and for this reason keeps asking 'who wishes to address the assembly?'" (Aeschines 1.27). Plato has Socrates assert that the Athenians will listen to anyone advise them on the management of the polis: "a carpenter, a blacksmith, a leather-worker, the passenger on a ship or its owner, a rich man or a poor one, high-born or low-born" (*Protagoras* 319d).

Athenian Democracy

The Pnyx was the heart of Athens' direct democracy: government not just by representatives voted into office by the people, but policy proposals made, discussed, and then voted upon by the people themselves (always remembering that "people" in this context means male citizens). In a famous apocryphal debate about styles of government, the proponent of democracy speaks approvingly of the way it grants *isonomia*, equality before the law. While this is a familiar bedrock of democracy for us as well, the speaker goes on to name a more unexpected feature of the system: "political office is won by allotment, and held strictly accountable" (Herodotus 3.80). In other words, if you're a male citizen, you could be chosen by lot at any point to serve in one of many different positions in the government. The council, the smaller body that set the agenda for the assembly and oversaw the day-to-day running of the city, consisted of fifty men chosen by lot from each of Athens' ten tribes; these ten groups of fifty divided the year into ten equal periods, and traded off taking full responsibility for the city during their period. Allotted positions had the term of a single year, and you would undergo rigorous scrutiny before and after in case you were tempted to use the position for your own profit, or in case any of your fellow citizens wanted to argue that you were not lawfully eligible. But the radical underlying assumption was that any man in the demos had the capacity to manage the affairs of the polis, and allotment guaranteed that experience in governing positions was spread widely through the demos.

The historian Thucydides, who will be one of our most prominent sources for the events of the year, gives us an extended meditation on democracy in the form of a speech over fallen soldiers delivered some fifteen years earlier. Here Pericles, prominent politician and military leader, lays out the aspects of Athens he assumes will inspire pride in his audience:

> Because our government operates with a view to the many rather than the few it is called a democracy: and under the laws it provides equality for all in their private disputes . . . each man is honored in public affairs not for his standing and wealth as much as for his excellence. Nor if anyone has some good ability to offer to the polis is he prevented by poverty or obscurity. . . . We associate privately without offending each other, and in public affairs we fear to break the law, obeying the men currently in office and most of all the laws themselves: in particular those established to help victims of injustice, as well as those unwritten norms that everyone agrees are shameful to break . . . for we alone consider the man who isn't involved with politics not peaceable, but useless; we correctly judge and carefully consider public business. We do not think that what's harmful to action is debate, but rather failing to instruct ourselves thoroughly in advance of whatever we need to accomplish. (Thucydides 2.37–40)

For Pericles, the great strength of Athenian democracy was in the wide participation it allowed, encouraged, and inspired. An education in this system produced citizens who were invested in the success of the city as much as in their own private affairs, who were experienced with weighing costs and benefits, advantages and disadvantages of given policy, and who could be trusted to vote for the best course of action for the community as much as for their own personal welfare. After all, the homonym for Pnyx that means "packed" also means "well put together, strong" as well as "shrewd, wise."

The speech Thucydides has given us sparks patriotic feeling for more than just the political system. Pericles connected his rhetoric about the excellence of the democracy to praise for those who had died fighting for it in order to inspire their fathers, brothers, sons to continue that fight. In an arresting metaphor he exhorts the demos to "gaze every day upon the power of the polis and fall in love with it" (Thucydides 2.43), that is, he directs them to look at and then feel desire for Athens' power. The decisions and actions of the demos in 415, when Pericles had been dead a dozen years, show us that that desire was still a powerful force in the city. How, exactly, could the demos gaze daily at the power of Athens? What would they see from their perch on the Pnyx hill to excite their desire?

If they were sitting toward the back of the area at its highest point, they could turn and look over their shoulders to the southwest and see the Aegean. Piraeus, Athens' port, was some three miles distant, and there rows of long, narrow ship sheds lined the harbors. The sleek wooden ships within, called triremes, were the engine that drove Athenian naval power. Two long walls connected the port to the city, and the city itself had secure walls surrounding it visible from the Pnyx: Athenians were not only protected from land attacks, but their naval strength ensured they could deliver supplies to the city for as long as necessary if they were ever besieged. Turning back toward the speaker's platform, the men seated on the Pnyx could look beyond it down to the bustling Agora, and see goods on offer from around the Aegean, the fruits of Athens' prominence as a trade center. Or they could shift their gaze to the right, and admire the spectacular temples of the Acropolis rising to the east. These temples, some still under construction in 415, had been financed in part by the massive supplies of silver stored within the Parthenon, delivered to Athens by allied (or, in fact, subject) cities. For while the Pnyx represented Athens' internal system of direct democracy, the triremes, walls, market, temples that the demos could gaze upon from their vantage point on the Pnyx were the visible signs of Athens' power over other cities: the power of the Athenian empire.

The Athenian Empire

In Greek this empire is simply called *arkhē*: "rule" or "sovereignty." Athens' rule was over some hundred and fifty city-states, mostly much smaller than

Athens, situated on islands in the Aegean or those Greek cities that dotted the northern and eastern Aegean coasts. Originally part of the alliance against the Persian invasions of the early fifth century, these Greek states all contributed either ships or money, first to the war and then to the postwar defense against Persia. Athens' leadership in this alliance was in part a function of its massive contribution of its fleet of triremes to the effort. Sparta, the premier land power among the Greek states, ceded its own role in leading the alliance very early: it was traditionally unwilling to have its leaders or military forces stray far from home for very long, and continuing operations in Asia Minor after the war necessitated this. So Athens, from 478, assumed leadership. Eventually, most of the other cities shifted from contributing and manning ships to simpler payments of silver which, after the middle part of the century, were deposited on the Acropolis in Athens. From there the money found its way into Athenian pockets as Athenian carpenters continued to build the triremes and Athenian oarsmen manned them, gaining valuable expertise in rowing and maneuvering the swift ships. Men like these would have been well-represented in the assembly, and would have had an interest in voting for policies that bolstered the empire, a reliable source of their livelihood.

Unlike the imperial powers of the modern era, for the most part Athens did not exploit the natural resources of what are called the subject allies, although the timber and silver mines in the northern mainland areas were attractive, and sometimes Athenians did occupy parts of these allies' lands. Nor did it, as Rome would, absorb them into a unified territory with shared citizenship and identity. Instead, the empire functioned in part like a protection racket. The Athenian navy patrolled the Aegean and made sure the Persians didn't interfere with the Greek cities on the coasts and islands, and in exchange these cities contributed substantial annual sums to Athens.

In addition to the security their navy provided, though, Athens also exercised a degree of economic and even political control over the tributary allies. They compelled the cities in their empire to use Athenian coinage. This facilitated trade, but also guaranteed profits for the Athenian mint. Certain types of legal dispute between Athenians and the allies had to be settled in Athenian courts before Athenian juries. Cities periodically chafed under these restrictions and struggled under the financial burdens of the assessed contributions. If they tried to withdraw from the alliance, however, Athens would direct its far superior military power against them, and force them back in on worse terms. After such unsuccessful rebellions Athenians sent to these cities small garrisons of their own citizens, who appropriated agricultural produce from the defeated people's lands.

The demos, gazing from the Pnyx at the triremes and temples that embodied Athenian power, were driven by desire for the maintenance of this arkhē. That desire and the energy it produced became hallmarks of the Athenian people. Thucydides has Corinth, an enemy, characterize the Athenians as innovative and restless, ceaselessly and energetically pursuing their desires: "for them alone there is no difference between hoping for and possessing whatever they set their minds to through the speedy attempt of anything they can imagine" (1.70). Hope and desire are double-edged impulses for Thucydides, however. A little later in the work, he places a less positive view of these impulses in the mouth of Athenian speaker: "Hope and desire . . . the latter leading and the former following, the latter hatching a plan and the former suggesting it can succeed, are mostly harmful; and although they are invisible, they are more powerful than the terrors we see" (3.45). While it may be part of that human nature Thucydides sees as constant over time, desire without limits leads to danger.

Thucydides indicates plenty of resentment in the Greek world toward Athens as ruler of this empire. He tells us that they were "harsh and exacting" (1.99) in assessing and collecting the allies' financial contributions, and he has several speakers, both from Athens and other Greek cities, claim that Athens acted as a tyrant toward the cities it ruled. Pericles himself makes this claim: "for you hold [the empire] as a tyranny, which it seems unjust to have taken, but highly risky to let go" (Thucydides 2.63).

The charge of tyrannical behavior against Athens is of course ironic on two counts: first, because Athens' position had grown out of its valiant fighting to prevent all the Greek states from coming under the tyrannical rule of Persia; and second, since it set such a high value on, and evinced such a great pride in, the equality of all its citizens before the law in the operation of its own democracy. In fact many aspects of the democratic polis were explicitly adopted in reaction against the rule of tyrants Athens had experienced in the sixth century, and were designed to prevent their rise in future. The institution of ostracism, whereby any man who seemed to be amassing too much power or influence with the demos could be voted out of Athens for a ten-year period, was aimed precisely against anyone ruling as tyrant. The curses at the opening of an assembly meeting may have included curses on anyone who aspired to become a tyrant himself or install another. How could this fiercely antityrannical city itself act as a tyrant over other Greek states?

The first answer to this question is simply that equality before the law was not a concept that could be easily transferred from a city's own politics to relations among cities. Under what law could cities be equal? Power was the only relevant factor: perhaps the reason Pericles exhorted the demos to gaze upon its signs and conceive a desire for it. Where there was no single community that could agree to law, only power could guarantee safety, and the desire for greater power had no natural limit.

Another element played into the charges of tyranny leveled at democratic

Athens: class conflict within the city and its allies. While we tend to see democracy as a good thing, most of the authors we have from this period were decidedly hostile to the system. The word "demos" is often used by elite authors to designate not "the people" in general but rather the poor majority. Aristocrats saw democracy as the rule of the poor over the rich. While "oligarchy" literally means the "power of the few," in fact those "few" were always the wealthy, and they preferred ruling to being ruled: for them, perhaps, "Pnyx" did signal "stifling" rather than "wise."

There was constant simmering tension in Athens and elsewhere between those who favored expanding the power of the many and those who sought to limit it. In many Greek city-states, both within Athens' empire and beyond, friction between democrats and oligarchs led to outbreaks of civil war during the last quarter of the century. Historians call this kind of conflict by its Greek name: *stasis*. Thucydides gives an extended and chilling account of how stasis played out first on the island state of Corcyra in 427, and subsequently in many other cities:

> Many brutalities occurred in the cities through stasis, things which have happened and will happen again, as long as human nature is the same. . . . For in peace and good times both cities and individuals make better judgments, because they haven't been trapped by constraints. But war, taking away the easy availability of day-to-day needs, is a violent teacher, and brings the impulses of most people into line with their circumstances. And so there was stasis in the cities . . . the ties of faction meant more even than those of family, because fellow partisans were readier to run risks without excuse: for these coalitions did not support existing law, but opposed the establishment through their desire for power. The pledges they made toward each other were strengthened not by sacred law so much as some common crime. Desire for more and love of honor were responsible for the beginning of all these things: and these in turn produced that zeal created when men descend into rivalries. For those prominent in the cities pursued their own advantage while paying lip-service to the common good with appealing terms on both sides—preference for the political equality of the masses on the one side, or moderate aristocracy on the other . . . and those citizens in the middle, either because they refused to participate, or through resentment of their survival, were crushed. (3.82)

This continuing and dangerous class conflict throughout the Greek world would become visible in Athens in 415, and we will return to it in the coming chapters. It can also shed some light on the paradoxical notion of Athens holding the empire as a "tyranny" over the allied states. We have seen indications of resentment at Athens' "harsh and exacting" demands for tribute moneys, the occasional appropriation of land, and some interference in domestic affairs of the tributary allies, but most intriguing is the fact that Athens repeatedly supported or even installed democracies in these cities. It is thus plausible that feelings about the Athenian empire among its subjects were class-inflected, and what we are hearing in the complaints about tyrannical behavior is coming from the elite. The poorer citizens in the allied cities found steady work rowing along with Athenians in the navy, enjoyed the goods in the marketplace that easy trade encouraged, and had a powerful protector of their own political rights at home. The elites on the other hand were most responsible for coming up with the tribute moneys, and more likely to find themselves on trial before hostile Athenian juries. They are most likely to have chafed under the rule of the Athenians. We hear frequently the language of "freedom" and "slavery" in the context of relations with Athens. Yet it's important to keep in mind that here "slavery" does not mean the actual nonfree status many in the Greek world had; rather it means a lack of complete autonomy in domestic politics. That Athens sometimes set up democratic governments in allied cities then will be described as "enslaving" only by the wealthy whose oligarchic rule has been ended. Allies who rebelled from the empire were almost always also engaged in oligarchic revolution at home.

As the power of arkhē was desirable to Athenians, its growth was a threat to other states, and in particular it would bring democratic Athens into conflict with oligarchic Sparta and its allies. Like Athens, Sparta had been a leader in the fight against Persia, but soon after the war, as we have seen, ceded leadership of the effort to Athens. Sparta now had its own set of allies, which we refer to as the Peloponnesian League: a collection of mainland cities loosely bound to it in bilateral agreements. Based on the mainland, rather than the islands or coasts, mainly speaking the Dorian rather than Ionian dialect of Greek, primarily oligarchic rather than democratic in individual constitutions, the Peloponnesian League stood in absolute contrast to the Athenian empire. It watched the latter's expansion of power and influence with increasing suspicion. Between 460 and 445 the two alliances had fought an intermittent war, and then signed a peace treaty that was supposed to last thirty years. In less than half that time they were at war again: a war that would stretch on until Athens' defeat in 404.

The Peloponnesian War

All but the youngest of the citizen men on the Pnyx would have fought land battles or rowed ships in what we now call the Peloponnesian War. The first half of this conflict had lasted from 431–421, and is called the Archidamian War, after the Spartan king who began it. But it might equally have been called Periclean. It was Pericles who persuaded the Athenians to fight rather than cede to Spartan ultimatums concerning Athenian policy toward specific cities. In any individual case, it wasn't obvious that holding firm was worth the devastating war that could follow, but Pericles' case was broader. Any demand the Spartans made signaled that they were unwilling to accept the Athenian empire as equal to the Peloponnesian League, and giving in meant "slavery."

Pericles won the day, and the war began. His strategy was to count on Athens' huge monetary resources, accumulated mostly from the tribute of the allies, and its naval power. Those Athenians who lived on farms in the Attic countryside relocated to within the walled city and allowed the Spartans to ravage their fields. The city filled up with refugees from the countryside, but control of the sea meant that they could import food, protect the people within the fortifications, and wait out the poorer Peloponnesians. If they maintained control of their empire and its revenues, Pericles predicted, their naval strength and wealth would prevail. He also insisted that further expansion of the empire under these circumstances was a mistake. The Athenians' best strategy for preserving the power of their rule was to concentrate on what they held rather than stretching themselves to extend it. But others had different ideas about the dynamics of that power.

Pericles did not expect the war to continue for as long as it did, but war is notoriously unpredictable, as Thucydides is fond of reminding us. At the beginning of the second year of the war, a highly contagious and deadly plague struck the city when all its inhabitants were crowded within its walls, by some estimates wiping out as much as one third of its population. Reserves of both treasure and manpower were severely depleted by the extended conflict, and Pericles himself died of the plague in the third year of the war. The Athenians fought on until a fragile peace was agreed with the Spartans in 421, but the terms of this treaty were never fully enforced.

As we return to the Pnyx on a spring morning in the year 415, we recognize a city that had fought long and hard to retain its power in the eastern Mediterranean. Preserving the empire had always been the unquestioned goal, both in fighting the Archidamian War and, finally, in agreeing to the peace. The successors to Pericles had disagreed with his strategies for accomplishing that goal. They were ready to consider expanding Athenian arkhē, while he had been convinced they should rather focus on guarding the resources they had. All, however, had agreed upon the central importance of the empire in the interest of Athens. The demos was still fired by the love of power Pericles had cultivated; the question was only how best to maintain it.

Sicily and the Lure of the West

On the Pnyx that morning were ambassadors from Egesta, a small city in western Sicily which had petitioned the assembly for military aid the previous autumn. Egesta had an existing alliance with Athens as the basis for this request, although we know little either about its terms or when it was first agreed. A tantalizing if barely legible inscription survives that implies a date of either 458 or 418, while Thucydides places the alliance in the 420s. Whatever the date, we know that the Athenians had been interested in territory to the west for some time before 415.

Sicily and the southern half of the Italian peninsula (an area known later as Magna Graecia) had long held both Greek and non-Greek cities. Compared to rocky Attica, this area was rich in grain and timber. As war with Sparta looked likely back in the 430s, Athens was intent on preventing those resources from reaching the Peloponnese. Using them to augment their own empire's assets must have been tempting too. Increasing tensions between Athens and Sparta were closely watched in the west as well. Was it safer to align with one or the other of these superpowers, or remain neutral? In 433, a city called Leontini was one of those that allied itself with Athens.

Six years later, well into the Archidamian war, an embassy arrived at Athens from Leontini requesting aid in a conflict with the much more powerful city of Syracuse. Syracuse was part of Sparta's confederacy, although it had not yet taken part in the war. Athens likely viewed aid to Leontini as a useful way to ensure that this remained the case. Thucydides claims that the real reason they committed forces was "to prevent the import of Sicilian grain to the Peloponnese and to make a preliminary trial of whether it might be possible to make Sicily subject to Athens" (3.86): already in 427, then, some in Athens thought expansion of the empire to the west was an attractive option. The assembly voted to send twenty ships to aid the Leontinians, and soon afterward reinforced these with forty more. They made alliances with several other cities in addition to Leontini in Sicily and Italy, but their operations were sporadic and inconclusive. After four years, the Athenian force of sixty ships had been unable to bring a decisive end to the conflict. Syracuse made peace not only with Leontini, but all the other cities of Sicily as well, and the Athenians were sent home. Syracuse had convinced the rest of the Sicilian cities that Athens was a greater threat to them all than any were to each other. Whether or not Athens was really aiming at controlling all of Sicily at this point, that was certainly how it looked to the Sicilians. The Athenian response only confirms it. They had been appalled at this end to the campaign, and in one of the impulsive moves characteristic of the demos they had voted to fine and exile the leaders of the force, convinced that only bribery could have prevented it from conquering the whole of Sicily. This gives an idea of how easy they thought that conquest was going to be.

After the Athenians left Sicily in 424, stasis had broken out in Leontini. The oligarchs there had joined forces with Syracuse to fight against their own people, and had exiled the democrats. Some of these Leontinians therefore now joined the embassy from Egesta requesting Athenian aid against Syracuse. Both relied on earlier alliances with the Athenians. Both saw Syracuse as a growing threat in Sicily, and sought to convince the assembly that unchecked Syracusan power allied with Sparta could threaten Athens as well. The Egestaeans and Leontinians had made this case on the Pnyx the year before, and the Athenian assembly had been open to the argument. But they were cautious. Sicily was a long way off, so committing any very substantial force was an expensive proposition. The Egestaeans had promised that they had plenty of resources available to pay Athenian expenses, but the Athenians needed more evidence that this was true. In the fall of 416, then, they had dispatched envoys to Egesta to investigate the resources available, and take stock of what would be necessary to win the war with Selinus and Syracuse.

These envoys had now returned home, and they gave their report to the assembly that morning. It was glowing. The Athenians had seen with their own eyes vessels filled to overflowing with gold in the town's treasuries, and they had dined nightly off gold and silver dishes. Every house they had been invited to seemed heaped with extraordinary wealth. The Athenians had long discouraged such display of private riches as inimical to the egalitarian ideal of their democracy, so the conspicuous nature of Egesta's wealth was all the more astonishing to them. The Egestaeans had brought with them this time sixty talents in silver: enough to pay the crews of sixty ships for a month. The report and the sight of the silver were graphic reminders of the legendary abundance of Sicily.

Thucydides records for us a debate at an assembly that happened four days later, in which two generals reconsider the decision the demos came to at this assembly. In the next chapter we will investigate the issues that those men raised, and their own personal stakes in the outcome. The historian does not, however, tell us anything about this first debate other than the final proposal they voted on. As the men assembled on the Pnyx considered whether to commit forces to the Egestaeans and Leontinians in Sicily, what would the salient issues have been?

The issue of available resources in the city must have been high on the list: ten years of war had put considerable pressure on the stores of silver piled on the Acropolis. The Athenians had been unprepared to commit their ships and men the first time they were asked, needing stronger proof that the promises of resources were grounded in reality. Now they seemed to have that assurance. As it would turn out, the Athenian envoys had been badly misled about the wealth of Egesta. Thucydides tells us that the same gold and silver vessels had been secretly passed from one house to the next to create the illusion of general riches, and that silver items deposited in the temples had seemed more valuable than they really were. The Athenians at the assembly, however, were easily convinced of the great prosperity awaiting them in Sicily. Any initial arguments that had been made against sending ships to Egesta on the grounds that it would be too expensive were neutralized. The conflict would pay for itself.

There were other arguments to be made in opposition, however. First of all, the Athenians had their own past to consider. Leontini had made the same arguments back in 427, and the Athenians had assented; they had sent the same sixty ships that Egesta was asking for now. Yet they had failed then. Sixty ships had not been able to inflict decisive defeat anywhere, and the many Sicilian towns had seemed more interested in pursuing local rivalries than in uniting under Athenian leadership. Later, when the stasis started in Leontini, the Athenians had sent an ambassador to see if a coalition of willing cities could be assembled to fight Syracuse. But he had met with no success, and had sailed home. What led anyone to expect that this time would be different? Past experience in Sicily surely argued against the proposal.

Another reason to be cautious about the undertaking would be a matter of scale. The Athenian empire was almost entirely limited to an area one or two hundred miles from the city itself. The most distant outposts, on the Black Sea, were certainly more remote, but the empire included strong allies much closer to these positions. Sicily, and particularly the western edge of Sicily where Egesta lay, was much farther away. Even as the crow flies Athens was almost six hundred miles from Egesta, and the sea-route was longer. Should an emergency arise at home the fleet could not be recalled quickly, and should the fleet in Sicily require aid it could not arrive with any haste.

The third argument to be made against heeding the Egestaeans' call would be the state of affairs much closer to home. Besides the drain on resources caused by the recent war, the plague had inflicted a huge loss of manpower. The farmers who had been persuaded to wait out Spartan invasions within the walls of the city had seen their land ravaged, undoubtedly with lasting damage to olive trees and grapevines. Six years of peace had restored some of these resources. The orchards and vineyards were beginning to recover. The peace was unstable to be sure, but it was peace. A war of choice at this particular moment seemed foolish and reckless. The real threat to Athenian security was arguably the neighboring Peloponnese. Would the treaty with Sparta signed in 421 hold? Had the Spartans and their allies learned to tolerate the Athenian empire, or were they simply waiting for a better opportunity to destroy it once and for all? Additionally, the tributary allies of the empire were always restive and ready to revolt if Athens were distracted. If a substantial portion of the fleet sailed off to the western end of the world, the city's security was at risk. Renewal of hostilities might be inevitable. The best way to prepare was to wait at home, guarding and building the resources that would be necessary to fight again.

Past experience in Sicily, the sheer distances involved, and instability at home pushed against the proposal. Yet each of these three arguments could be turned around and made to fuel the desire for conquest. After all, if the Athenians had been able to send sixty ships to Sicily while engaged in a full war with the Peloponnesians, how risky could it be to do so now that there was peace? This time they would have the advantage of already knowing many of the cities. This time the Syracusans' interference in Leontini would make others much more inclined to join with Athens to defeat them. And if renewed war with Sparta was inevitable, then gaining influence in Sicily would be the best possible way to prepare for it. It would provide a new and rich source of timber for ships and men to row them, allow the Athenians to squeeze the Spartans' food supply from the west as well as from the east, and deny them the kind of naval assistance that could threaten Athenian dominance of the sea. Sparta and its allies ultimately would never tolerate Athenian power while they thought they could crush it. The addition of Sicily, or some part of Sicily, to the empire would effectively surround and strangle the Peloponnese. The balance of power would be altered for good, and the empire would be entirely secure. The terms of the peace of 421 stipulated that both parties return territories they had added during the war, but it did not preclude adding others. Was the best way to secure the empire simply to guard current possessions against possible rebellion, and use their superior resources to wait out any threat from the Spartans? Or was it rather to expand westward, effectively pressuring the Spartans into a position of permanent tolerance of Athenian power?

The best-known indication we have that the Athenians in this period were favoring a more aggressive policy of westward expansion is the case of Melos, a small island off the Peloponnesian coast, west of most of the islands controlled by the empire. The word *mēlon* in Greek means "apple," and Greek mythology associates apples with desire. It was on Melos that a sculpture of Aphrodite, goddess of desire, was ploughed up by a farmer in the nineteenth century. The statue lost her arms in a scuffle over ownership. We know her today as the Venus de Milo: the Aphrodite of Melos. One of her lost arms held an apple, perhaps a pun on the island where she was carved. Aphrodite's desire for that apple had ignited the Trojan War. Athenian desire for Melos would also lead to conflict.

The previous summer, the Athenians had sailed into the harbor at Melos accompanied by both land and sea forces. In introducing the episode Thucydides is vague about their precise motivation. The Melians were Spartan colonists but had been neutral in the earlier war; at some point however the Athenians had "raided their island and forced them into open hostility" (5.84).

Why? Evidently because they felt that their empire needed to control all, not simply most, islands, even those to the west of their normal territory. Before commencing hostilities, Athenian ambassadors met with the Melian ruling elite to discuss terms: they wanted Melos to enter the empire as a tribute-paying ally. The Athenians asked to address the full assembly of the people, but the Melian oligarchs would not allow this; they knew too well the attractions of Athenian protection for the demos. The assembly might well vote in favor of Athenian alliance. The oligarchical council admitted the Athenian envoy to negotiations behind closed doors only.

Thucydides has left for us a remarkable account of these negotiations in what is known as the Melian Dialogue; a translation of the text follows this chapter. In form, it is unlike anything else in his history. It is closer to drama, or Plato's dialogues, than to the normal set speeches he records in other contexts. There is no consensus among scholars as to whether it is a complete fiction, composed purely to give the historian a space to consider the dynamics of imperial power, or whether it does in fact reflect arguments that were made on each side. In either case, it is startling in the brutality with which it sets out the issues. The Athenians do not sugarcoat their motivations in the aggressive expansion of their empire. As Thucydides had suggested at the very outset of his narrative of the war, they are driven purely by security and self-interest. The logic of imperial power demands that it make no exceptions. Gone is any trace of Pericles' strategy: it is in failing to expand that the empire creates real risk for itself. The Athenians refuse to allow the Melians to use arguments founded on common notions of justice since "what you call justice exists only between equals" (5.89). In the end, the Melians still refused to join the Athenians as tribute-paying allies. The empire's forces laid siege to the city, and it fell some months later, betrayed from within. The Athenians executed all men of military age whom they caught, and sold all the women and children into slavery.

Thucydides does not record for us any debate at Athens over whether to invade Melos, nor about what to do with its population once it fell, although the brutal treatment of Melos is not different from that voted for rebelling cities earlier in the war. We do not know whether the decisions were contentious or popular. But Thucydides' elaborate account of the incident implies that for him it was a significant indicator of the direction in which Athenian policy was heading, a direction that in his assessment led inevitably to the decision on Sicily he reports immediately afterward.

The easy victory over Melos was only months in the past that morning in the spring of 415. On the Pnyx a proposal was made that the Athenians should send sixty ships to Sicily—twice the number they had sent to Melos, and the same number they had sent to Sicily back in 427—under joint command. The three leaders would be Nicias, a well-regarded and exceptionally fortunate leader whose name was associated with the treaty of 421, a second highly experienced general called Lamachus, and the much younger but charismatic and passionate Alcibiades. The more delicate decision, though, was not the number of ships nor their commanders, but their mission. The official topic before the assembly had been the request of the Egestaeans, but the arguments in favor of honoring this request revealed other advantages to sending the force to Sicily. The exiles from Leontini joined the Egestaeans in the request; surely there was an obligation to them. And what of the other, vaguer, notions of the advantages of western conquest? The proposal that finally came to the vote at the end of the meeting gave plenty of latitude to the expedition's leaders. The Athenians would send sixty ships to Sicily, under the command of Nicias, Lamachus, and Alcibiades; they were to help the Egestaeans, to restore Leontine exiles upon gaining any advantage in the war, and "to order all other matters in Sicily as they should deem best for the interests of Athens" (Thucydides 6.8).

The chair had the herald read out the proposal in its final form, and then put the matter to a vote. The Athenians voted with their hands at this period. If meetings, as they very occasionally did, had gone on so long that the light was failing, the vote had to be postponed until the following day so that the hands could be seen. It is hard to imagine counting six thousand hands, and we assume that most debates produced a majority that would be clear from a look at the voters. In this case, the yeses had clearly prevailed. The Athenians were going to Sicily.

Primary Source Interlude

The Melian Dialogue (Thucydides 5.84–116)

[84] The following summer, Alcibiades sailed to Argos with twenty ships, and captured three hundred Argives still suspected of favoring the Spartan cause. The Athenians settled them on neighboring islands that were under Athenian authority. Against the island of Melos, the Athenians sent thirty of their own ships, along with six from Chios and two from Lesbos, carrying a force of twelve hundred Athenian hoplites, thirty Athenian archers, and twenty mounted archers. With them went fifteen hundred hoplites from the allied islands.

The Melians were Spartan colonists, and unlike the other islanders were unwilling to submit to Athenian authority. At first, the Melians remained neutral, but when the Athenians raided their island they were forced into open hostility.

The Athenian generals were Cleomedes, son of Lycomedes, and Teisias, son of Teisimachus. After bringing their troops into position, but before launching any offensive action, these generals sent envoys to negotiate with the Melians. The Melians received the envoys, not in front of the assembled people, but in closed session with the island's chief magistrates.

[85] "Since we are not bringing our case before the people," the Athenian representative began, "there will be no occasion to seduce them with long speeches that present no opportunity for rebuttal. We know that this is why you have brought us to speak in front of this select audience. This being the case, I suggest that we dispense with the speeches altogether and engage in something more in the nature of a debate. This would give you the opportunity to respond to our arguments point by point. Does this strike you as a reasonable method of proceeding?"

[86] The Melian representative replied: "We have no objection to the ground

rules you propose. But your hostile actions belie your reasonable words. We know that you come here as both judge and jury. We know that there are only two possible outcomes: war, if we prove the justice of our cause and refuse to submit; and if we choose to submit, slavery."

[87] **Athenians**. If your purpose in assembling is to calculate possible outcomes, or to discuss anything beyond how the present crisis bears upon the security of Melos, there is no point in further discussion. But if your sole object is to secure the survival of Melos, we can proceed.

[88] **Melians**. Under the circumstances, it's understandable that we would want to consider all our options. But since our main concern is for our survival, let the debate proceed as you have suggested.

[89] **Athenians**. In that case, we'll dispense with the long speeches. We won't press the claim that we have a legitimate authority over you based on our former defeat of the Persians, or that we have come here seeking satisfaction for some wrong you have done against us. These arguments are unlikely to convince you. At the same time, as I expect you know, you won't persuade us with the argument that Melos, though a Spartan colony, never took Sparta's side in any act of aggression against Athens. Let's have no illusions between us. We both know that, for all practical purposes, what you call justice exists only between equals. In the real world, where there's an imbalance of power, the more powerful do what they can, and the less powerful do what they must.

[90] **Melians**. In which case, since you've made expediency rather than justice the basis for our proceedings, we suggest you think of your own position before you set aside all consideration of justice and equity. One day you yourselves may be judged by the precedent you set with us.

[91] **Athenians**. We are not concerned with any such hypothetical situation. Your argument would not apply in dealing with an enemy like the Spartans, who are our equals in power. It would apply only if one of our former subjects were to find itself in a position to pass judgment on us. We're willing to take that risk. We have clear objectives on this occasion: to serve the interest of Athenian authority and establish our control over Melos without incident, and to discuss how Melos might maintain its safety and stability in a manner advantageous to both parties.

[92] **Melians**. How would it be as advantageous to us to be slaves as it is for you to be rulers?

[93] **Athenians**. Think of your own advantage: unless you submit to us now, you will suffer a fate worse than slavery. Spare us the trouble of having to destroy you.

[94] **Melians**. Then you refuse to accept our neutrality? You refuse to consider us friends instead of enemies, and allies of neither side?

[95] **Athenians**. It's not that it would harm us to have you as enemies, but that accepting friendship would be interpreted by our subjects as a sign of weakness on our part. Having enemies is a sign of strength.

[96] **Melians**. Do your subjects consider it reasonable that you make no distinction between a sovereign people like the Melians, and those who, either as your own colonists or as insubordinate allies, have made themselves subject to your authority?

[97] **Athenians**. Such a distinction would be lost on them. The relevant issue here is power. If our subjects see an island like Melos allowed to maintain its independence, they will assume the island must be powerful, and that Athens refrains from attacking out of fear. Leaving aside the side benefit of enlarging our empire, the subjugation of Melos would benefit Athens by demonstrating that the weakest of the islands does not, in fact, have any power over us, and that we are still masters of the sea.

[98] **Melians**. Let's come back to the advantages of accepting our neutrality. Since you've taken considerations of justice off the table, and force us to consider only what is in the interests of Athens, let's consider how to align our interests, and come up with a course of action that can be to our mutual advantage. Consider this. If you violate our neutrality, will it not lead other neutral peoples to conclude that you also intend to take similar action against them? What result can there be but to drive more allies to the side of the enemies you already have, and make reluctant adversaries out of those who never had hostile intentions toward you?

[99] **Athenians**. We don't have to worry about the mainland. The mainland Greeks don't see any threat to their freedom. They'll be slow to take precautions against us. It's the islanders that we're worried about: those like you who claim their independence, and hold out against our complete dominance over the sea. These are the people who are more likely cause trouble for us and for themselves.

[100] **Melians**. When you are willing to go to such great lengths to preserve your empire, and your subjects are equally determined to free themselves, surely for us it would be the height of cowardice not to risk everything to preserve the freedom we still possess.

[101] **Athenians**. Not if you take a reasonable view of the matter. This isn't a contest between two equals to determine which one has the most courage. It isn't simply a question of saving face. It's a question of saving your skin. It's about knowing when to back down from confrontation with a more powerful opponent.

[102] **Melians**. But as often as not, wars are decided by chance, rather than by the relative numbers on either side. In any case, we know that as soon as we submit to you, we immediately abandon all hope. As long as we keep up the effort, there's some hope we'll be left standing at the end.

[103] **Athenians**. Hope is certainly a comfort to those in your situation. And if you have other resources to back it up, it might just save you from complete destruction. But only a fool marches out to face certain death armed with nothing but hope. Don't make that mistake now, not when your lives are hanging in the balance. And don't make the other common mistake of banking on some miracle to save you when all else has failed.

[104] **Melians**. We know how difficult it is for us to contend both against your power and against chance, even if the odds weren't stacked against us. But we're willing to take the chance that we still find favor with the gods. The gods will see that we honor our bond with them in opposing those who violate the bonds that exist between men. And as to what we lack in strength, our alliance with the Spartans will make up the difference. The Spartans are bound to come to our aid out of a feeling of kinship and a desire to avoid disgrace. Our confidence is not entirely misplaced.

[105] **Athenians**. As to the good will of the gods, I don't think we'll run into trouble there. We make no claims or pursue any actions against you that go beyond any established custom either human or divine. For in the case of the gods we believe, and in the case of humans we know that it has always been in their nature, wherever they have the power, to rule. We did not set this precedent, nor are we the first to make use of it. It was true before our time, and it will be true for generations to come, and we follow it knowing that if you or any other peoples were to possess the power that we now have, you would do the same. When it comes to the favor of the gods, we have no reason to fear that

we'll come up empty-handed. And as to your expectation that the Spartans will be shamed into helping you, we bless your trusting nature, but we don't envy your foolishness. When it comes to themselves and the laws of their own land, the Spartans are really excellent people, and much could be said about their conduct toward others, but all in all I think we can sum them up by saying that they consider good whatever they find pleasant, and just whatever they find advantageous. Such is the frame of mind on which you now irrationally base your hope of rescue.

[106] **Melians**. All the more reason for us to trust that the Spartans will find it in their best interests not to betray Melos, which is their own colony. Such an action would give the advantage to their enemies, and cause their friends in Greece to write them off as untrustworthy.

[107] **Athenians**. Then you don't understand that it's safe to do what's expedient, but dangerous to do what is just and good. And danger is just what the Spartans hope to avoid.

[108] **Melians**. But this is exactly why we think they will undertake these risks for us, and with more of a sense of security than for others: both because our proximity to the Peloponnese makes it easier for them to act, and because we are more faithful than others to the ties of our common blood.

[109] **Athenians**. The security of their allies is not foremost in the minds of those who have been called to offer military assistance. Their foremost consideration is the relative strength of the opposition they will face. This is especially the case with the Spartans. They have so little confidence in their own resources that even when they attack an enemy close at hand they only do so with the help of many allies. It's unlikely they would send troops to an island when our navy controls the sea.

[110] **Melians**. But they would have others to send. The Cretan sea is wide, and it will be harder for you to patrol than it will be for those wishing to elude you to slip through your blockade. And if the Spartans should fail at this, they would turn against your land, and against all of your remaining allies whom Brasidas didn't attack. Then you will be fighting not to subdue a foreign land, but to protect your own land and that of your allies.

[111] **Athenians**. Something of the kind may happen to you, as it has to others who have tried, and you will find out that never once have the Athenians backed away from a siege out of fear of what others might do. But we notice that,

although you claim that security is your first priority, in this entire discussion you have never mentioned a single thing you can count on to provide security. You expect that the future will strengthen your hand, while your available resources, compared to ours, are too small to give you any chance of success. It would be the height of foolishness if you don't look around you and come up with a more sensible response to your present circumstances. For surely you will not be influenced by that false sense of honor that proves most destructive to those who find themselves in shameful situations that could have been foreseen. It is so often the case in these instances that men are so carried away by their so-called honor that they allow themselves to fall into even greater dishonor through their own recklessness than they would have had they trusted to luck. You will guard against this, if you consider your options wisely, and don't consider it beneath you to accept the terms the greatest city in Greece offers you: to keep your own territory and become tributary allies, and, when faced with choosing between war and security, not to insist on the worse choice. Those who stand up to their equals, come to good terms with their superiors, and act moderately toward their inferiors—those men are sure to prosper. As we leave you to deliberate, think about these things, and keep in mind that you are deliberating about the fate of your country: you have one country, and whether it stands or falls depends on the one choice you make.

[112] And with that the Athenians withdrew from the conference. And the Melians, in closed session, reached a decision in keeping with their earlier statements, and told the Athenians: "We have not changed our position, Athenians. We will not in so short a time deprive a seven-hundred-year-old city of its freedom. For our security, we will put our trust in the favor of the gods, which has saved us up to now, and in the assistance of men, which will come from the Spartans. We entreat you to let us be friends, with no enmity on either side, and to depart from this country after agreeing upon terms convenient for both parties."

[113] This was the answer the Melians made. But the Athenians broke off negotiations, and said: "It would appear from the outcome of your deliberations that you are alone in considering future prospects more certain than what appears before your eyes, counting on vague possibilities as if they were already assured. You put your hope entirely in the Spartans and your own luck. You stake everything on this, and so you will lose everything."

[114] With this the Athenian envoys returned to their camp. As a result of the Melians' refusal to submit, the Athenian generals made immediate preparations for war, and their divisions prepared to lay siege to the Melians. Leaving both

Athenian and allied forces to blockade and besiege the island by land and sea, the Athenians planned to return later with most of their army. Meanwhile, the troops left behind on Melos maintained the siege.

[115] At this same time, the Argives made an incursion into Phleiasia and lost eighty men in an ambush by the Phleiasians and Argive exiles. At Pylos the Athenians plundered the Spartans, and the Spartans, though they fell short of renouncing the peace treaty and going to war, announced that any other of their people who wished to could plunder the Athenians. The Corinthians, for reasons of their own, declared war on the Athenians. But the rest of the Peloponnese was at peace. Meanwhile, the Melians made a nighttime raid against the Athenian lines near the marketplace, killing as many men and taking as much food and supplies as they could before falling back quietly. After this incident the Athenians made improvements to their watch. And so the summer came to an end.

[116] The following winter the Spartans intended to invade Argos, but the offerings at the border were unfavorable to safe passage, and so they withdrew. This caused the Argives to suspect the loyalty of some of their own people. They arrested some, and others fled. And at the same time, the Melians took another poorly defended part of the Athenian line. As a result, reinforcements arrived under the command of Philocrates, son of Demeas, and the siege was strengthened, and some act of betrayal among the Melians caused them to surrender and put themselves at the mercy of the Athenians. The Athenians slaughtered all the young men of military age, and enslaved the women and children. They occupied the island, and eventually sent five hundred Athenians to establish a colony on Melos.

CHAPTER 2

Symposion

Alcibiades, Nicias, and Eros

The famous clarity of the daylight and the jutting prominence of its hills make Athens a city of views. As Nicias and Alcibiades, just chosen to lead the expedition to Sicily, made their way down from the Pnyx into town, they would have looked over the low rooftops of the neighborhood called Melite to the temple of Hephaestus on its hill above the Agora; or at the rocky Areopagus, with the Acropolis and its dazzling temples looming behind, and the even higher Lykabettos rising behind these, outside the city walls. Men headed in the opposite direction, down to the harbor rather than into town, could see the sparkling ocean three miles away, vivid in the afternoon sunshine. The conspicuous high points in Athens offered vistas over houses, shops, taverns, and streets to the sea or the mountains beyond the city. The streets offered reassuring glimpses of the high temples and rocky crags.

But after sunset everything was different. Without a moon, the narrow streets were pitch black—a disorienting maze of alleyways and blind house walls. If you were out after dark, you (or your slaves) carried your own torches along to light your way, and hoped you wouldn't encounter anyone who wished you ill. Athens did have a police force of sorts at this period: public slaves imported from the barbarian Scythians. Yet as far as we can tell this force functioned only to keep order at public meetings and trials, not to patrol the streets by night. Under these circumstances it is perhaps less peculiar that Athenians habitually carried coins, if they had them, in their mouths rather than in some more easily grabbed wallet or pouch. Comedy and particularly oratory of the fourth century paint a vivid picture of the sorts of things that might go on after dark: from the anonymous snatching of a victim's woolen cloak, to boisterous house-breakings or kidnappings of disputed prostitutes, to full-scale gang assault or attempted murder. One of the more disarming stories Plutarch tells us about

Pericles involves his treatment of a detractor who has spent the day harassing him in the Agora, and then follows him home, continuing the abuse. As it is after dark by the time they reach Pericles' house, he kindly directs a slave to accompany his tormentor back to his own house, lighting his way with a torch and presumably protecting him from the dangers of the night streets.

We think of nighttime crime largely being committed by poorer people against richer ones, and among strangers. Such muggings likely did go on in Athens, but we have little record of them. Instead, the assailants we hear about in legal speeches are frequently wealthy young men, roving the streets in drunken gangs. A speech by Demosthenes includes the tantalizing detail that such gangs gave themselves obscene, sexually aggressive names (*Ithyphalloi*, or "hard-ons," being the most unambiguous example) and boasted of stealing or fighting over flute-playing girls who could be hired for sex or entertainment. Athens had a surprising degree of tolerance for the lawless behavior of wealthy men in their twenties and even thirties, particularly if they were drunk (a regular excuse), particularly if it was dark. Wine and darkness were inflammatory, and youth itself was inflammable. Who could expect the self-control of older, colder blood to rule their behavior? Just what aberrant behaviors these packs of drunken men could get up to would become particularly crucial in a matter of weeks. At that point, the focus of attention would turn from the dark but public streets where the results of the drinking played out to the lamplit private dining rooms where it began. For these gangs of wealthy and intoxicated young men were engaging in the only publicly visible portion of a *symposion*, hereafter called "symposium" from its more familiar Latinized name.

In the last chapter we investigated the demos: the body of male citizens gathered on the Pnyx whose desires drove the vote to send forces to Sicily. Now we turn to the wealthy upper crust of that larger citizen body. It was this much smaller group of men who tended to speak at assembly meetings. As Pericles had in the generation before, they were the ones responsible for kindling the desires in the demos that had just resulted in their vote to send forces to Sicily. Were these elites motivated by the same love for the power of the city, the same belief that imperial power was best secured by territorial expansion?

These more prominent figures were tightly connected in a web of friendships, rivalries, and enmities. Their private relations and public interactions were deeply entangled. Nicias and Alcibiades, who had just been appointed to lead the Sicilian Expedition, were two such figures. Between them they would instigate much of what played out later that year and beyond. (The third general, Lamachus, was of a poorer background and we hear much less about him, so our focus will remain on the more prominent two.) To understand the relations between these men, as well as the motives and choices of each, we need a sense of the elite culture they emerged from and performed within. We begin with an activity favored by Alcibiades and his aristocratic friends, but pointedly rejected by Nicias: the symposium.

Symposium

The symposium, literally "drinking together," was something more formalized, with more standardized features, than just a drinking party. The gathering normally included some fourteen to twenty men (and only men; wives wouldn't have been present although prostitutes were often part of the entertainment). Departing from the normal Greek practice of eating while seated, symposiasts reclined on couches arranged in a square along the walls of the *andrōn* or male quarters of the house. After a meal, a symposiarch, the "leader of the drinking-together," was elected or appointed. He poured out a libation to the gods, and the drinking commenced. The symposiarch would determine the ratio of wine to water and the number of rounds, as each symposiast drank precisely the same amount as everyone else, at the same time. Greeks always drank their wine, which was much stronger than ours, diluted with water. Only barbarians drank it straight, and they could go mad as a result. The wine was mixed in a large vessel called a *kratēr*, and the nature of the symposium shifted as more kratērs of mixed wine were consumed. A comic fragment from the following century has the god Dionysus say "I mix three kratērs only for those who are wise. One is for good health, which they drink first. The second is for desire and pleasure. The third is for sleep, and when they have drunk it those who are wise wander homewards" (Eubulus, fragment 93).

During the drinking, there were various forms of entertainment. Occasionally there would be elaborate performances involving dancers or acrobats. Xenophon describes a dancer somersaulting in and out of a ring of swords, or juggling giant hoops. Depictions of symposia in vase-paintings as well as texts also include flute-girls, who performed on the reed pipe called the *aulos* and doubled as prostitutes (perhaps after that second "desire and pleasure" kratēr). But frequently the guests themselves were the entertainment, playing games or taking turns asking riddles, telling jokes, or speaking on a set topic. Like the drinking, this conversation unfolded in a regulated manner. This ordered speechmaking gave rise to the word's more familiar sense, in English, of an academic gathering to discuss a single issue.

Perhaps the best-known account of a symposium is Plato's dialogue of that name. Although it was written some thirty or forty years later, it purports to describe an occasion around the time we are focusing on: the winter of 416. At the house of Agathon, a hot young tragic poet, a group of men gather for a small party in celebration of his victory in a tragic competition. First, in direct opposition to all expectations for a symposium, they decide against regulated drinking because they are all hungover from the previous night's festivities. Then, they send the flute-girls away to the "women's quarters." And then they decide that they should each in turn, "from left to right," give a speech in praise of the god *Erōs*, or desire. We hear five of these speeches, each taking a new approach to the topic, and each entertainingly written in a style evoking what we know of the speaker. Agathon himself, for instance, gives a speech replete with poetic wordplay and the balanced phrases made popular by contemporary rhetoricians; Erixymachus the doctor gives a scientific take bristling with medical jargon. The comic poet Aristophanes tells an absurd but endearing fable about originally spherical humans being split down the middle and consequently spending their lives yearning for their missing half. Socrates characteristically avoids giving a traditional speech and instead reports a dialogue in which he presents Eros as the driving force that impels us toward The Good: philosophy itself, in other words.

While Plato's *Symposium* explicitly marks itself as so atypical as almost to be an anti-symposium, it points negatively, as it were, at some characteristic features. The absence of regulated drinking is notable; the guests decide to drink "for pleasure" meaning that each will drink just what he wants, rather than the expected practice in which the symposiarch orders rounds. The conventional flute-girls are sent away. The set speeches, on the other hand, seem to be more typical, although of course more elaborate and accomplished than what we might expect from extemporaneous toasting. In two aspects in particular, they likely do reflect normal practice. First, Plato carefully has each speech pick up on something from the last, effectively capping its predecessor. This competitive element to the proceedings reflects an important thread of aristocratic relations. Even within a friendly social group, rivalry and competition are never far submerged.

Second is the element of the erotic: while the flute-girls whose presence suggests the possibility of sex have been excluded, the speeches bring the idea back in the rarified form of meditations on eros (remember that second kratēr: eros and pleasure). Notably, the speeches all ignore or downplay heterosexual desire, and focus on the homoerotic. Athens, perhaps even more than the rest of the ancient Greek world, organized space and activity with a very high degree of gender segregation; men largely spent their time with other men and women with women. The ideal of human beauty, as evidenced by classical art, was the young male body. Lyric poetry and vase-painting from the sixth century show that a man's attraction toward a youth was considered equivalent to, and often coexisted or alternated with, attraction to a woman. This is not to say that what we think of as homosexuality was more common in Athenian society than it is today; indeed, the Athenians did not seem to think in the same categories of sexuality at all. Rather, the meaningful differences they saw were between the active and the passive, the "lover" and the "beloved." That an older man, even while he was married and enjoying sex with his wife, should be a lover of a younger one struck nobody as odd or blameworthy. But the sexual part of the attraction was not thought of as mutual. The boy's role was to "gratify" his lover in exchange for the wisdom and experience (or, in other cases, gifts or resources) the older man could impart. These could constitute a political education, or a balder offer of power or influence in the public sphere. When the youth had matured, he would in turn start eyeing beardless adolescents in search of his own beloveds. Should a pair stay together over an extended period of years, or if the beloved returned the desire of his lover, they were stigmatized; the younger partner in particular would be seen as dangerously effeminate. While there is some evidence from art that lover-beloved pairs could be the same age, texts are silent on this possibility. It is certainly well outside of established norms.

While this way of thinking about active and passive sexual desire is common throughout our sources, the specific practice of sustained attention of lover to beloved was likely much more common among the elite than the masses. It was wealthier men, after all, who had the leisure to spend their days at the gymnasium gazing at youth exercising naked, and engaging them in political or philosophical dialogue. Like the symposium itself, the homoerotic desire nurtured there could be the object of bemusement or suspicion to the lower classes.

These two aspects of Plato's *Symposium*, competition and eros, were closely connected to each other in the elite society we are examining, and much more explicitly part of politics than our culture tends to acknowledge. Older men competed for the attention of the most desirable younger ones; these in turn could leverage their attractions into political influence. Perhaps the most famous (or infamous) instance of this is the career of Alcibiades.

After Socrates has finished his speech on Eros, the intellectual evening is suddenly and dramatically interrupted:

And not much later they heard from the courtyard the voice of Alcibiades, who was very drunk and yelling loudly. He kept asking where Agathon was and ordering the servants to lead him to Agathon. And so the flute-girl and some others of those with him, supporting him, led him in, and they stood him up in the doorway. He had been festooned with a shaggy sort of a crown of ivy and violets, with lots of streamers on his head (*Symposium* 212)

This is a nice introduction to Alcibiades, but before we turn our focus to him we must note what he's doing. Garlanded and intoxicated, he and his drinking companions have left the private dining room where they started their evening's drinking. They have commenced the *kōmos*, the informal drunken parade through the streets that was the final stage of the symposium. Remember the comic fragment mentioned above told us that the wise go home after the third kratēr, but everyone else continues drinking. The poet lists the increasingly negative effects of the fourth through tenth kratērs, for those drinkers not wise enough to stop after three. These include shouting and anger, and finish with insanity. Kratēr six is designated "kōmos." It was these roving bands of komasts who were responsible for the acts of violence that made walking the dark streets of Athens risky (kratēr seven: black eyes; kratēr eight: legal summonses). The point was simply to demonstrate their power and superiority over anyone not part of their own group. The Athenians had a name for this sort of behavior: *hubris*; the Greek, as we'll see, has a slightly more specialized meaning than our own general sense of arrogance. We hear about hubris repeatedly in connection with the figure who just showed up at Agathon's symposium: Alcibiades.

Alcibiades

Much of our information about both Alcibiades and Nicias is collected by the Roman-era biographer Plutarch, who wrote in the second century CE. While Plutarch is thus some five hundred years later than our period, he had access to many sources we no longer have, and provides many vividly characterizing (if perhaps not literally true) anecdotes. Most of what follows about both figures is taken from Plutarch's *Lives*.

Alcibiades was born in 451, so in 415 he was in his midthirties, very young to have achieved the degree of political prominence he had at the time. Athenians had a healthy suspicion of youth, and while you could attend (and speak at) the assembly as soon as you completed your military training at the age of twenty, service on the council, juries, as well as all magistracies was available only to those over thirty. Alcibiades had been elected general already in 420 and thus held the office as soon as he was legally able to. This was surely in part thanks to the prominence of his family. He traced his ancestors back to the Homeric hero Ajax. He was related through his mother to the famous Alcmaeonid clan, a family strongly associated with the expulsion of the tyrants and the formation of the democracy a century earlier. Pericles himself, another famous Alcmaeonid, became Alcibiades' guardian on his father's death. But in addition to his glorious pedigree Alcibiades clearly had his own talents. He was an exceptionally able public speaker, a skill that would take you a long way in Athens. He was wealthy, although evidently never quite wealthy enough for his own ambitions. Perhaps most famously, he was astonishingly, knee-weakeningly gorgeous, with the kind of charismatic personality that attracted anyone he talked to. In a society where older men competed to become the lovers of beautiful youths, the young Alcibiades was the most desired of all, and clearly knew the power that gave him. Plutarch tells us that "he had a golden shield made for himself, bearing no ancestral device, but an Eros armed with a thunderbolt" (*Life of Alcibiades* 16). Alcibiades' talent for kindling eros in others, both for his own beauty and more generally for Athenian wealth or power, would have a lasting impact on Athens.

As flamboyant a figure as this will in any circumstances be polarizing, but the traditions surrounding Alcibiades are extraordinary by any measure. His prominent part in highly consequential events, along with the exceptional nature of his life and personality, made him a figure of abiding interest in his own lifetime and beyond, and the ancient sources that allow us to reconstruct his life are both remarkably rich and highly biased both for and against him. He would be hailed as invincible popular leader, exiled in disgrace, recalled as beloved savior of his city, then exiled a second time before his spectacular death at the hands of barbarian enemies. During his periods of exile he transferred the power of his personality to other lands, where he became beloved first among the Spartans and then the Persians. He possessed a peculiar ability to adapt to different customs and enchant even those who should naturally have been hostile to him.

Plutarch's account of his life is filled with striking anecdotes, many of which are probably fictions, but which add up to give a sense of his personality and the power he exercised over his contemporaries and those who came after. A single example: as a young boy, we learn, Alcibiades objected to practicing the aulos (a double flute), because playing it distorted his attractive face and because, unlike the lyre, it did not permit one to perform words and music together. The aulos, said he, "is for the Thebans; since they," unlike the eloquent Athenians, of course, "don't know how to converse." The result of his boyish revolt was general. All boys refused to learn the aulos if Alcibiades wouldn't, and Plutarch maintains that the instrument was dropped from the standard curriculum as a result. The story illustrates his intense pride in his good looks, his propensity to ignore general norms that weren't to his liking, and his persuasive influence over those around him. All these would remain potent aspects of his personality throughout his turbulent life, and all would have disastrous consequences for the city of Athens.

Plutarch contrasts Alcibiades' considerable talents for politics and public life with the excesses of his private affairs, mentioning in particular the *hubrismata* (hubristic acts) associated with drinking parties. Once, as in Plato's

Symposium, he leads a kōmos from his own party to another. In this case the second symposium is that of one of his many hopeful lovers. He has declined the invitation to this one, but arriving there drunken from his own he sees gold and silver vessels on the tables, and directs his slaves to take half of these back to his house. Outraged by this behavior the guests claim that their host has been treated with hubris, but the host, besotted by Alcibiades, points out that at least he left them half rather than taking them all. Hubris, then, is associated here, as in our comic fragment, with the aggressive acts of drunken young aristocrats. It's worth looking more closely at this impulse and where it comes from.

Hubris, Honor, and Shame

We learn to associate hubris with tragic heroes, and the word is often translated with the charmingly archaic phrase "overweening pride." But "pride" does not necessarily imply a victim, while hubris, at least in the context of Athenian law, does. What precisely was meant by the word is still the subject of debate, but some connect it to the system of honor and shame that drove much elite behavior in Athens. On this definition, hubris is the intentional attempt to dishonor another, to detract from another's honor for the pleasure of the superiority you feel in doing it. This view has its basis in Aristotle's *Rhetoric*, where, connecting shame to anger (ninth kratēr: anger), he says that "hubris is doing and saying things at which the victim incurs shame, not in order that one may achieve anything other than what is done, but simply to get pleasure from it. . . . That is why Achilles says when angry: 'He dishonored me; for he has himself taken my prize and keeps it'" (1378b). Anger springs from shame. The imposition of shame on another is an act of hubris.

Of course Aristotle uses Achilles for an example. What more familiar icon could there be of an angry young aristocratic hothead obsessed with his own honor? The Homeric system of honor (*timē*) is purely external. A prize (*geras*) is awarded in recognition of excellence in battle, but in a very real sense, the prize *is* the honor. When Agamemnon takes Achilles' prize (which happens in this case to be a woman), he has also taken Achilles' honor. Note that Achilles' true abilities as a warrior, the source of his excellence, are unaffected. But honor itself is fully externalized: the communal recognition of individual value. Besides being external, honor is highly competitive. Achilles' loss of timē is Agamemnon's gain, and vice versa. While all the kings who fought at Troy were honored by their own people, it mattered a great deal who had the most honor.

While the Greek world had changed between the time of Homer and the fifth century, the concept of honor still had enormous power. Its locus had shifted somewhat from the battlefield, however. First, the concept could be applied to entire communities: remember the Athenians' admonition to the Melians not to be motivated by self-destructive considerations of timē:

> For surely you will not be influenced by that false sense of honor that proves most destructive to those who find themselves in shameful situations that could have been foreseen. It is so often the case in these instances that men are so carried away by their so-called honor that they allow themselves to fall into even greater dishonor through their own recklessness than they would have had they trusted to luck. (Thucydides 5.111)

Just as the concept could be extended to full cities, in Athens it could operate on new levels of society. Aristocratic individual combat had given way to the much greater importance of the middle class hoplite phalanx of men fighting in an unbreakable line, and the poorer oarsmen manning the navy's triremes. This development likely drove the increasingly democratic constitution of the city. Yet even in this egalitarian context, the concepts of timē and geras adapt themselves to the context of the polis. In Athens we see this already in the sixth century, in the words of an early political reformer: "I gave to the demos as much geras as is fitting, neither taking away from their timē nor giving them too much" (Solon, fragment 5). The old Homeric terms of military excellence and social valuation now indicate political power. And while there are obvious gradations of this power—you don't want to give the people too much geras— the principle that they, too, participate in this economy of honor has been established. By the fifth century, the generic term for an office or magistracy was timē, and the legal term for being without citizen rights was the negative version of the word: *atimia*.

We saw in the last chapter how Athenian pride in the honor arising from participation in the polis was evident in Pericles' funeral oration: "each man is honored in public affairs not for his standing and wealth as much as for his excellence. Nor if anyone has some good ability to offer to the city is he prevented by poverty or obscurity" (2.37). In contrast to the era when timē and its fruits were available only to a small aristocratic minority, Pericles praises a society where honor and power are shared among the entire citizen body, and status is determined purely by ability and diligence, not birth and wealth. Yet the reality of politics in Athens did not match up perfectly with Pericles' stirring rhetoric. Most of those who were elected general or served in other offices continued to come from a limited set of propertied families. And honor continued to drive much of their behavior, both public and private. Alcibiades in particular seems to have been defined by his burning desire for honor: it is undoubtedly from this characteristic that the anecdotes about his hubris derive.

Thucydides calls him *philonikōn* (a lover of victory), while Plutarch calls him *philoprōton* (a lover of being first, or preeminence), and says that the people "were forever giving the mildest of names to his transgressions, calling them the product of youthful spirits and *philotimia*" (love of honor). This driving force in Alcibiades' personality and career is clearly evident in his relationship with Nicias, the man the assembly had voted to join him as leader of the Sicilian Expedition.

Nicias

Nicias could not have been invented to better contrast Alcibiades: he was older, cautious, excessively religious, a self-styled recluse while Alcibiades was young, bold, recklessly blasphemous and a dazzling socialite. Nicias lacked his rival's family connections. We know only the name of his father and none of his ancestors before that time, in stark contrast to Alcibiades' long and prominent pedigree.

In 415 Nicias would have been in his midfifties, with a well-established reputation as both soldier and statesman. He had served as general with success several times in the conflict with Sparta. As the generalship was one of very few offices in the Athenian democracy that was elective rather than allotted, his successive terms in that office prove that he had some popularity among the people. He certainly had name-recognition. This was enhanced, of course, by his military success, but he never could have been elected general in the first place had he not achieved a degree of fame through other means. What made Nicias most conspicuous among the Athenians was his wealth, and the uses he put it to.

Nicias derived a very substantial income from huge numbers of slaves who worked the silver mines in Laurium, a district in the southern part of the Attic peninsula. The silver mines there were owned by the city of Athens, and the revenues, along with the tribute from the empire, were a major part of civic finances. But the city did not actually run the mines. Instead, it leased mining interests to individuals who were wealthy enough to own the slaves who did the actual mining. Nicias was one of these. His income from the thousand slaves he owned who worked the mines was about one hundred and sixty-five drachmas a day, or up to ten talents per year. The silver mines weren't his only source of income, but with this revenue alone he controlled an amount of wealth that was eye-popping in contrast to the regular wage earner in Athens, who brought home a drachma per day or less. In other words, Nicias' holdings brought him in a single day the same income a middle-class artisan would earn in six months.

Now the public display of wealth that had signaled honor before the democracy was a delicate matter during the fifth century. The kind of egalitarian ideal expressed in Pericles' funeral oration exerted pressure against extravagant or conspicuous display of personal wealth. Elsewhere Thucydides tells us that "the rich [did] their best to assimilate their way of life to that of the common people" (1.6). Luckily there was a mutually beneficial avenue for public displays of extravagance: the *leitourgia*, usually Latinized to liturgy. The liturgy, literally "the people's work," was essentially a tax on the very wealthiest families of Attica. Perhaps 5 percent of the citizen population, or somewhere between three and seven hundred families, were subject to liturgies. Under this system, dozens of recurring public expenses were assigned to individual wealthy men on a rotating basis. Many of these obligations were religious in nature. Athens was famous for its lavish and frequent festivals to the gods, including dramatic, musical, and athletic competitions, all of which had to be paid for. Some military expenses were parceled out this way as well. If you were an Athenian of the liturgical class, then, periodically the relevant archon (magistrate) would come tell you that this year it was your turn to foot the bill for one of the choruses at some festival or another, or for fitting out and maintaining one trireme for a year. This seems to us like a cumbersome system; paying a predictable income tax would be easier. But the liturgy was one of the only avenues that allowed, even encouraged, the otherwise problematic public display of private wealth. Particularly spectacular outlays on festivals or ships meant excellent publicity for any aspiring politician, and juries were more sympathetic toward a defendant who had shown his love of the city through such outlays of his personal fortune. Thus, the liturgical system allowed the demos to benefit from the wealth of the aristocracy, as well as allowing elite competition for honor, power, and prestige from their contributions.

Nicias made excellent use of the liturgical system for gaining public honor. The festivals he financed were extraordinary, spectacular, memorable, and thus his name was linked with piety as well as generosity and public spirit. When it was his responsibility to send an Athenian chorus to Apollo's sacred island of Delos, he constructed a richly decorated bridge of ships that could stretch to the shore from a nearby island. He deployed this in the night, so that his chorus could process, singing, onto Delos as the sun rose—a memorable spectacle and one that signaled Athens' power and wealth to all the celebrants assembled from other states.

Nicias' public expenditure for the citizens of Athens was complemented by a rigidly guarded private life. Plutarch tells us that he refused to dine with his fellow citizens (unlike Alcibiades, he was no symposiast), and indeed would stay home, if he had no public business, with his doors bolted. The anecdotes that cluster around him imply that his devotion to the city was so extraordinary that he dealt with public matters even while bathing or dining. In fact, the only activity we ever hear about in relation to Nicias' private life is his obsessive interest in prophecy and prophets. Even here, evidently, his public claim was that he consulted these in the interests of the city. There were rumors, though, that he slipped in questions about his mining interests as well. All sources agree that he was excessively interested in divine prophecy, and terrified of doing anything not condoned by some prophet or other. This superstitious caution was admired by the people, and made another notable contrast with his more impulsive fellow general Alcibiades.

In 415 Nicias had already had a distinguished military career; he served as general with considerable success throughout the theater of war during the first conflict with the Peloponnesians, and had been responsible for the capture of Cythera, one of the westernmost islands in the Aegean. Most recently he had been instrumental in negotiating the fragile truce with the Spartans in 421, which we therefore know as the Peace of Nicias. It was this that had brought him up against Alcibiades.

Alcibiades' family had held the position of *proxenos* of Sparta—a sort of unofficial ambassadorship based on family friendships with elite members of other states. Although he was only in his twenties during the first part of the war with Sparta (431–421), he was eager to take on this role, and thus felt his honor at stake when the Spartans were more inclined to deal with the older and more established Nicias. Evidently simply because it was Nicias rather than himself who arranged the peace treaty in 421, Alcibiades put all his energies into sabotaging it. He double-crossed an important Spartan embassy that had arrived to cement details of the treaty, thus publicly dishonoring Nicias. Then he brought Athens into an alliance with Argos, which would inevitably lead back into conflict with Sparta. His political skill in all this was manifest. But also disturbingly evident was the fact that he seemed to operate with no principles other than advancing his own personal position. The consequences for his city were quite clearly secondary to his need to best his rival Nicias.

This kind of public competition for honor among the elite drove the Athenian democracy as surely as economic competition drives our capitalist systems. Like economic competition, though, in completely unregulated form it carried uglier consequences. We've had glimpses of these in the stories of the kōmos turned violent; it was intentional dishonoring of rivals that led drunken aristocrats to fight in the streets. Once the competitive impulse was activated, there was no restricting it to the beneficial public forum of advice to the demos or liturgical generosity. Hubris, the intentional shaming of a rival, was not just unpleasant behavior. It was the logical consequence of a system prizing individual honor above communal solidarity, of a society which benefits from and therefore fosters aggressive competition for honor among its elite. And hubris, as Sophocles reminds us in a famous line from the *Oedipus the King*, begets the tyrant. The impulse to shame rivals can only finally be satisfied when no rivals remain, with the supremacy of one man.

In chapter 1 we encountered Athens' anxiety about the democracy's vulnerability to tyranny. The prominence and obvious ambition of Alcibiades clearly set off alarms among some; Plutarch tells us that "the reputable men of the city looked on [Alcibiades' behavior] with loathing and indignation, and feared his contemptuous and lawless spirit. They thought such conduct as his tyrant-like and monstrous" (*Life of Alcibiades* 16). Remember that one check the city had against prominent individuals rising to tyranny was ostracism; it is not surprising that Alcibiades should have been a target of this. A year or less before 415 an ostracism was voted; among the obvious candidates at the time were Nicias and Alcibiades. Plutarch claims that part of the moving force behind the ostracism was a man called Hyperbolus. Hyperbolus was agitating for the ostracism because, Plutarch asserts, if he could get rid of either Nicias or Alcibiades he thought he would be able to challenge the remaining one for preeminence in the city. However, "when Nicias and Alcibiades became aware of his baseness, they took secret counsel with one another, united and harmonized their factions, and carried the day, so that neither of them was ostracized, but Hyperbolus instead" (*Life of Nicias* 11). This was, Plutarch tells us, the very last ostracism ever held in Athens, allegedly because the institution itself had been "treated hubristically" by being applied to such a contemptible figure. Perhaps the blatant manipulation of the process suggested that it was no longer serving the democracy as intended. Rather than the demos selecting the candidate, it seems, organized "factions" subverted the intent.

Hetaireiai

Since Athens had nothing like what we think of as political parties, it is reasonable to wonder what Plutarch meant by implying that Nicias and Alcibiades each had his own "faction" who could be counted on to band together and vote against Hyperbolus. This question brings us back to the symposium, for one plausible answer to it is in the grouping called a *hetaireia*, from the word *hetairos* or "comrade," often translated as simply "club." We start hearing of hetaireiai quite early in the fifth century. They seem to have been smallish groups of about fourteen to twenty, and to be primarily associated with drinking parties. Thus they would have been precisely the kind of group we saw drinking and conversing at symposia, and engaging in the kōmos at the end of the evening. These groups could be purely social; the gathering Plato describes, making speeches in praise of Eros, clearly enjoys intellectual conversation.

But they could also have political uses. Fellow members of hetaireiai could be counted on to support each other in the law courts and assembly.

We assume that these groups, like the symposia they attended, were mostly a feature of the elite classes in Athens, and this inevitably made them the object of suspicion for the masses. In chapter 1 we saw the ongoing tension between democratic and oligarchic factions that erupted into stasis in many cities during the last quarter of the century. Thucydides claimed that in stasis "the ties of faction meant more even than those of family, because fellow partisans were readier to run risks without excuse" (3.82). The word "faction" here translates *hetairikon*, or "a hetaireia-like thing." That these groups could be involved in revolutionary plots would become clear in Athens four years later in 411, when they helped instigate a brief oligarchic coup. As their ambitions become more dangerous they are also referred to as *synomosiai*, a word meaning "bound together by oath." Already in the 420s there was anxiety about this. The word is frequently used in Aristophanes, generally hurled by leaders of the demos against their suspected enemies among the elite.

Yet even those hetaireiai not involved in political activity could, in a different way, seem problematic to the demos. If such gatherings of wealthy men were not actively plotting against the democracy, they could be encouraging withdrawal from it. This was an equally dangerous position, as far as true democrats were concerned. Remember that Socrates' speech about Eros had radically redefined the force commonly associated with sexual desire to mean a different drive altogether, an impulse that drew you toward a fully abstract concept of Beauty. What Socrates lays out in his discussion of Eros is a structured path toward pure philosophical contemplation. While this path proceeds through attention to political institutions, its ultimate goal is to move away from them. The message is clear, if implicit: politics is no fit occupation for the truly good person, and while Eros may lead you there, you must be careful not to get stuck at that inferior level.

When the drunken Alcibiades shows up in Plato's *Symposium*, after the speeches on Eros are finished, he gives as his contribution to the festivities a speech on Socrates himself. Most interesting for us, as we consider the fateful events of 415, is what this speech tells us about Alcibiades' relation to Socrates. Alcibiades uses the language of hubris repeatedly in his speech to playfully assert that Socrates' treatment of him deserves this name. He claims that Socrates is the only man before whom he feels shame (and remember, hubris has as its aim the shaming of another). But unlike the Aristotelian definition of hubris, where the shaming has no cause other than to make the man who shames another feel superior to him, Socrates' treatment of Alcibiades very clearly is aimed at improving him. The dynamic is complicated and deserves to be teased out carefully. Here Alcibiades recounts the supernatural, even god-like, effect that resides in Socrates' arguments:

> [Socrates] however, has often changed my outlook and made me think that the life I lead isn't worth living. . . . You see, he forces me to admit that I busy myself with Athenian politics when I'm far from perfect and should be doing something about myself instead. . . . What happens is that although I'm perfectly aware of the inescapable force of his recommendations as to what I should do, yet as soon as I'm away from him, I get seduced by the timē of the masses. (216a–c)

Note that Plato has Alcibiades describe himself just as Plutarch would: obsessed by timē. He laments that Socrates wants him to focus on his own virtue before being active in Athenian politics. Indeed, Plato has Socrates make this argument elsewhere and repeatedly, to all sorts of people in addition to Alcibiades. It doesn't tend to strike us as anything but high-minded, even if we are not prepared to follow the admonition ourselves. But it may have sounded different to an ordinary Athenian, for whom political participation was the central tenet of the democratic system. In his funeral oration Pericles claims:

> An Athenian citizen does not neglect the state because he takes care of his own household; and even those of us who are engaged in business have a very fair idea of politics. We alone consider the man who isn't involved with politics not peaceable, but useless. (Thucydides 2.40)

Important here is the combination of public and private interest and expertise. Staying out of politics is not simply a neutral choice, but a negative one. The word "peaceable" translates the adjective *apragmon*, literally "inactive." We have many indications that toward the end of the fifth century some wealthy men, perhaps frustrated that they were unable to wield the political power in the democracy they felt entitled to, simply withdrew from politics. The term given to this lack of action is *apragmosyne*. It is a term used positively by the elite, who contrast it unfavorably with *polypragmosyne*, "busy-bodiness" "meddlesomeness" or excessive interest in other people's affairs. But here Pericles gives us the demos' view: the apragmon man is not the peaceful innocent, but rather is useless, even harmful, to the city.

From this perspective, Socrates' constant admonitions that people should stay away from politics could well seem antidemocratic. Plato's *Symposium* is of course intended to give its (likely elite) audience a favorable view of Socrates, to show that he had tried constantly to educate Alcibiades out of those dangerous tendencies that would in the end prove so damaging to Athens. The scandals that would break later in the summer of 415 involved symposia where groups of the elite got up to shockingly impious and politically suspect activities. Plato wants to open the dining room door on such an occasion to show us how virtuous it actually was. There is no plotting political revolution or desecrating the city's gods. But his very effort at exoneration implies the popular suspicion such parties must have occasioned among the demos at large, and offers a glimpse of the kind of philosophical teaching that spurned the political engagement which the demos considered their patriotic duty.

The focus on Eros at the Symposium is, we saw, typical of symposia and yet ultimately very different. Rather than the second kratēr's anticipated kind of eros, this was a highly intellectualized and ultimately completely nonsexual one. But as we saw in the last chapter Pericles had also removed the term from the physical drive, to attach it to patriotic feeling itself: "gazing every day on the power of the city," he urges his audience, "become its lovers" (2.43). Eros, Pericles tells us, should have a public version, rather than either the private homoerotic attachments of the elite symposiast, or the philosophical contemplation of Beauty advocated by Socrates.

The small groups of elite men who gathered in private for symposia, and who sometimes caused trouble engaging in their kōmos at the end, could spark anxiety in the demos for various reasons. What did they talk about in private? Could they be plotting antidemocratic activities? Or simply refusing to engage with the affairs of the polis like good patriotic citizens? And while the competition and rivalry among individual aristocrats was usually in the service of Athens, what happened when it erupted beyond those constraints? Could the excessive desire for honor driving such rivalries end in tyranny? Such was the stew of social forces just under the surface of that democracy we saw voting in favor of sending forces to Sicily at the end of the last chapter.

The Second Debate on Sicily

The rivalry between Nicias and Alcibiades is audible, if we are attentive, in the debate on the Sicilian Expedition Thucydides recounts for us. This is not the initial debate the assembly held, which we considered in the last chapter, but a second one that occurred four days later to discuss logistics; excerpts of his account follow this chapter. Nicias, the historian tells us, was alarmed at the Athenians' assumptions about easy conquest in the west. Alcibiades evidently was already taking victory in Sicily for granted and moving ahead to schemes of advancing into Libya. The older, more cautious Nicias therefore asks that the assembly reconsider the decision to sail, and lays out the dangers he sees in undertaking the expedition. The current truce with Sparta is fragile and the Athenians should not "grasp at an expansion of our empire before the one we already have is secure" (6.10). Subduing Sicily is a much larger and more difficult enterprise than anyone realizes. And while he does not name Alcibiades, he clearly attacks him as interested in private gain rather than public good, and too young to be in such an important position.

Alcibiades' response gives a vivid sense of the man he was. Impulsively and proudly he embraces Nicias' criticisms and turns them to his advantage. His private extravagance brings fame to the city, and his youthful energy will enhance its greatness. The best way to protect the empire is by expanding it, leveraging alliances like the one with Egesta. This was how the Athenians achieved their empire to begin with, and expanded it to its current size. Nicias' suspicion of youth seeks to divide the generations that are stronger working together. Athenian unity will easily overcome the fractured Sicilians.

The sentiment in favor of the expedition was clearly strong. Alcibiades' powers of persuasion were great, and the optimistic forecast of success he painted was a powerful inducement. Nicias, seeing the way emotions were tending, adopted a different strategy. Instead of trying to dissuade the assembly from the enterprise altogether, he sought to substantially increase the force that he would command. Thucydides claims that his hope was still to put off the assembly with the scale of expense they were undertaking. But the crowd only became even more feverishly excited at the prospect of what looked like certain victory from overwhelming force. "An eros for the expedition gripped Athens," remarks Thucydides (6.23).

In using this expression Thucydides may well want us to think back to Pericles' admonition to Athens that they should become "lovers" of the city's power. The logical extension is an eros driving toward dreams of distant conquest and imperial expansion. Small wonder that it was Alcibiades, whose golden shield depicted Eros, and who inspired desire in so many, who kindled that passion in the demos.

Primary Source Interlude

The Second Debate on the Sicilian Expedition (Thucydides 6.8–26)

[8] Early the following summer, the Athenian envoys arrived from Sicily, and with them the Egestaeans, who brought with them sixty talents of unminted silver as a month's pay for the sixty ships they intended to have sent. The Athenians called an assembly, and when they heard from the Egestaeans and from their own envoys the tempting but false reports of how much treasure was available both in the temples and in the public treasury, they voted to send sixty ships to Sicily under the command of Alcibiades son of Cleinias, Nicias son of Niceratus, and Lamachus son of Xenophanes, to aid the Egestaeans against the Selinuntines, to assist in resettling Leontini if the opportunity should arise in the course of the war, and to do in Sicily whatever might be most to the advantage of Athens.

On the fifth day after this, a second assembly was called to vote on outfitting the ships as quickly as possible and on giving the generals whatever they might need for the expedition. But Nicias, who had been chosen against his will to lead the expedition, thought the city had made the wrong decision and was embarking on so massive an undertaking as the conquest of Sicily on the flimsiest of pretexts and with little preparation. He came forward in the assembly and made the following recommendations in an effort to change the minds of the Athenians:

[9] "This assembly has been called to consider the preparations necessary for the expedition to Sicily. To me, at any rate, it seems like a good idea to reexamine whether it is best to send the ships and allow these foreigners to tempt us into a war of choice when we have spent so little time considering the magnitude of the situation. It's true that I give less thought than other men to personal risk, although in general I think a good citizen ought to give some

thought to his own interests, since such a man will, for his own sake, think about what is best for the state. It's also true that I stand to gain honor from such an undertaking. But I have never in my life gone against my better judgment for the sake of popularity, nor will I now, but I will say what I think is best. I know your character, and know that my words would have little force if I advised you to hold onto what you actually have and not risk it on uncertain prospects. Instead I will argue that you are making haste at an inopportune moment to bring about something that is not so easily accomplished.

[10] "I assert that you leave behind many enemies here in Greece in your eagerness to sail to Sicily and add to their number. Perhaps you think you can rely on the existing treaty, which even while you are still at peace is a treaty in name only—as the conduct of certain people here and on the other side has shown. But if you are defeated anywhere with a sizeable force, your enemies will be swift to attack, first of all because their own misfortunes forced them to accept the treaty, which made it more of a disgrace for them than it was for us. . . . And it is likely that, if they find our force divided, as we are now rushing to divide it, they would join forces against us with the Sicilians—an alliance that in the past would have been more valuable to them than any other. We ought to consider these things, and not put the city at risk when its situation is already uncertain, or to grasp at an expansion of empire before the one we already have is secure. The Thracian Chalcideans who have rebelled against us for so many years are still unsubdued, and the loyalty of others on the mainland remains in doubt. We rush to the aid of the Egestaeans as allies as soon as they are wronged, but we have yet to punish those rebellious states who for a long time now have been wronging us.

[11] "If we subdue these rebellious states closer to home, we might hold onto them. But if we defeat the Sicilians, they are too far away, and there are too many of them for us to rule without difficulty. It is foolish to set ourselves against an enemy who, even if defeated, could not be held. And if we fail, we will be worse off than we were before. . . . Therefore, if we are wise, our effort will not be on behalf of foreigners like the Egestaeans in Sicily, but we will keep a sharp eye on the Spartans and their oligarchical machinations.

[12] "We must also remind ourselves that recently we have had a brief respite from plague and war, which gives us the opportunity to replenish our resources and refresh ourselves, and that it is right for us to spend these bonuses here in Athens, and not on foreigners who ask for our assistance. It is to their advantage to spread falsehoods and expose others to danger while they themselves provide nothing but empty words, and then either to fail to show proper gratitude or

drag their friends down with them, depending on whether their cause succeeds or fails.

"Someone, pleased with himself at having been chosen to command, encourages you to make this expedition. Ask yourselves: is he thinking only about his own profit? Is he a young man, too young for such a command, who wants to be admired for the race horses he breeds, and who eyes a generalship to support his extravagant lifestyle? Don't let a man like this enrich himself at the city's expense. Keep in mind that such men take from the public and spend on themselves. This is too important a matter for such a young man to rush into making a decision.

[13] "When I see the kinds of men he has surrounded himself with, I am afraid, and I in turn call on more senior members of this assembly, if they find themselves sitting next to one of these men, not to be shamed into voting in favor of the war out of fear of being considered soft. Do not, as these men do, pine after distant prospects, but remain firm in the knowledge that success is more certain to result from forethought than from eagerness, and stand up against these men in the hour of your country's greatest danger. Vote to observe the current satisfactory boundaries between ourselves and the Sicilians—the Ionic gulf if we sail along the coast, the Sicilian sea if we cross by open sea—and leave them to work things out for themselves. Tell the Egestaeans, since they started the war against the Selinuntines without Athens, to finish it by themselves. And in the future, make no alliances, as we used to do, with those who depend on us for protection, but are useless when we need them."

[15] This was the speech of Nicias. Of the Athenians present, most recommended launching the expedition and not reversing the earlier vote, but some spoke on the other side. The one promoting the expedition most vigorously was Alcibiades, son of Cleinias, who wished to oppose Nicias because he was a political opponent, and because he remembered the accusations Nicias made against him, and most of all because he was eager to secure the command and, if he succeeded in capturing Sicily and Carthage, to add to his own wealth and reputation. Because he had a reputation to maintain among the Athenians, he lived well beyond his means, running up debts on horse breeding and other extravagances. This contributed not a little to the later downfall of the Athenian state. For many Athenians, alarmed at his habit of putting himself above the law and suspicious of his motives in everything he did, stood in opposition to what they saw as his autocratic tendencies, and although he couldn't be faulted for his management of the war, they chafed at his private conduct and handed the leadership over to others, and in a short time caused the downfall of Athens. But at the time of the debate, Alcibiades came forward and made the following remarks:

[16] "I am the best choice to be your leader, Athenians—I have to start this way, since Nicias has attacked me—and at the same time I think I deserve the honor. I am being called out for things that bring honor to my ancestors and to myself, as well as benefits to the state. Because of my exceptional performance in the Olympic games, the Greeks concluded that our power, far from being reduced as they had expected, was even greater than it actually was: because I entered seven chariots—more than any private individual had before—and my chariots placed first, second, fourth, and made us look like winners. It is the custom for such accomplishments to be honored, and at the same time to create the impression of power.

"As my reputation in the city has been through sponsoring choruses and providing other services, I have naturally been envied by the citizens, but in the eyes of foreigners such distinction shows strength. It is not useless folly when a man, at his own expense, benefits not only himself, but the state as well. Nor is it unfair for a man who has reason to think highly of himself to set himself above other men. . . . I know that, during their own lifetimes, such men, and all who have achieved distinction for something, have a poor relationship with other people, especially with their equals. But when they are gone, future generations claim them as kinsmen, and their city boasts that they never harmed anyone and did good for everyone. I have striven for this kind of distinction. I have been railed against for my private life, but stop to consider whether anyone has managed the business of the state better than I have. . . .

[17] ". . . Don't be afraid of this situation. As long as I am young and vigorous, and as long as the luck of Nicias holds out, use both for your own benefit. Don't revoke the decision to send an expedition to Sicily on the grounds that you will meet a superior force. Cities with large but diverse populations are prone to revolutions and upheavals. No one feels invested in his country either through military service or property ownership. Every man makes arrangements to take what he wants from the community by persuasion or by insurrection, and tells himself that if something goes wrong, he can always settle in some other country. Such a mob can't be expected to come to a consensus or join together for a common purpose. It's more likely they will come together piecemeal, whenever it pleases them to do so—especially if, as we have heard, they are experiencing a state of stasis. . . . From all reports, things over there will be as I have said, or even easier—for we will have many barbarians who out of hatred for the Syracusans will join in attacking them. If you plan accordingly, this expedition will cause no inconvenience here at home.

"It's been said that if we launch this expedition we leave ourselves exposed to our enemies. Our fathers faced the same enemies, and the Persians besides, and built an empire based on naval superiority alone. The Peloponnesians have never been more helpless against us than they are now. Even if they are strong enough, and prepared to attack us whether or not we launch the expedition, they can't harm us with their navy. The part of our navy we leave behind is more than a match for them.

[18] "What plausible excuse can we give for holding back and not coming to the aid of our Sicilian allies? We must come to their aid as we promised, and not object that they have never done the same for us. We did not ally ourselves to them so that they could help us here in Greece, but so that by causing trouble for our enemies in Sicily they might prevent those same enemies from attacking us here. This is how we won our empire, and how all empires are won: through the prompt offer of assistance to anyone, barbarian or Greek, who has asked for our intervention. . . .

"It isn't possible for us to decide at what point our empire has reached its limits, but it is imperative, since we have gotten ourselves into this position, that we set our sights on acquiring some territories, and refuse to let others go, since we run the risk of being ruled by others if we do not rule them. You cannot regard inactivity in the same light as others do, unless you change your customs and behavior to be like theirs.

"Therefore, having calculated that we will increase our own power through this intervention, let us launch the expedition, and deal a blow to the pride of the Peloponnesians by setting sail against Sicily in disregard of the current truce. At the same time, we will either rule all of Greece, with the addition of the territory won there in Sicily, or we will destroy the Syracusans, in which case we will have done a favor for both ourselves and our allies. Whether we end up occupying Sicily or sailing home, our navy will provide cover. Even against all of the Sicilians combined we will still be masters of the sea. Don't let the isolationism of Nicias influence you, or be swayed from your purpose by the disagreement he sets up between the young men and their elders, but in your time-honored fashion, as your fathers did, with young and old acting together to raise the city to this height—in this same way, strive to advance the city further. Know that youth and age can do nothing without each other. Know that simplicity, moderation, and discernment are strongest when their forces are joined. Know that if it remains inactive the city will wither, in this case as in others, and its skill in all things will decay, but with every accepted challenge it multiplies its experience and increases its capacity for self-defense—not hypothetically, but with actual results. My conclusion is that the surest way for an interventionist country to destroy itself is to adopt a policy of nonintervention, and that it is always best for a people's established customs and character to shape its policy, with as little innovation as possible."

[19] These were the arguments Alcibiades made. When the Athenians had heard him, as well as the Egestaean and Leontinian exiles who came forward to remind them of their treaties and to plead for aid, they were even more eager than before to launch the expedition. And Nicias, knowing that he would not be able to sway them with the same old arguments, but perhaps might dampen their enthusiasm with the size of the operation he was proposing, came forward again and addressed the assembly.

[20] "Since I see that you are overpowered with the urge to make this expedition, Athenians, I hope these things will turn out as we want, but for the present let me give you my assessment of the situation. According to my intelligence, the Greek cities we plan to attack on this island are large and numerous and not subject to one another; they have no need of a revolution to win their independence, and they certainly aren't looking to exchange their current freedom for the rule of Athens. . . . But the main advantages that they have over us are that they have an abundance of horses, and grow their own grain instead of relying on imports.

[21] "Against such a force we will need more than a small naval detachment: if we want things to go as planned we'll need a significant land force as well to prevent their cavalry from cutting us off from the land, especially if the cities are alarmed and combine their forces, and we are left with no allies but the Egestaeans to defend us with cavalry. It would be dishonorable to be forced into a retreat, or to send for reinforcements later because we didn't plan appropriately from the beginning. From which I conclude that we must set out with a sufficient force, knowing that we are planning to sail far from our own territory, to a strange country where we will be unable to depend, as we have in the past, on a short supply chain from friendly territory. For the four months of winter, it will be difficult even for a messenger to get through.

[22] "It is my recommendation, therefore, that we take a large contingent of hoplites, made up of our own citizens, allies, client states, and whatever Peloponnesian mercenaries we can pay, or persuade, to join us, as well as archers and slingers, in order to hold out against their mounted troops, and to back the entire effort with naval superiority. This is the surest path to success. . . . And what we will especially need are funds, since you can be sure the Egestaeans have inflated their account of the funds they have on hand.

[23] "Even if we arrive with a force not only equal to theirs—except, perhaps, in the number of ground troops—but even superior to them in every respect, we will still have a hard time defeating them and managing a safe withdrawal. . . . For

this reason I would prefer to leave nothing to chance, and prepare thoroughly for all contingencies before setting sail. This is the safest strategy, both for the city as a whole and for our fighting men. If anyone thinks otherwise, I will step aside and leave the command to him."

[24] Nicias made this speech thinking that he might dissuade the Athenians with the magnitude of the undertaking, or, if he were forced to go to war, to set out with as much strength as possible. But the Athenians, far from letting the prospect of a massive mobilization dampen their enthusiasm, became even more hawkish. Nicias' plan had backfired. They accepted his recommendations, and were convinced there was no possibility of failure. An *eros* for the expedition gripped Athens. The older men were convinced there was no stopping so massive a force, and the men of fighting age welcomed a chance to see the world, and had no doubt of coming home safely. The masses who made up the bulk of the army saw an opportunity for steady pay, now and for a long time to come. So pervasive was the feeling in favor of the expedition that if any man had his doubts, he held his tongue for fear of being thought anti-Athenian.

[25] Finally one of the Athenians spoke up and told Nicias not to keep hedging, but to come out and say what forces he needed the city to authorize. Nicias reluctantly said that he would rather have the opportunity to consult with his joint commanders, but he estimated that no fewer than a hundred triremes were needed—supplied as far as possible by the Athenians themselves, and supplemented with those sent by the allies—and a total of no fewer than five thousand Athenian and allied hoplites—more if possible—and Cretan archers and slingers and whatever else was necessary to equip such a force.

[26] When the Athenians heard this, they wasted no time in voting the generals full powers over the size of the deployment and the management of all aspects of the operation, keeping in mind the best interests of the Athenians. And so the preparations began. The allies were notified and the troop rolls were drawn up. The city had recovered from the plague and a decade of war. A new generation had reached fighting age and the city's coffers were full on account of the truce. All the pieces were in place.

PART 2

DISSENT?

While the debate and decision-making in the assembly of Athenian citizen men show us direct democracy at an impressive scale, the large majority of people living in Athens were not on the Pnyx for either of the two debates, let alone in private dining rooms for elite symposia. In the following two chapters, we expand our focus to consider the rest of the city as preparations for the Sicilian Expedition get underway. Thucydides asserted that "an eros for the expedition gripped Athens," but if the mutilation of the herms could be seen as an attempt to sabotage it then some must not have shared that passion. Retrospectively, in the wake of the expedition's defeat, some events in the months beforehand seemed like harbingers of the debacle to come, or even muted warnings against it. As we move from the spring to the summer of the year, we can explore some places where opposition to, or at least a certain queasiness about, the coming military venture may be evident.

As in Part 1, in Part 2 we begin our examination focusing on public activities before moving into private households. In both realms, and for the people associated with each, religious practice becomes a crucial part of life and community. Chapter 3 (Theatron) investigates the City Dionysia, the larger of the two main religious festivals in honor of the god Dionysus. In the citywide celebration lasting five days, participants and spectators included citizens, foreigners, and even slaves. Three days of dramatic performances formed the climax of the festival including, in 415, the premier performance of Euripides' *Trojan Women*. Did that original audience see the play the way modern audiences have, as a powerful argument against war?

From the massive and varied audience in the theater of Dionysus, we move in chapter 4 (Oikos) into the private houses that packed the space within the city walls, and consider the lives of the women who managed them. While the realm of the household is often imagined in stark opposition to the world of the polis, we investigate here the various ways in which the interests of the city and household intersected. We also reconstruct in this chapter the social networks women had among themselves and perhaps across status lines as well. Family and civic religious practice offered opportunities for social bonding. Would this population of women have opposed the coming war? And if so, how might we find traces of their voices?

CHAPTER 3

Theatron

The City Dionysia and Euripides' Trojan Women

Nestled on the south slope of the Acropolis was the theater of Dionysus: a circular orchestra (literally "dancing place") with a low stage building in back. The stone seats still on view in the hillside above are later additions. In the late fifth century, temporary wooden bleachers were erected for the plays. The audience seated in all but the lowest positions had a spectacular view beyond the theater. To their left, mount Hymettus loomed in the southeast, and to their right sparkled the deep blue bay of Phalerum: the mountains and sea that represent uncivilized wilderness in the Greek imagination. The massive audience itself, on full view during the daylight performances, completed the setting. Behind the stage building was the sacred precinct of the god Dionysus, who presided over and helped to judge the tragic and comic competitions that were held in his honor. Each tragedy and comedy enacted in this space, then, inescapably set the words, choices, and deeds of the individual actors in the context of the untamed natural world, the human community, and the transcendent gods. All these elements are fundamental to Athenian drama. Nature, community, and the divine form the constant limits tested by the actions of individual humans.

In the same early spring that the Athenians fell in love with the idea of conquering Sicily, many men who attended the debates on the Pnyx, along with others who had not, sat in this theater and watched the original performance of Euripides' *Trojan Women*. Starting with the Women's Peace Party production of this tragedy, which toured the US in 1915, pacifists in the English-speaking world have deployed it as an impassioned argument against war. How would average Athenians have responded to the performance, in the wake of the brutal victory over Melos the previous fall and with the coming summer's expedition against Sicily on everyone's mind? Could it have made them troubled by the city's decisions, or goaded them to reconsider? To answer this question, we need to pause and investigate the experience of theater in Athens. For while we still read, perform, and watch these plays, and while they can still resonate powerfully after twenty-five hundred years, the relationship of theater to our society is, in practically every respect, radically different from what it was in ancient Greece. At the heart of these differences is the place of ancient drama within civic religion, and in honor of the god Dionysus. Let's start with the god, and then return to the notion of civic religion.

Dionysus

Associated specifically with viticulture and wine, Dionysus was also a nature god more generally, especially connected to the life force itself. In the Attic countryside, he was depicted wearing a black goatskin, and was occasionally even horned himself. He is conventionally accompanied by bands of sex-crazed satyrs or sileni, ithyphallic men with goat tails. His worship often involved the display of giant phalluses as well as the consumption of much wine. Like the intoxication he effected, Dionysus produced both great pleasure and much darker and more frightening impulses, and this double nature is everywhere in his mythology. His birth itself fused sex and violence, life and death, power and weakness. Semele, daughter of the king of Thebes, asked her lover Zeus to make love to her as he did to his immortal wife. Zeus' essential form was a thunderbolt, however, dangerous for a mortal woman. Semele was simultaneously inseminated and vaporized in the process. Zeus rescued the embryo, transferred it to his thigh, and bore the child Dionysus himself.

Because of Hera's jealous hostility toward her husband's love child, Zeus hid the baby in an undisclosed but exotic eastern location, to be raised by nymphs. Many of Dionysus' myths therefore involve his return to Greece, where he is paradoxically at once native (as son of a Theban) and foreign (as invader from the East). This collapse of normally opposing categories is itself characteristic of Dionysus: youthful and somewhat effeminate, he combines masculine and feminine qualities; as a shape-shifting god he appears as beast (often bull) as well as human. But the conflation of categories extends beyond the god, because to worship Dionysus is to drink in the god himself, in some senses to become him. His ecstatic female followers are called *bacchae*, the feminine plural form of one of his own names, Bacchus. To worship Dionysus is to lose your individual identity, to merge with something radically different. This is a powerful but profoundly terrifying experience, and the myths of Dionysus' advent invariably tell of resistance. But resistance to this force of nature is futile, and appalling violence and destruction result from it. Most famously, in Euripides' masterpiece the *Bacchae*, the Thebans' rejection of this "new" god results in the maddened Agave (Semele's sister) leading a throng of women to tear her own son Pentheus to pieces.

Civic Religion and the City Dionysia

Perhaps it was the powerful but unsettling experience of lost and altered identity that made drama, where participants take on new roles or watch others take them, central to the worship of Dionysus. Both major festivals celebrated in his honor in Athens culminated with days of dramatic performances. This is not to imply, however, that the plays were viewed as enactments of religious ritual in the way we would think of that term. For we can return, now, to the notion of "civic religion" mentioned above, and note how it signals the degree to which obligations to the gods were inseparable from the interests of the city. The five-day celebration of the City Dionysia superseded all public business, because it was the public business. The festival combined religious rituals such as animal sacrifice with elements that seem to us strictly political. But there is no indication that Athenians would have thought of these two areas as separable from each other. Clearly the celebration of this and the many other festivals on the civic calendar, all requiring extravagant resources and skilled artistry, simultaneously honored the gods and fostered Athenians' pride in their powerful city. This is why getting a sense of the "civic" part of the equation is as important as the "religious" aspects when we seek to understand the effects on the audience of tragedy in general and Euripides' *Trojan Women* in particular.

Preparations for the City Dionysia started months before the early spring when it took place. Oversight and management of the festival was the responsibility of one of the ten archons in charge of affairs in the city. He chose the three tragic and five (possibly pared back to three during wartime) comic poets from among those who sought to present their plays at the festival. We don't know anything about this process except that it was known as asking for, and being awarded, a chorus. For the chorus was the primary expense, and the most anticipated part of the spectacle, of drama in the fifth century.

Each tragic poet needed a *khorēgos*, "chorus-leader," the wealthy man who undertook to fund the production as a liturgy. He would hire a *didaskalos*, "teacher," sometimes the poet himself, to choreograph and direct the plays, and he would pay for the upkeep of the chorus of fifteen young men during their rehearsals. Perhaps "training" would be a better word for this intensive process. Choral dance was highly athletic and involved exactly synchronized movements, often in rectangular formation. It is not surprising, then, that the men performing in choruses were excused from military training or service. The skill of maintaining your position in the choral line while wearing the head-covering theatrical mask was very like what was demanded of hoplite soldiers, whose helmets obscured their peripheral vision, fighting shoulder to shoulder in the battle line known as the phalanx. A late source reports that Socrates claimed "those who honor the gods most suitably with choruses are the best at war" (Athenaeus, *Deipnosophistes* 14.268E–F). Of course tragic choruses sometimes acted the roles of women, but in tragic performance all roles, male and female, were portrayed by male actors.

Choreographing and rehearsing the chorus and actors for the tragedies and comedies, then, would have occupied a significant amount of time and resources for many months before the festival. Additionally costumes, masks, props, and scenery had to be prepared and paid for. But while we focus on the dramatic performances when we think about the City Dionysia, these were not the only part of the festival that required elaborate planning, preparation, and expense. The other major competition at the Dionysia was the dithyramb, where choruses of fifty danced and sang hymns to Dionysus. Each of Athens' ten tribes prepared a dithyrambic chorus of men and one of boys to compete at the Dionysia. A thousand Athenians, in addition to over a hundred involved in the tragic and comic choruses, thus would have been occupied rehearsing in advance of the festival—a not inconsiderable percentage of the citizen body as a whole. And of course there were animals to be purchased for sacrifice, and the great *pompē*, or procession, to be prepared.

We know the least about the parts of the festival that took place before the dramatic competitions. At some point the cult statue of Dionysus was removed from its seat in his temple below the theater and placed in a temple outside of the city on the road to a village called Eleutherai. Then a procession of young men escorted it into Athens and positioned it in the front and center seat in the theater, so that the god himself could watch the performances. Either before the festival proper or in its first days the *proagōn* ("preliminary contest") occurred, at which each of the dramatic poets, with the actors and chorus of the year's productions, appeared on the stage of the smaller roofed performance hall next to the theater to announce what his plays would be about. Presumably this event functioned like a movie trailer for the upcoming productions. The smaller audience of the proagon would learn something of the plots of the plays to come, and word would spread. The dithyrambic competitions must also have occurred during the first day or two of the festival. But the main event was the pompē: a massive parade of animals to be sacrificed, city officials, the dramatic and dithyrambic performers in elaborate and expensive costume, and floats bearing giant phalluses brought from all over the empire. The procession culminated with the sacrifice of the animals in the temple of Dionysus and the distribution of the meat for an enormous public feast.

Animal sacrifice was fundamental to the religious practice of the Greeks;

the act of killing, dividing, cooking, and consuming an animal brought the community into correct relations with the gods and its own members. At its core it enacted what it was to be human, occupying the middle level between slaughtered animal and honored god. All animal sacrifice shared a set of ritual actions. The animal was led to the altar, where it was sprinkled with water and then barley grains. Some of the hairs from its forehead were snipped and thrown onto the fire blazing at the altar as a preliminary rite. Large animals were then struck on the back of the neck as women standing around raised the ritual cry *ololugē*; the stunned animals' throats were cut, the blood was collected in bowls and poured over the altar. The animal was then opened and the entrails removed. Portions of these would be roasted on spits and consumed by the central participants. Sacrificial butchers skinned and jointed the carcass (the skins, and perhaps other by-products, would be sold to offset the costs of the sacrifice); the tail of the animal and the thigh-bones, covered with fat, were placed on the altar fire as offering to the god. The rest of the meat was cut into equal portions for distribution to the participants in the procession, and then generally to the people of the city, to be consumed at home or perhaps in neighborhood feasts. The enormous scale of the sacrifice at large festivals like the Dionysia could allow twenty thousand or more to have consumed the meat.

We also hear of komoi, exactly like those at the end of a symposium, as part of the Dionysia. Given the strong association between the god and wine it is natural that drunken bands of revelers, perhaps after the sacrificial feast, would have roved the city through the night. The crowd that filled the theater at dawn for the main event surely included many who were hungover and sleep-deprived. But not all of them. It was a large and diverse audience, so we can imagine a wide range of people there, and this is important to remember as we try to excavate the response that the *Trojan Women* generated. Estimates on the seating capacity of the theater vary widely, from six thousand on the low end up to as high as twenty thousand. The audience was primarily citizen men, for whom the city distributed a dole toward the cost of a ticket. But it also included many who would not have been allowed to speak or vote on the Pnyx: visitors from Greek cities around the Athenian empire, noncitizen immigrants who lived in Athens (called metics), children, perhaps even some slaves and women.

This enormous and varied audience presented the city with an irresistible opportunity for self-promotion, and we know about three civically oriented events in particular that preceded the performances. After a sacrifice to purify the space of the theater and a libation poured out by the ten generals (including, in 415, Lamachus, Nicias, and Alcibiades), the annual tribute, in talents of silver, was carried into the theater for the crowd to gaze at. The dazzling wealth and power of the city was thus displayed for citizens and subjects alike. This exhibition of the empire's strength in resources was accompanied by another, as the sons of Athenians who had died in battle paraded into the orchestra in full armor. These war orphans had been brought up at state expense, and the armor for them to fight for Athens as their fathers had was also a gift from the city. The young men were invited to take places of honor at the front of the theater. The message was powerful: Athens nurtures and honors its men, just as they pledge their lives for Athens. Finally, the names of men who had greatly benefited the city were read out and the rewards given them, sometimes a crown or garland, were proclaimed; Demosthenes (who received such a crown) argues that the force of this was "to spur all those listening to do good for the city" (*On the Crown* 120).

The audience waiting for the first of the dramatic performances at the theater of Dionysus, then, had spent days celebrating the god with spectacular parade, solemn sacrifice, joyful feast, raucous revel, and choral song and dance. At the same time the astonishing wealth of the city itself had been constantly before their gaze. By one estimate the outlay for the Dionysia at this period, combining public and private liturgical expense, could have been as high as thirty talents: a sum that could have paid for a fleet of thirty triremes to defend the empire for a month. The Dionysia was a prime opportunity for the Athenians to follow Pericles' exhortation to gaze upon the power of their city and become its lovers. How might watching the tragedies that formed the climax of this festival complicate that desire?

Tragedy

Most of us encounter Greek tragedy for the first time as words on a page. We know some of the stories. Possibly we are familiar with the Homeric legends of Troy and the heroes on both sides of that war. These and other familiar characters and plots form the backbone of tragedy. But reading the drama, especially in English translation, allows us to gloss over what is most alien to us about it. Like Dionysus himself, the drama associated with him is hybrid in its very nature. Tragedy was born, Aristotle theorizes, when a chorus-leader broke off and addressed his chorus. The second and third actors came later, but it is this fundamental division between the original, central chorus and the individual speaker that gives tragedy its form. The actors generally speak quite straightforward Greek in the Attic dialect of their Athenian audience, using an iambic meter that closely approaches the rhythms of natural speech. The chorus, on the other hand, dances and sings, using a different and more archaic-sounding dialect, and often highly dense, complex, allusive language. These two opposing elements sometimes cross over and trade features. The chorus-leader will take part in dialogue, speaking and using the more familiar meter and dialect, while the actors, at moments of heightened emotion, will sing in the more complex lyric meters. But overall, like a musical, the drama consists of speech and song, which alternate in regulated and predictable ways. A prologue spoken by an actor alone, or in dialogue with another, is followed by the *parados* or entrance song of the chorus. Once the chorus has danced its way into the theater it almost always remains throughout the drama and its odes, or *stasimons*, alternate with dialogue scenes ("episodes") among the actors. At the end of the play, the chorus dances out again to its exit song, or *exodos*, and the drama is over.

We read the lines of the chorus rather than listening to their song and watching their dance. Their language is difficult, and in a very different register from that of the actors. Often they are providing background or mythic parallels, or commenting on the emotions they feel as witness to the actions of the play. If you just skip over the choruses, as generations of students have discovered, you follow the plot of the play just fine, and directors of modern productions frequently omit the chorus, or reduce it to a single voice, speaking only the dialogue lines. But for the Athenians, the chorus was equally if not more important than the actors. Remember that the archon's choice of which tragedies to produce was known as "awarding a chorus." Choral singing and dancing was a central part not only of religion, but also traditional education. The numbers involved in the dithyrambic and dramatic choruses just at the Dionysia, as we've seen, were considerable. But this was just one festival. Choruses formed part of the spectacle and offering to the gods at dozens of festivals throughout the year. Most citizen boys and men would have at least passing experience with choral dance, and while our evidence is weaker for women in Athens, they danced as well in many Greek cities. We cannot have any sense of what tragedy was like for its original audience without making ourselves focus on the chorus as intensely as on the actors.

This hybrid nature of tragic form, comprising song as well as speech, and performed by coordinated group as well as individual actors, replicates and partially overlaps with some other characteristically duplex aspects of the plays. The myths that provide tragic plots almost always portray the suffering of powerful and ambivalent individuals, but their actions are seen to some degree through the ways in which they affect those around them. Thus the formal combination of actor and chorus embodies the relations and tensions between individual and community that are at the heart of many tragedies. Less explicit than this common theme, the tragedies also maintain a curiously doubled perspective on space and time. While the mythic material is almost always removed from Athens in space (tragedies are most frequently set in Troy, or on the Peloponnese, or, notoriously, at Thebes), and is set in the legendary past, issues, ideas, and rhetoric from the Athenian present form a simultaneous undercurrent to a great deal of the action. This temporal double vision is likely related to the formal and thematic split between one and many— the individualistic epic hero finds himself, in tragedy, in relation with the more recent collective that is the polis. Euripides in particular is fond of setting myth and its glorious heroes against a more modern and familiar reality, using one to illuminate and critique the other. Experienced audiences would have been ready to hear resonance of contemporary issues against the backdrop of ancient myth. In 415, aspects of the Trojan War on display in Euripides' tragedies would plausibly remind the audience of conflicts closer to home.

Finally, the effect of tragedy upon its audience, insofar as we can reconstruct it, had a sort of doubleness to it as well. Plato and Aristotle, writing in the following century, stress the emotional response tragedy elicits (although they differ notably on whether that's a good or a bad thing). The extreme nature of tragic action, the heightened language along with the music and dance, produced intense emotions in the mass audience, and there are numerous stories of the tears, groans, and other uproar that offered witness to these emotions. But Aristophanes, a comic poet contemporary with late fifth-century tragedy, seems rather to emphasize the intellectual, moral component of the works. The best tragedian, he claims, is the one most able to make the city better. Tragedy forces its characters into impossible situations, constrains them to make choices between equally terrible actions; frequently it stages debate between competing or conflicting goods. What must be done when obligations to the city clash with the needs of the household, or when individual honor endangers community security? These characteristic tragic dilemmas allow probing examination of assumptions about what is good, pious, just. Perhaps in unsettling contrast to the powerful loyalty to the city evinced in the opening ceremonies discussed above, tragedies often seem to us to expose tensions and contradictions beneath the city's values and ideals. A day at the dramatic festival offered a workout for both the intellect and the emotions. From this potent combination sprang the intense tragic pleasure that brought the massive audiences flocking into the theater.

Euripides and His Tragedies

We are now equipped to consider the audience of 415, squeezed onto their bleachers along with friends, neighbors, and army buddies; also present, even if in smaller numbers, were metics, representatives from the empire's allied cities, possibly some slaves and women. They have witnessed the spectacular display of the year's tribute and the parade of war orphans. Perhaps some were sons of friends or family. They have heard the names of civic benefactors and (if

Demosthenes is right) perhaps some have warmed with patriotic ambitions. They gaze around at the enormous crowd, squint into the sun rising over Hymettus, and settle in for some drama from that most controversial of the three most famous tragedians, Euripides.

As mentioned, each tragic poet presented three tragedies at the festival. Decades earlier these trilogies had often been linked in plot, although Aeschylus' *Oresteia* is our only complete remaining instance of this; in the latter half of the fifth century playwrights had abandoned the practice to present three unrelated tragedies. But in 415 Euripides seems to have been experimenting with linked if still independent plays. He is the playwright most known for his innovation. Might he have been employing it in the service of some larger message to his audience about the looming war?

The biographical tradition about Euripides paints him as a dyspeptic recluse, contemptuous of the ignorance of his fellow men, and bitter that they failed to appreciate his art sufficiently. He left Athens, supposedly in disgust and despair, soon after 408, and went to stay at the Macedonian court of Archelaus. There he lived briefly until he was torn apart by Molossian hounds in divine retribution for his blasphemous writings. While scholars are skeptical about the hounds, the skeleton of this account is still often presented as historical. There is something that appeals to us in the idea of a lone genius, unappreciated by his contemporaries. Perhaps lurking beneath this romantic notion is the little thrill of feeling smarter than the Athenians; we see what they could not in our appreciation of this unhappy but brilliant poet. We can recognize and accept the harsh truths about politics and life that his audience did not want to hear.

But most of the details in the biographical tradition come from his own plays or comic satire, and his prominence in Aristophanes and other comedians implies fascination and popularity more than rejection. When news of his death reached Athens, Sophocles publicly donned a cloak of mourning, and brought his actors and chorus onto the platform at the proagon without their festive crowns as a mark of respect for his fellow poet. The crowd then present wept their loss, and the Athenians erected a cenotaph in his memory. This anecdote, along with records of successful revivals of his plays through the fourth century, casts doubt on the image of a deeply unpopular and bitter Euripides. By 415, Euripides was sixty-five years old, and his tragedies, innovative as they often were, had been regularly performed at the Dionysia for over twenty years.

While many in the theater would not have attended the smaller proagōn at the beginning of the festival, when the plots of the plays were revealed, word would have gotten around. By now everyone would have known that all three of Euripides' tragedies involved the Trojan War: its prelude, a moment during the fighting, and its aftermath. We have only fragments of the first two plays, but can reconstruct at least the outlines of their plots.

Alexander, the title character of the first tragedy, was the young prince of Troy whose seduction (or abduction, depending on which version of the story you prefer) of Helen would ignite the Trojan War. While pregnant with him, his mother Hecuba had dreamed that she gave birth to a burning branch. This was correctly seen as an omen that her baby would have ruinous consequences. In an attempt to avoid these Hecuba and her husband Priam, king of Troy, exposed the child. Unknown to them, though, he was rescued and raised by shepherds. The tragedy *Alexander* focuses on an episode of his young manhood, when he returns to his parents' palace ignorant of his own identity. Other shepherds have accused him of hubris, but he defends himself successfully in a trial before the king. Priam finds him innocent and rewards him by allowing him to participate in a ritual set of games. In a strange repetition of the earlier attempt to kill him in his infancy, his success in these games so threatens another of Priam's sons that he and Hecuba plot to kill this brilliant young shepherd. They are dramatically prevented at the last minute by the revelation of his true identity as their son and brother. The audience knows that all the decisions in this story ended up enabling the destruction of Troy: the decision to expose the baby rather than killing it outright, Priam's decision in the youth's favor, and the discovery of his identity that prevents his murder the second time, will all conspire to allow Paris to steal Helen and bring war and devastation to Troy. Not just once but repeatedly the Trojans have, but fail to take, the opportunity to prevent the coming war. Yet the audience surely felt sympathy for Alexander, intense suspense as he faced death, and relief at his rescue. The next two plays, however, would vividly show the destructive repercussions of his survival.

We have much less of the second tragedy, *Palamedes*, than we do of the first. It takes place near the beginning of the Trojan War and focuses on the Greek side. Odysseus, jealous of Palamedes' reputation for wisdom, frames him for treason. In a trial scene Palamedes gives an eloquent self-defense, but the prosecuting Odysseus is the more persuasive speaker. Palamedes is condemned to death. His brother sends word to their father back in Greece, and the tragedy foretells the vengeance he will take when the Greek ships return from Troy. If the *Alexander* left the audience with the impression that the Trojans were in some sense responsible for the war to come, the *Palamedes* left no very savory impression of the Greeks. Jealousy over status and prestige, and treachery in their protection, were clearly common to both sides in this conflict. Both victors and vanquished in the Trojan War will face horrific consequences.

As the audience awaited Euripides' third tragedy, then, they were not simply admiring the precision of the dance or the haunting melodies of the choral songs, but also contemplating themes and patterns emerging from the first two dramas. In both plays, fierce competition for the rewards of elite status and reputation had threatened to erupt into violence. In both, a plot had been hatched to further the agendas of those who saw their positions at risk. Perhaps most unsettling was how what looked like reasoned debate over a course of action led in both plays to a problematic decision. For anyone looking for resonances between these themes and the issues of the moment, connections would not have been difficult to find. We've already seen the extent to which the personal rivalry between Nicias and Alcibiades lurked behind their positions on the Sicilian Expedition. Pericles had proudly extolled the virtues of democratic debate: the Athenians were accustomed to thinking of elite rivalry and agonistic decision-making as beneficial to the polis. Might the *Alexander* and *Palamedes* have cast a new and troubling light on these assumptions?

The *Trojan Women* opens with an old woman in rags prostrate in the dust of the orchestra and a god high on the roof of the stage building above her. A god at the opening of a play is unusual. More frequently they entered, sometimes conveyed by the stage machinery, at the end; that's where we get our expression *deus ex machina*. This unexpected god identifies himself as Poseidon, friend of the Trojans. He is angry at the Greeks not only for their victory over Troy, but for their impious treatment of its sacred places ("Every god's altar is now drenched in blood. The city's king, Priam, is himself lying slaughtered at the steps of Zeus' altar, inside his very own palace. The altar of Zeus, the protector of his palace!" 15–17). He identifies the woman still prostrate below (and unaware of his presence) as Hecuba, queen of Troy, and tells us that she is grieving the loss of her husband and all her sons in the war. She and the other Trojan women are awaiting the departure of the Greek army, not yet knowing to which commander they have been awarded as slaves.

Having fulfilled the prologue's function of letting the audience know when and where they are, and who the figure is on stage, Poseidon starts to exit. But then there is another surprise. Athena, Poseidon's rival, enters and asks if the two can put aside their grudge. The first exchange between the two actors alerts the audience to who the entering figure is, but the Athenians certainly recognized their tutelary goddess from her spear and helmet, as they had recognized Poseidon from his trident. The famous competition between Poseidon and Athena for precedence over Athens was depicted on the west pediment of the Parthenon just above and behind the audience sitting in the theater, so the two figures and their mutual antipathy would have been familiar to everyone.

While Athena had supported the Greeks throughout the long siege, and had been instrumental in hatching the plot that led to Troy's final defeat, she has now come to seek aid from Poseidon in punishing them. Astonished, he asks her "how can you leap from excessive love to excessive hate?" She is angry, she tells him, because of the Greek treatment of her temples. For the second time the victorious army's sacrilegious behavior is marked, and now its deadly consequences are set forth in detail: Poseidon will roil the Aegean Sea and fill the shoals around Delos and the other islands with corpses. The imagery was frightening and immediate for Athens with its naval empire. Many of the thousands in the theater had personal experience of sea travel, and knew the terrors storms at sea could threaten. That shipwreck could be the consequence of impious behavior in military victory was much more immediately applicable to their own lives than it can be for a modern audience.

Having settled the terrible fate to come for the returning Greeks, the gods leave the roof of the stage building. Hecuba stirs and begins alternately to lament over her losses and attempt to rouse herself to face them. She calls the chorus of Trojan women to grieve with her and they dance in, mourning their own fates, and wondering where in the Greek world they will be sent. They worry that it will be Corinth or Sparta; they hope that it might be the famous and fortunate Athens, in one of Euripides' common offerings to the local pride of his audience. They are even drawn to the possibility of a home in Sicily, heralded for its crowns of excellence! But they remain focused on comforting their queen. They will stay on the stage with Hecuba through the full tragedy, as she is faced in the four succeeding episodes with the consequences, each more harrowing than the last, of her city's destruction.

Each of these four episodes centers on a confrontation with some aspect of Hecuba's loss. First her daughter Cassandra, then her daughter-in-law Andromache, then Helen herself, the cause of the war, enter the stage for a scene. Each leaves Hecuba more defeated and despairing than they found her. Finally, the Greek herald Talthybius enters with the corpse of her grandson, Andromache's child Astyanax. Odysseus (who in later tragedy tends to be more slippery and villainous than Homer makes him) has persuaded the Greeks to kill the child, to prevent his wreaking vengeance on the Greeks for their treatment of Troy. In the heartrending final episode, Hecuba prepares the body of this small boy, who had been the last remaining male of her line, for burial on the shield of his father, her dead son Hector. Then she and the chorus process off the stage, to the thunderous sound of Troy's towers collapsing in the conflagration she dreamed of back at the opening of the *Alexander*.

Audience Response

Reading this summary, or even the full play, gives only a pale impression of the strong emotional effect it can create. A performance will be more effective, even one without music. But the full production that first audience would have seen, including choral song and dance and the anguished musical keening of the actors, must have been gut-wrenching. Plutarch tells us that the fourth-century tyrant Alexander of Pherae, a notoriously brutal character who terrorized his own people and others, once left a performance of the *Trojan Women* halfway through because, as he later told the principal actor, he was ashamed to be seen weeping for Andromache and Hecuba when he had never pitied any man he murdered. Aristotle calls pity and fear the most tragic of emotions, and goes on to tell us that Euripides is the most tragic of the poets. The *Trojan Women* is arguably Euripides' most pity-inspiring play. It is precisely the intensity of the pity we feel for the women of Troy that has given this tragedy its reputation as an antiwar play. Over the past hundred years productions abound whenever military conflict is brewing or in progress, and urge audiences to consider the fates of noncombatants. In the Athens of 415, male citizens had just voted in favor of a major military expedition in a distant land across a dangerous sea. Would the tears they shed for the women of Troy nudge them to reconsider their choice? What about those in the audience who hadn't been part of that debate, but who would face the consequences of the decision?

The pity we feel for the women in the play is intensified by Euripides' use of a kind of utterance that would have been familiar to his audience from their lives: funerary lament. One of the few areas in which women's voices were regularly heard in public was in this context. Women were intimately involved with rituals for the dead, and their mourning cries and songs were a traditional part of burial ceremony. Yet from early on the city sought ways to limit these voices, evidently for two diverging reasons. First is the possibility that female voices of lament would paralyze male resolve to face danger for the city. As they do in the lyrics and dialogue of the *Trojan Women*, funeral dirges often contrast the unfortunate plight of the survivors with their happier past. The focus, that is, is as much on the gap the dead man has left behind as on his qualities. Women mourning their men killed in war would focus attention on their own plight as survivors, and might make it more difficult to get other men to participate in the city's military. A character in Aeschylus' *Seven against Thebes* warns the women of the chorus, who are expressing fear of such loss during a battle, that they will weaken the men's resolve to fight. This response to female lamentation, for the ancient audience as for us, would indeed push against military conflict. Perhaps this was the reason that the city appropriated the burial of war dead, and replaced the traditional individual laments of female relatives with an official funeral oration for all, given by a man chosen by the city. This was the occasion for the oration of Pericles' we have been using to get a sense of the city's ideals; his strategy of moving focus from the war dead to the glorious city they fought for is common in these orations. Insofar as soldiers and oarsmen in the audience linked the Trojan women's plight to the possibility that their own wives or daughters could face the same fate, they might experience hesitation about the expedition to come. If they connected the pitiable figures on stage to the women of Melos, sold into slavery after their city fell to the Athenian siege the previous year, perhaps they were moved to feel regret for that decision.

But there was a second, more pressing danger attending prominent and emotive lamentation: that it could provoke its hearers to anger and vengeance. This response to female lamentation is also well-attested in tragedy. In all the plays concerning the Orestes myth, his sister Electra incites him to vengeance against their mother Clytemnestra by prolonged and emotional lamentation over their murdered father Agamemnon. Limiting the opportunity for such dangerous voices to be heard in public removed one source of instigation to dangerous blood feuds in the interests of civic solidarity.

The female voices of lament so prominent in Euripides' *Trojan Women*, then, evoke not only pity for the central figures, but anger against their victimizers. Modern productions tend to structure this pity and anger as purely pushing against whatever war is on the horizon: the Greek soldiers are despicable, the cause of the war is questionable, its consequences horrific. The audience emerges at the end of the tragedy emotionally exhausted but safely reaffirmed in what was likely their initial assumption: that "war is not the answer"; perhaps they are ready to turn their outrage against the government currently contemplating or conducting war.

But a slightly different response would have been equally plausible in 415. Could the audience's rage toward those responsible for the women's fates be channeled into a desire for retribution, rather than an attempt to stop war? Avenging the destruction of Troy would be nonsensical in any literal sense, of course. But as was the case with the first response, this one depends on the audience feeling parallels between events on stage and in their own experience. The Sicilian Expedition was to be launched in support of the Egestaeans and the Leontinians against Syracuse, and Thucydides tells us that the Egestaeans were descended from the Trojans. Anger on behalf of the Trojans could well intensify motivation for the defense of their descendants. Additionally Syracuse, just a few years ago, had depopulated the city of the Leontinians just as the tragedy showed the Greeks doing to Troy. If the anguished keening of the women in the theater roused the audience to feel anger and thirst for vengeance, that could as well energize them for the fight to come as deter them from it.

The ambiguity of the tragedy's effect is traceable elsewhere as well. Consider the lines that would most explicitly have evoked the Athenians' immediate situation. These come from Cassandra as she attempts to persuade her mother that even though the Trojans lost the war, they are still more fortunate than the victorious Greeks. She contrasts the sorry fate of those fighting far from home, buried in foreign soil, with the glory of those defending their land against invaders. Nicias' argument against the Sicilian Expedition, that protecting the city was preferable to pursuing conquest in distant lands, could well have occurred to some in the audience as they listened to Cassandra. Yet every Athenian over the age of thirty-five would also remember vividly the perspective of their own besieged city. They and their families had watched from Athens' walls as the Spartans invaded and ravaged the surrounding land through the early years of the Peloponnesian War. The glorification of defending one's city against such invaders could have stirred patriotic pride in past victories as plausibly as anxiety about future defeats. That the villainous Helen and Menelaus are repeatedly marked as Spartan throughout the tragedy would only increase this resonance.

One other moment in the play is often cited as a reference to the Athenians' current world. Hecuba, grieving for Astyanax, proclaims

> What should be
> the epitaph inscribed on your tomb?
> This child the army of the Greeks killed out of fear?
> Such an epitaph ought to bring shame on Greece. (1188–92)

Might that small defenseless boy evoke in the audience the tiny island of Melos, destroyed by the Athenians out of fear of letting it remain neutral? Perhaps. But within the play the image can have a quite different resonance.

The scene before Astyanax's burial presents a trial, just as the two earlier tragedies had. Menelaus comes to retrieve Helen from among the prisoners, and Hecuba, concerned that her beauty will deter her husband from punishing her, asks to speak against her. Helen then responds in her own defense. The episode is very different in tone from the rest of the tragedy, allowing a break from the high emotion that precedes and follows. The core of the argument between the two women is the question of the causes of the war: who or what, exactly, is at fault for the terrible destruction we have been watching? For Hecuba, Helen is personally responsible, just as at several earlier moments in the play people have spoken of her the sole cause. In Hecuba's account Helen is the subject, rather than object, of desire: she fell in love both with the handsome Paris and the wealth of Troy. Following Paris from Sparta she ignited the long war. In her own defense Helen also blames eros, although in her account she is a passive victim of Aphrodite. In general, Greek myth connected desire to war in the love affair between Aphrodite, goddess of desire, and Ares, god of war. Desire in myth has an irresistible force. No wonder, perhaps, that Thucydides chose to describe Athens' decision to invade Sicily as the product of eros.

The trial ends with Menelaus judging Hecuba's argument to be the right one: Helen is at fault, and he vows to kill her as punishment. Both Hecuba and the audience know, however, that he will fail to do this. Desire for Helen's beauty will overcome him once again, and she will suffer no consequences for the years of carnage and ruin she set in motion. In the *Alexander* and the *Palamedes*, trials had led to troubling results. This time, Euripides suggests, the decision made after debate is the correct one, but it nevertheless will fail to achieve the correct outcome.

In addition to Helen's claim to have been victim of Aphrodite, she makes another significant argument: that the Trojan War was not Aphrodite's, but Hecuba's fault. Helen reminds the audience of what they had seen a few hours before in the *Alexander*: Hecuba and Priam knew that Paris would cause the destruction of Troy. They should have killed him when they had the chance. When Hecuba caresses the broken body of her small grandson and rails against the Greeks for the "barbarity" and cowardice of the deed, she mocks the "fear" that drove them to it, but leaves out what it was they feared. We know, though—the Greek herald Talthybius told us when he announced the plan to Andromache. In killing Astyanax, the Greeks sought to prevent vengeance for the destruction of Troy. They sought to prevent a future war in retaliation for the past one. In other words, in hurling Astyanax from the towers of Troy, the Greeks have done precisely what Hecuba was unable to do with Paris: kill a son to prevent a future war. The body of the boy forces us to recognize what it looks like to kill a child as an act of preemption. Even to stop all that bloodshed, the price seems too high. The play seems emphatically to deny that there is any reasonable human means to prevent war. It certainly shows us the many terrors of defeat. But the lesson may well be not to lose.

The audience at the City Dionysia of 415, like any mass audience, will have had varying responses to the play. We've seen how the tragedy might have moved some to shrink from war, but could equally have stirred patriotic fervor in others; the preceding days and rituals of the festival would, as we have seen, have nudged them in that direction. Women possibly reacted to the dramas differently from men, and those who had lost fathers, husbands, or sons differently from those who had not. Some passages of the tragedy had special resonance for those with the experience of being displaced, or for parents who had buried children. But it seems unlikely that any would leave the theater thinking anything different about war from what they already knew: it is an inevitable part of life with devastating consequences for the losing side.

The opening of the *Trojan Women*, as we've seen, had like the closing of the *Palamedes* reminded the audience that things didn't go so well for the victors of the Trojan War, either. Both elite competition in advance of the fighting and blasphemous behavior in its course, particularly mistreatment of sacred places, was what got victorious armies into trouble. The play might have suggested to many Athenians not so much that the Sicilian Expedition was a mistake, as that it was imperative to ensure the commander was the type of man who would never commit an impiety. In this they could be confident about Nicias, but perhaps less sure of Alcibiades.

There were three tragedies from each of two other poets at that festival of 415. One of these was Xenocles, who had a reputation for staging monsters with spectacular special effects. We have only the titles of the tragedies he produced that year, from which they seem to have been more narrowly focused on great men and their clashes with gods and society. They must have been very different from the palace intrigues, trials, and lamentations of Euripides' set, but they, too, may well have had contemporary resonance in light of Athenian fascination with the individual power of the charismatic Alcibiades. When all the performances were over, the ten judges, one chosen by lot from each tribe, cast their votes among the three poets who had been awarded a chorus that year. The best guess about how this obscure process worked is that they each inscribed their choice for best tragic poet on a ballot and threw it into an urn. From these ten ballots, the presiding archon picked five; the poet who received the most votes of these five took first place, the one with the next most took second, and the remaining poet took third. If the five votes first chosen didn't yield a clear first-prize winner, two more ballots were chosen; if there were still a tie, ballots would be chosen one at a time until it was broken.

The system seems bizarre. A poet could conceivably get first prize with only three votes out of ten, even if a different poet got all seven remaining votes. Yet the lottery was very much a part of democratic life in Athens. It was felt to cut down on the possibility of bribery, and at the same time to give the god a say in the process. Dionysus, remember, or at least his cult statue, had been escorted to a seat in the front row of the theater at the opening of the festival. Perhaps the system also allowed a degree of face-saving for the losing productions; after all, they might actually have had more votes than the victors. It certainly might account for some known decisions which seem inexplicable to us. Sophocles' great *Oedipus the King*, after all, received only second place. This year it was Xenocles who got the winning votes first; Euripides had to be content with the second prize. The much later author Aelian, whom we can thank for dating the *Trojan Women* to this year, was clearly scandalized by this decision:

> Xenocles (whoever he was) was *first* with *Oedipus* and *Lycaon* and *Bacchae* and *Athamas* as satyr-play. After this Euripides was second, with *Alexander* and *Palamedes* and the *Trojan Women* and *Sisyphus* as satyr-play. Isn't that ridiculous? That Xenocles won, and Euripides was defeated, and with those plays! The judges were either intellectually incapable of a proper decision, or else they were bribed.(*Varia Historia* 2.8)

The day after the City Dionysia finished, an assembly was held in the theater to examine the conduct of all the officials, and to ensure that nobody had any complaints about the way in which all parts of the festival had worked. It must have felt like a pretty sparse crowd after the thousands of bodies that had squeezed in for the plays, and those who spoke seemed somewhat colorless after extremes of emotions expressed in the days before. Slaves were already pulling down the temporary seating erected for the festival, and picking up the trash. In the Agora, men skipping the assembly were chewing over their favorite odes and episodes with the metics and those foreigners who hadn't already cleared out of the city. And in women's quarters, mistresses with their slaves were humming the catchier cadences of the lyrics and odes of the *Trojan Women*.

Primary Source Interlude

Euripides' Trojan Women, *excerpts*

In the tragedy's prologue, the god Poseidon agrees to help Athena wreak vengeance on the Greek forces for their treatment of the sacred places of Troy. Hecuba laments her fate, then calls the chorus of enslaved Trojan women to come join her in grieving. In the first episode, the Greek herald Talthybius arrives to escort Hecuba's daughter Cassandra to Agamemnon, the Greek king to whom she has been awarded. Here Cassandra tries to console Hecuba by arguing that the defeated Trojans were in fact more fortunate than the victorious Greeks.

365–405.
Cassandra.
[12 lines omitted]
I will show you that this city is more blessed
than the Achaeans. I am filled with the god,
but I can still speak objectively. The Greeks,
for the sake of one woman and her lust,
hunted down Helen and lost the lives of thousands.
Their wise leader, to gain the things he hated,
gave the life he held most dear, trading the pleasures
of his own home and children for his brother's wife,
who left home willingly and without being forced.
And when they beached their ships beside Scamander,
they died and died, and not even to win back
their own lands and homes. The ones who went to war
never saw their children again, nor did their wives'
hands shroud them, but they came to lie in a foreign land.
The situation was the same for the Greeks at home.
They died bereft, childless in their own homes

because they raised their children for others. There is
no tomb they can visit to make their offerings to the dead.
You can see how worthy the Greeks are of praise.
It's best to keep quiet about some things that followed:
the muse does not intend my song to be a list of scandals.
But now consider the Trojans, and how gloriously
they died for their country. Those who fell to the spear
had friends to carry their bodies back to their own houses,
and were buried in the soil of their own native land,
and their own wives were there to wrap them in their shrouds.
Those who survived a battle were able to live another day
in their own homes, but the Greeks enjoyed no such pleasures.
And now consider the case of Hector, which you find so distressing.
In death he enjoys a reputation as the best of men,
and it was the coming of the Greeks that made this possible.
If they had stayed home, his excellence would have gone unnoticed.
Paris married Zeus' daughter. If he hadn't, no one
would have paid any attention to his marriage. A sensible man
will avoid war, but if it comes, the city attaches no shame
to a good death, only to the man who dies ingloriously.
So you see there is no need for you to pity your country, mother,
or my marriage bed, for by going as Agamemnon's bride
I will destroy both your enemies and mine.

After Talthybius leads Cassandra off stage, the chorus sings their first ode.

First Stasimon

Chorus.   [*strophe*
Put into my mouth, o Muse,
a new song, a lament for Ilium,
tuned to the sound of women weeping.
For now I lift my voice to sing of Troy,
and how the Argives' wheeled contraption trapped
Trojans in their town, how the gold-trimmed horse
disgorged the armored Greeks within the gates of Troy.

The people rose and shouted from a rocky place:
"Your troubles are over, Troy, go now
and bring this wooden image to the temple

as a tithe to Zeus' daughter, guardian of Troy."
Young and old, the Trojans filled the streets,
rejoiced and sang, and little knew
the gift they praised would give them to their doom.
     [*antistrophe*

To the city gates of Troy
the Phrygians were rushed along en mass
to bring this image made of mountain pine—
this ambush fashioned by the cunning Greeks—
to offer Troy's destruction to the goddess.
With ropes the Trojans towed it like a ship
to anchor at the blood-stained altar of Pallas.

And so the darkness fell on all their labor and rejoicing.
The night was full of the piping of flutes,
and the strains of Phrygian music,
and the young girls danced together and sang
a chorus of celebration, and in all the houses of Troy
the fires blazed and dwindled to a glow of coals
as the unwary Trojans settled down to sleep.
     [*epode*

I was there in the chorus
circling the temple, singing hymns
to the mountain-dwelling daughter of Zeus,
when a blood-chilling cry echoed through Pergama.
Frightened children hid among their mothers' skirts.
Ares released the ambush, according
to the plan of Pallas Athena,
and around the altars of Troy there was slaughter.
So many young husbands left headless in their beds,
so many mourning wives who went as war brides with the Greeks,
taking nothing with them
to remind them of their homeland but their grief.

*In the episode following this ode, Andromache (wife of Hecuba's son Hector)
enters; the two women are interrupted by Talthybius who delivers the news
that the Greeks, persuaded by Odysseus, will kill Andromache's child Astyanax.
Talthybius takes the child away. In this final scene he returns with the body and
the women prepare it for burial.*

1123–1250
Talthybius.
Hecuba: the last ship of the Greeks is prepared to sail,
loaded with all there was left to plunder.
Neoptolemus, son of Achilles,
has heard some news of banished Peleus,
some alarm that makes him set a course for Thessaly.
There is nothing left to keep him here.
He will take Andromache. It made me weep
to hear her praying to the tomb of Hector,
begging that her dead child be buried—
your Hector's son, who had the life crushed out of him
when he was thrown from the walls of Troy.
The Greeks feared this great bronze shield
that Hector carried before him into battle, and she
begged that it not be taken as plunder back to Greece
to stand in the bedchamber she'll be forced to share,
but that it serve as a sepulcher for her child.
She asked that her son be given into your arms and,
with whatever small means you have at your disposal,
that his body be prepared for burial. Her master's haste
prevents her from placing her child's body in the grave.
When you have arranged his body for burial,
we will spread the earth over him, and then set sail.
Do what is required of you as quickly as you can.
But there is one task I have taken off your hands:
as I crossed the Scamander, I washed the corpse
and cleaned his wounds. And now I will go
and break the earth for his grave, so that working together
we can make short work of it, and be on our way.

Hecuba.
Set Hector's bronze-rimmed shield on the ground.
The sight of it pains me. You Greeks—
your spears are more penetrating than your minds.
He was a child. Why did you fear him?
Why the need to devise new forms of slaughter
for a child? Were you afraid he would rebuild Troy,
this fallen city? Even when great Hector was alive,
we still died by the thousands. Now we have nothing,
and you were afraid of a little child? I despise fear

when it involves the abandonment of reason.
O dearest one! You came to such an unlucky end.
If you had died defending the city in the full
flower of youth, as a husband and a godlike king,
you would have been blessed, if such things are blessings.
You looked forward to these things, and knew them
in your soul, but you never enjoyed the fruits
of your knowledge. Poor child, the walls of the city
that cradled you, crushed the fair head your mother
loved so much, covered with so many kisses.
Your skull was shattered, and—. It's too shameful.
Your hands, so like the hands of your father, are limp.
Your dear mouth, so full of brave words, is silent.
You deceived me when you tugged on my dress and said:
O grandmother, I will cut a lock of my hair for you,
and with my friends I will honor your grave with feasting,
and make an offering of prayers. But it is I,
a homeless, childless old woman, who buries you, a child.
Oh! The times I held you, and nursed you, and
lay beside you as you slept—all gone! What should be
the epitaph inscribed on your tomb?
This child the army of the Greeks killed out of fear?
Such an epitaph ought to bring shame on Greece.
But you shall inherit your father's bronze-backed shield
if only as a casket. O protector of Hector's well-turned arm,
you have lost the one who took care of you best.
The mark he left on your armstrap is dear to me,
the exquisite bronze rim, salted with the sweat
that fell from Hector's brow in the midst of battle.
Come, bring burial attire for this poor little corpse,
though our fate has left us with little enough to give him.
          Take whatever I have.
Only a fool thinks present prosperity
is enough to grant him security for life. This is the way
of fortune: it is a faithless companion, and can't be relied upon.
No man can ever be insulated in his good fortune.

Chorus.
Out of the spoils of Troy, these women bring
garments to dress the dead for burial.

Hecuba.
O child, your grandmother adorns you with gifts of your own—
but not as she would have had you been victorious
over other young men in contests of horses or archery.
Helen, hateful to the gods, has robbed you of these things
and of your life, and destroyed your entire house.

Chorus.
Ai! Ai! My heart
breaks for you, it breaks
for the great lord of the city
who would have been.

Hecuba.
These are the fine Trojan garments I should have given you
when you married the finest woman in Asia. And you,
once victorious mother of a thousand triumphs, Hector's
beloved shield, receive this crown. Your death is not
the body's death. It is more fitting to honor you than
the weapons of the clever devil Odysseus.

Chorus.
Ai! Ai!
The earth will receive you,
child, a bitter loss.
Lament, mother.

Hecuba.
Ai! Ai!

Chorus.
A song of mourning.

Hecuba.
Oh!

Chorus.
Oh, unbearable suffering!

Hecuba.
I will doctor your wounds with bandages,

a wretched doctor—I have the name, but not the skill.
Your father will tend to you among the dead.

Chorus.
Strike, strike your head—
give it a beat of lamentation—
io!

Hecuba.
O dearest women.

Chorus.
Hecuba, speak to your friends. Speak.

Hecuba.
The gods thought of nothing but making me suffer—
and Troy, hated above all other cities.
We made our offerings in vain.
If the gods had not overthrown us and tumbled
our city to the ground, we would have disappeared
and gone unremembered in the songs the poets
pass on to future generations.
Go, bury this poor little body in the tomb.
He has been dressed well enough to meet the dead.
I think it matters little to the dead if given costly gifts.
These things are the occasion of empty boasting for the living.

CHAPTER 4

Oikos

Athenian Women in and out of the Household

After a day's tragic performances at the Dionysia, the audience would sit back for some comic relief. Four years after the events we're examining, the comic poet Aristophanes produced what perhaps remains his most famous comedy: the *Lysistrata*. Like Euripides' *Trojan Women*, the *Lysistrata* is popularly produced today as an antiwar play, but unlike the tragedy, the comedy makes its antiwar message absurdly explicit.

Aristophanes has the women of Greece, led by the title character, hatch a successful plot to bring an end to the war between Athens and Sparta that had resumed two years earlier in 413. The younger wives in both Athens and Sparta stage a sex strike, and the older women of Athens take over the Acropolis to control the flow of the resources stored there. Once the plot is underway, an Athenian official shows up to put a stop to the nonsense. He harangues the throng of protesting women occupying the high point of the city; this is just like that other time, he says, when a meeting of the assembly to discuss the Sicilian Expedition was disrupted by someone's drunken wife yelling "oh! Adonis!" from her roof.

The official is comparing Lysistrata's plot to stop the war within the play to something the audience is evidently expected to remember from their own lives, something that happened in 415, as the assembly debated preparations for the Sicilian Expedition. What could that something be? Is it plausible that the notion of a plot by the city's women to oppose a war was not simply a figment of Aristophanes' fertile imagination, but was inspired by something that had really happened? What is the official talking about? To answer this question, we need to ask more, turning from the world of men we have focused on thus far to that of their mothers, wives, and daughters. What were the lives of Athenian women like? Can we think of them as a coherent bloc with unified interests? If so, were they likely to have opposed the Sicilian Expedition? And if they did, how might they have made that opposition audible to the city at large?

The attempt to excavate women's attitudes in classical Athens immediately runs up against the challenges of interpreting our source material. There are no extant texts from this period written by women, and the male-authored texts must be read with careful attention to the ideologies and assumptions that shape them. This chapter, then, will necessarily venture outside of the specifics of what happened in 415. It is impossible to form conclusions about the likelihood of female dissent to public policy that summer without at least a partial look at the culture and society the women were part of.

To begin with: why would the women have had any concerns about politics at all? One of the comic premises on which the *Lysistrata* rests is the absurdity, in the Athenian male imagination, of women taking charge of civic affairs. In the exchange between the official and Lysistrata he repeatedly objects to the very idea of taking orders from women, while Lysistrata patiently explains how the women intend to make peace using the skills of woolworking and household management they usually practice at home. As the scene progresses, the women push on the official the emblems of their femininity, the veil and the wool-basket, and enjoin him to keep silent while they carry on with their successful management of the city. The (hilarious!) gender role-reversal is complete.

Women and the Oikos

Discussion of women's lives in classical Athens commonly starts with this division between men's running of the polis and women's concern with the *oikos*, a word meaning the physical "house," the resources belonging to it, and the group of people within it who made up the "household." We'll need to take a deeper look at the associations between polis/men on the one side and oikos/women on the other, the assumptions that underlie it, as well as the places where the opposition breaks down, to understand what the possibilities were that would allow women to react to and be heard in the polis from their positions in the oikos.

One of the most detailed accounts we have of an elite woman's responsibilities in her oikos is from an author called Xenophon, a contemporary of Plato who also wrote some dialogues starring Socrates. In the *Oeconomicus*, a treatise on household management, Xenophon has Socrates recall a conversation he once had on this topic with a wealthy and well-regarded man called Ischomachus. Having encountered him waiting for some foreign visitors in the Agora, Socrates had asked how he had time for such things, given his stellar reputation for running his large estate. Ischomachus tells him that he leaves the bulk of affairs in his house to his wife, who manages them very well for him. Amazing! says Socrates. Where did she learn to do that? Did her parents teach her? Oh no, replies Ischomachus. "What could she have known when I married her, since she wasn't fifteen years old when she came to me, and in the time before that she had lived such a protected life that she saw and heard as little as possible, and asked the fewest questions?" (*Oeconomicus* 7.5).

Ischomachus goes on to tell Socrates in some detail about what he had taught his wife when they were first married. We don't hear how old he was himself at this point, but traditionally Athenian men married when they were about thirty: twice as old, then, as their young brides. This large age gap is evident all the way through Ischomachus' conversations with his bride, although he is generous enough to acknowledge that when he gives her his first lecture she is "already manageable and domesticated enough to participate in a discussion" (7.10). He starts, conveniently for us, with theory. Her role in the oikos, he claims, arises from the natural functions of male and female, and thus the natural reasons for marriage. He explains that the gods have established the link between male and female so that they can have children. But humans, unlike other animals, need oikoi, houses. The products they get from work outside (like farming and herding) must be protected inside, as must their infant children. Thus humans need to work both outside and inside, and the gods in their wisdom have made men especially good at being outside (because they are stronger and more tolerant of heat and cold), and women especially good for what goes on inside (because they have greater affection for babies than men do, and because their greater share of fearfulness makes them better guards).

This division of labor between men and women, and the spaces they occupy as a result, is presented as divinely ordained and thus "natural"; the arrangement also coincides with *nomos* ("law" or "custom"), so that the community can use it to distribute honor and shame. "For it is more honorable for a woman to remain indoors than to go outside, and it is more shameful for a man to remain inside than to take care of the work outside. If anyone does something contrary to the nature the god gave him, it is quite possible that his disorderliness will not escape the notice of the gods and that he will pay the penalty for ignoring his proper work or doing a woman's work" (7.31). The word "disorderliness" here translates *atakton*, normally used of soldiers not properly stationed in their battle line; a man working inside the house or a woman working outside, Ischomachus implies, has deserted the post where the god stationed him, and is subject to punishment accordingly. Just as in the army, the safety and well-being of all depends on everyone holding their assigned position. Women are not only primarily concerned with the affairs of the oikos. They are, in a sense, confined within it, since venturing outside is divinely sanctioned.

Ischomachus goes on to detail exactly what his wife's responsibilities will be. She will manage all the produce of an extensive estate (both storing and tracking the agricultural produce and supervising the production of food and textiles within the house), she will nurse the slaves if they become ill, train the women in woolworking and housekeeping, reward the good and punish the bad. In all this Ischomachus develops an elaborate simile comparing his wife's role to that of the queen bee in a hive. This all seems like a tall order for a fourteen-year-old girl. In some households the husband's mother, if she were still alive, would have taken these responsibilities and the bride could have learned them gradually while assisting her mother-in-law. Perhaps Ischomachus has obscured the presence of his mother to magnify his own role in instruction, and thus to emphasize his crucial part in the smooth running of his household. Or perhaps the girl did need to take over the role of "queen bee" from the moment she arrived in the new house.

Thus far Xenophon's Ischomachus has, in unusually explicit ways, laid out for us the ideology we began with: the close association of women with the oikos, and men with concerns outside of it. As we investigate how plausible women's possible opposition to war in 415 might have been, we must confront the issue of women's seclusion not just to the house, but within it. A little later in the *Oeconomicus*, we find Ischomacus showing his young wife "the women's quarters, separated by a bolted door from the men's" (9.5).

Other texts as well imply the separation of sexes within the house, with distinct terms for the men's quarters (*andrōn*) and the women's (*gynaikonitis*). Does this mean that Athenian women were confined in remote, harem-style quarters, sheltered from the sight of any male? If this is the case, it would be hard to see how they could hear much about the impending expedition, or form opinions about it, let alone stage any kind of public reaction.

Stray anecdotes that come down to us from legal speeches vividly indicate how powerfully some form of segregation of women was idealized. In this passage from a prosecution speech, the narrator wants to inspire the outrage of the jury against his opponent, who had broken into his house when he was out:

> he came there at night when he was drunk, and having broken through the doors, he entered the women's rooms (*gynaikonitis*): my sister and my nieces were inside, who have lived so decently that they are ashamed to be seen even by their relatives. This man, then, was so hubristic that he refused to go away until people nearby and those who had come with him, considering that he was behaving monstrously in bursting in on young girls and orphans, drove him out by force. (Lysias 3.6–7)

The clear implication is that even within the household, among family members, these women would have been customarily separated from the men. Whether the speaker's sister and her girls were really "ashamed to be seen even by their relatives" is something we'll never know. What is clear, however, is that the speaker assumed that the jury would take their shame as evidence of their "decent" lives, and thus of his own probity as householder and citizen.

As the anecdote illustrates, elite Athenian men habitually present themselves as intent to keep women out of the public eye. Pericles, at the close of his funeral oration (that famous crystallization of Athenian democratic ideology we looked at in Part 1), turns from addressing the fathers and brothers of the war dead to their wives and mothers. His terse statement: "If I must add something about female virtue, for those who will now be widows, I'll point to the whole in this brief admonishment: your reputation will be great as long as you aren't inferior to your existing nature, and if your fame, for virtue or blame, is least among men" (2.45). The pressure to minimize women's "fame" is so great that women are conventionally never named in public while they are alive. Ischomachus never calls his young wife by name all the way through his extended conversation with Socrates, and Xenophon never names her anywhere in his account of the conversation. This paradox, that the very best reputation possible for a woman belongs to the one who has the least fame, points at another impediment to learning about women from our (elite male-authored) sources. A man's reputation depended in part on the invisibility of his wife. It's no wonder that effort is required for us to see her.

One way classicists cope with this challenge is to bring together evidence from different types of sources. We can see an example of how this works by combining archaeological evidence with the legal texts just quoted. This passage from Lysias mentioning women who were "ashamed to be seen even by their relatives" used to be offered as evidence for what was quaintly called the "oriental seclusion" of Athenian women. But archaeological remains of actual houses complicate the notion of a secluded, harem-like area for women, and can give us a more nuanced view.

The standard Greek house at this period stood in a block of houses that shared common exterior walls. One entrance from the street led, often by way of an anteroom, into an open courtyard. Off this central area were several rooms, some only accessible through another rather than directly from the courtyard. Some houses had a second story of rooms around the courtyard. The modern western practice of designating specific rooms for some activities (kitchen, living room, bedroom, etc.) does not align well with the distribution of objects found in excavated houses. Shifting light and temperatures more likely led members of the household to move their activities to the most appropriate available area at any given point in the day or year. As the open courtyard provided the best light, it is likely that a good deal of household work occurred there, and anyone moving from one room to another would have been visible from this vantage point, just as women or slaves weaving in the courtyard would have been visible to those in the surrounding rooms. While the male and female members of the oikos may have customarily slept in separate quarters, then, material remains do not support the notion that women were held in any sort of enforced seclusion from men within the house.

We have already encountered the one exception to this pattern: the andrōn, site of the symposium. Often more elaborately decorated than other living-spaces, this room is usually separated from the house's central courtyard by having a separate entrance nearer the main door, or else an anteroom. That way men reclining on the couches around the walls, carrying on their philosophical or political discussions over wine at the symposium, could not gaze out the door into the courtyard and catch sight of any household members there. This very exception shows how the structure of the house is designed to segregate those who live there from men who visit, rather than to keep the male and female inhabitants of the oikos separate from each other. For while it is inaccurate to think of women as sequestered from men within the oikos, it does seem, again at least in the elite class, that they were very carefully kept out of the view of men from outside of the family.

The andrōn, however, tends to be identifiable primarily in larger houses, which brings us to a major caveat. Returning to Ischomachus for a moment, we must be attentive to the very strong class bias in his pronouncements about the proper spaces for men and women. Aristocrats' income came from their large landed estates, and the management of such land required outdoor work. Similarly, business deals in the Agora or exercise in the gymnasium would go on outside. A large class of men, however, such as craftsmen (cobblers, potters, vase-painters, smiths) would have worked indoors. Ischomachus' formula implies that such work cannot be the province of "real" men, but is somehow feminized by happening inside. Similarly, many poorer women assisted with agricultural labor, or operated stalls outside in the marketplace. Aristotle famously says that strict regulation of women is not democratic, for "how is it possible to prevent the wives of the poor from going out?" (*Politics* 1300a). The dominant association of women with the oikos and men with the polis may apply generally to the concerns of most women and men in the city; but the strict spatial segregation can only have applied to families wealthy enough to afford it.

Clearly, then, the notion of a stark separation between the realms of men and the polis on one side and women in the oikos on the other doesn't give us an accurate picture of where and how all men and women in the city spent their time. Poorer people were far less segregated by gender than wealthier ones. But the opposition also distorts the complex ways in which the interests of the larger community, the Athenian polis, overlapped with and included the individual households it comprised. It's worth exploring in a little more detail some of the ways in which the polis was both concerned with and dependent upon those women who were largely associated with the oikos, for we need to understand the underlying assumptions in order to interpret our sources accurately. The three principal areas of interest here are the way in which Athenian citizenship was determined, the ideology that helped cement male reputation and political advancement, and the demands of civic religious practice.

Women and Athenian Citizenship

Ischomachus tells his young wife that he has married her to be a partner not just in bed, but "of oikos and children." Children, of course, result from sex whether it happens within or outside of marriage, but Athenian law very strongly distinguished between these two categories. In 451, Pericles enacted a law stipulating that only the children born from a legal marriage between two Athenian parents were Athenian citizens, and only Athenian citizens could inherit property from their parents. Children born outside these restrictions lacked these rights. In other words, the polis was careful to define, protect, and sustain the oikoi that in turn reproduced the citizen body.

Your status as a citizen was therefore dependent upon the status of your parents as legally married citizens. Under these circumstances, we might assume that the city would keep marriage records that could be used as documentary evidence in cases of dispute. But they didn't. Even in cases where documentary evidence existed (as it did for men's citizen status) court cases show a marked preference for adducing witnesses who could give eyewitness testimony to someone's presence and participation in the community of citizens. Evidently there was a greater suspicion that documents could be forged than that eyewitnesses, under oath, would lie. Proving your status, in other words, was dependent on your parents' appearance outside of the oikos. This was a straightforward proposition in the case of your father, but a much trickier one for your mother in a society where the ideal female was "ashamed to be seen even by relatives," where a man's reputation depended on the invisibility of his wife.

A legal and regular marriage, attested to by witnesses to the betrothal or dowry agreement, or neighbors who attended the marriage feast, was generally considered sufficient proof of the woman's citizen status. But in the absence of such proof, her status was open to attack, and the most common tactic was to claim that she was not a legal wife, but had been in a sexual relationship with the man on some other terms: as a concubine or *hetaira*.

While the lowest class of prostitutes were usually brothel slaves, hetairas were usually free but noncitizen women, often from some other Greek city. The most famous of them were witty and well-educated as well as beautiful, and men gave them "gifts" in exchange for the pleasure of their company, rather than predetermined fees for sex. The hallmark of a hetaira was that she dined out with a man, appearing publicly with him. A famous speech from the mid-fourth century prosecutes a woman called Neaera for pretending to be an Athenian citizen and trying to arrange the marriage of her daughter to a citizen. Again and again the speaker cites as proof of her noncitizen status the fact that she dined out with her "husband" like a hetaira. The accusation also asserted that Neaera was from the city of Megara and thus could not claim Athenian citizen status either for herself or her daughter. But the bulk of the speech concentrates not on Neaera's foreign origin, but on her behavior. Acting like a hetaira makes you a hetaira, and attending drinking parties with a man is something only a hetaira would do.

Here then was a strong motivation for those Athenian men who were of a class likely to be involved in inheritance disputes to keep their wives and daughters out of public contact with other men. Being seen with an unrelated man, even, or perhaps especially, if it was her husband, could be cited as evidence that she was not his wife but rather his hetaira. This could throw the children's citizen status into question, and block sons' inheritance of family property. The most effective way to guard against this possibility was for men to keep their wives out of the sight of unrelated men as much as was feasible.

Women and Male Reputation

Yet concerns about women's behavior, if known beyond the oikos, could have public ramifications beyond the specific question of citizenship status. A good example of how knowledge of events within the household might be exploited for political advantage brings us back to Ischomachus' young wife.

From a different text, which we will encounter again in chapter 6, we learn about a very different set of events concerning this woman. In a defense speech, a man called Andocides gives the name that Xenophon discretely withheld: Chrysilla. She bore Ischomachus a daughter or two and at least two sons. When her husband died, probably sometime right around 415, one daughter was married but the sons were still minors. Ischomachus' will stipulated that the daughter's husband, Callias, should become the boys' guardian. Chrysilla also joined her sons and daughter in Callias' household. Women were perpetual legal minors in Athens, so when one is widowed she generally moves back to her father's house if he is still alive, or else joins the household of one of her sons.

Callias was from a very wealthy and prominent family, and the holder of a hereditary priesthood in the cult of Demeter and Persephone. His mother was related to Pericles, and his sister Hipparete was married to Alcibiades. This oikos must have been a particularly desirable one for Ischomachus to marry his daughter into, and for Chrysilla and her sons to join on his death. According to Andocides, however, scandal erupted almost immediately. By his account Callias and Chrysilla had an affair and Chrysilla bore Callias a son. Andocides recounts the tale with obvious relish:

> [Callias] married the daughter of Ischomachus: having lived with her for less than a year, he took her mother, and this most worthless of all men lived with both mother and daughter, being priest of Mother and Daughter, and kept both of them in his house. (Andocides 1.124)

Now it is possible that what Andocides is peddling as scandal was nothing of the kind. It wouldn't be unheard-of for Ischomachus to have directed in his will that Callias divorce his daughter and marry his widow when he became guardian to his sons. On the other hand, Callias and Chrysilla may have fallen in love and had an affair once she moved into the house. She would have been much closer to Callias' own age than was her daughter. The point here, though, is that what went on with the women within Callias' oikos could furnish material useful to political enemies in the polis. We don't know how Andocides knew these details of Callias' home life, but his use of them to prejudice a jury against his opponent gives a particularly vivid illustration of the fact mentioned above. Dominant ideology demanded that a man maintain an oikos ordered along conventional lines. His public reputation could be shattered by dubious goings-on within the privacy of his household. In particular the behavior of the women under his care and control presented a vulnerability that could be exploited by his enemies. It is important to keep in mind this feature of Athenian elite ideology as we use these sources to draw conclusions about women's lives. Authors of this class will tend to mention women either to make themselves or their friends look good, or to make their enemies look bad. We need to be very careful about using such texts to determine women's actual experiences and interactions both in and out of the oikos.

Women and Civic Religion

The third area of Athenian life where the interests of polis and oikos substantially overlap is in the worship of the gods and the demands of civic religion. As was clear from chapter 3, maintaining correct relations with the gods was an essential part of polis obligations, and in many publicly funded festivals women's participation was essential. This could take the form of women participating alongside men, as they did in the Eleusinian Mysteries we will be hearing about later in the summer. But there were also several festivals organized and celebrated by women alone, apart from men, but also outside of their own households. The most famous of these, the Thesmophoria, will serve as an example of what these festivals were like and how important they were to the polis.

The Thesmophoria was celebrated early each autumn in honor of the goddess of grain and agriculture, Demeter, and her daughter Persephone. The famous myth tells that Hades, god of the underworld, abducted the young Persephone. Demeter roamed the world searching for her lost daughter, and in her grief made the earth barren. Finally Zeus relented and allowed mother and daughter to be reunited, but because Persephone had eaten pomegranate seeds in the underworld, she was tied to that region and had to return for a few months each year. These months are always unfruitful, while the earth blooms during the months in which she resides in the world above. We are so familiar with this story as an explanation of the seasons that we can overlook one of its remarkable features: the centrality it gives to the bond between mother and daughter. While the myth makes the traditional connection between human and vegetative fertility, its focus is not on birth but on the tragic separation and joyful reunion of Demeter and Persephone. The Thesmophoria combined these elements.

Only citizen women took part in this festival in Athens, and possibly only married women. While their husbands paid the bills in the form of liturgies, the women organized and arranged the festival, even evidently electing officers for the purpose called *archousai*, the feminine form of archon. Inscriptions and literary references indicate almost a shadow polis of women in this context. The festival lasted three days and during that time it completely displaced the business of the city. Neither assembly nor courts convened during the Thesmophoria. The women brought tents and provisions to camp, possibly on the Pnyx itself, during the festival. On the first day, they carried these provisions to the designated area and made preliminary sacrifice. On the second they imitated the grief of Demeter over the loss of her daughter by sitting on reed mats on the ground and singing laments, finishing, evidently, with *aischrologia*, "shame-speech" or ritual obscenity. On the third they reenacted the joyful reunion with a feast and celebration called "beautiful birth." The central event of the festival was the descent of a special group of women, called "bailers," into caves or some natural fissure in the rock. At some point before the festival, sacrificed piglets and phalluses made of dough had been thrown into these caverns, and at the Thesmophoria the bailers recovered their rotting remains and spread this sanctified (but undoubtedly disgusting) substance upon the altar for farmers to mix with their seed in the approaching sowing season. The women who did not descend in search of the remains stood around the entrance to the cave and yelled to scare off the snakes that evidently gathered there. Women celebrating the Thesmophoria are referred to as "bees," just as Ischomachus had compared his wife to a bee. Perhaps Ischomachus used the simile to signal his bride's obligations outside of, as well as within, his household.

In the Thesmophoria then, as in other all-female religious festivals, the well-being of the polis not only depended upon women, but on their sustained activity outside of their oikoi. A sharp, gendered separation between polis and oikos ignores a great deal of important overlap and crossover between the categories, as well as reasons our sources might be interested in obscuring our vision of women in Athens. Irregular activities within the oikos would have repercussions in the polis if they became known, because the polis had strong interest in monitoring the purity of the oikoi that constituted it. Class signaling, combined with legal vulnerability and the dangers of political attacks, all pushed the sort of men most likely to have authored extant texts to present themselves as having wives who usually stay out of public male view. At the same time, their wives clearly did operate outside of the household on marked occasions, for the benefit of the very city that demanded their invisibility at other times. And of course "the sort of men most likely to have authored extant texts" made up only a fraction even of the citizens, let alone the metics and slaves who also lived in Attica. It is manifestly not the case that public spaces like the Agora were devoid of women altogether, even if assembly or council meetings were all-male affairs.

"Women's Interests"

This brief introduction to gender norms in Athens has given us the beginning of an answer to the first question set at the opening of this chapter: "what were the lives of Athenian women like?" It has also equipped us to start thinking about the second question: "can we think of them as a coherent bloc with unified interests?" To what degree did women have opportunities to nurture anything like communal solidarity? Would the dividing lines of class and status that, as we have seen, left their traces in our source material, have been felt among the women of Athens as they were felt by the men?

For a limited case study in the kinds of ties among women likely in classical Athens we can return to Chrysilla. We know nothing of her birth family, but she will have formed close ties at least with her mother, and sisters if she had them, before she moved into Ischomachus' house. There, as mentioned, she may have found other women from her husband's family in residence: probably, if she were still alive, his mother, but also possibly other of his female relatives like sisters, sisters' daughters, even cousins. Remember that the speaker who called attention to the outrageous behavior of his legal opponent had his sisters and their daughters living in the gynaikonitis of his household. Before long Chrysilla would have had her own daughters as well. This set of women would have spent many hours in each other's company, tending to the obligations of the household Ischomachus set out for his new wife, and particularly spinning and weaving the textiles necessary to clothe everyone who lived in the house.

After Ischomachus' death, Chrysilla moved into Callias' household, and here again she would have lived with and fostered ties with his female relatives. His sister Hipparete, for instance, moved back to Callias' house for some time when her marriage to Alcibiades was unhappy. Marriages bound unrelated oikoi together, so the progression of Chrysilla from her natal family, to her marital, to the marital family of her children, was a common and natural way for women to form relationships outside of their immediate nuclear family. Because women were essential to household as well as civic religion, numerous rituals would have brought these women together to help each other celebrate weddings and births, and lament the dead.

Within a household and those related to it by kinship or marriage, then, women had ample opportunity to form and foster close ties. The usual absence of the men would only have strengthened these as women relied on each other for company. Others inhabited the household besides these relatives, though. Would there have been social relations of a kind between free women and their female slaves? The idealizing Ischomachus expounds upon the ways in which he and Chrysilla chose their housekeeper, a sort of head slave, evidently, and "taught her to be loyal to us by making her a partner in all our joys and calling on her to share our troubles" as well as making her "eager for the improvement of our estate, by making her familiar with it and by allowing her to share in our success" (Xenophon, *Oeconomicus* 9.12). Even without the idealizing, it was true that the economic well-being of a slave depended on the economic well-being of the household, and thus that a slave would have shared some interests with her mistress: both were economically entirely dependent upon the master of the house. Another text, a legal speech recounting a colorful tale of adultery and murder, allows us a glance at a young mistress whose slave-girl acted as go-between with her lover and facilitated their assignations. Can we fill in a kind of friendship between these two women? Does the stray allusion to the master's sexual interest in this slave-girl give grounds for seeing mistress and slave feeling common antipathy toward, and thus engaging in a conspiracy against, the master of the house? Or is the mistress more likely to have been hostile toward a girl she saw as a sexual threat? Presumably in Athens, as in other slave societies, a wide range of possible relations existed between mistress and slave woman. Sisterly solidarity in that context must have been the exception rather than the rule, but it couldn't have been impossible.

If we expand our search for networks among women beyond the kin and slaves within a set of related households, we might ask whether citizenship or social class were barriers to female friendships beyond the oikos. In men's minds, sexual jealousy is the major source of divisions between women. Mythical wives like Deianeira and Hermione are jealous of and feel threatened by the concubines that their husbands bring home from war. These figures of the tragic stage may have real-life analogs. Alcibiades' wife Hipparete was so offended by her husband bringing hetairas home that she temporarily went back to live in her brother Callias' house to register her objections. But if they were not competing for the attentions or resources of a single man, there does not seem to have been any bar to friendships between married women, whether metic or citizen, and noncitizen hetairas. It was men, after all, who had to worry about keeping those categories strictly separate, but that separation was effected by keeping the wives away from men, not other women. Provided they were out of the sight of men, what women did and with whom they socialized seems to have been of little concern. Remember that Athenian houses often shared walls in a continuous block. Slipping next door to chat with a neighbor or help out during a family occasion would not necessarily have entailed exposing yourself to public view or gossip. Both legal texts and comedies offer examples of friendships between one man's wife and another's hetaira, usually based on proximity. Neighbors were neighbors, and status was evidently not a barrier to friendship among women.

Some evidence available to us, then, supports the notion that women living in the city might have shared social ties even across class and status divisions. To be sure, there is also evidence that women cared about and maintained some boundaries. One of the penalties for a wife caught in adultery, for instance, was that she was barred from the public temples, clearly implying that other women could be expected to police their own festivals and enforce this status distinction. For some, unwillingness to share religious practice with a woman of an inappropriate class must have been a strong force. Legal texts occasionally imply that women were as concerned about status distinctions as their husbands. The speech against Neaera mentioned above asserts that if the jurors acquit, "the best women will get angry at you, because you thought that *she* was worthy of participating in affairs of the city and the gods along with *them*" (Demosthenes 59.111); again, though, this may be as much ideology as reality. That the lives of most women, whatever their status, were primarily occupied with producing and caring for children, preparing food or producing textiles, would have given them common experiences and concerns. Their most prominent opportunities for maintaining these social ties came from their crucial role in religious practice—both for the household and for the city. The rituals they practiced regularly brought them together with other women, both from their own oikos or their extended family, and from the larger community. It is in the context of civic religious celebration that women would have most easily made and fostered the ties with other women outside of their own households.

Let's return to the Thesmophoria, considering it now from the perspective of the women who took part rather than the city's interest in agricultural fertility. Women participating in the festival enacted cycles of human relations and transitions rather than planting and harvesting. During the lamentations on the second day, the women seated on the earth were playing the part of Demeter grieving for her lost daughter, but their emotions must have sprung from their own experiences of losing daughters to marriage, or simply of separation and loss. The bailers were playing the part of Persephone, descending into the earth and then returning, but here too they would have experienced in their own lives the departure from their familial homes into a new and possibly risky environment. And at the final celebration of "beautiful birth" all the women enacted the joyful response of mother and daughter reunited that resulted in the earth's fertility, exactly as the annual festival itself offered the opportunity for mothers and their married daughters to reunite, at least briefly, share the feast and catch up on each other's lives. The three days away from their husbands and individual households, ensconced in a community of women, must have offered a powerful emotional catharsis to Athenian wives, first evoking their grief in ritual lamentation, then channeling that emotion into the joy of the final day's celebration. In this pattern it replicated the emotional progress of funerary rites, which also moved from lamentation, in the home and at the graveside, to feasting and celebration afterward. Each occasion offered the opportunity for women to leave their household responsibilities and meet up with neighbors, friends, sisters, and mothers. This community of women slides below the radar of our male-authored texts, but it was a real and important feature of life in the city. It is not difficult to imagine that women used these occasions to discuss interests and issues that they shared with each other, or that they might have more in common based on their sex than they did with their husbands or sons. Might this wider community have shared common anxiety about the distant war their men had voted to begin? Did the women of Athens have reason to be pacifists?

To begin with it should be said that there is exactly no evidence from the classical period to support the notion that women were opposed to the violence of warfare on principle. There are in fact numerous examples of women participating in fighting, particularly in urban settings where they could be effective hurling missiles from rooftops or out of windows. War was a fact of life in the fifth century, and women's stake in defending their households was as great as their husbands'. Euripides' *Trojan Women* gives vivid evidence of the fate that awaited the women of defeated cities, and no free woman would advocate entering such slavery voluntarily as a price for avoiding war. But at the same time, there was a substantial difference between a defensive war to protect one's household and city, and the kind of offensive Athens was on the verge of launching. Cassandra's speech argued that a defensive war was more admirable than an offensive one, and while Euripides' emphasis in these lines is on the fate of the men, who get to live with their wives and children and then be buried in their native soil, it is possible that women would have shared the sentiment. Whether or not there was real affection between husband and wife, and many of our sources indicate that there was, at least eventually, a woman's lot would have been significantly harder in the absence of her husband or father. If he were wealthy, she would have had resources to live on, but would have been constrained in her ability to operate economically without him. If he were poorer, the absence of his daily wages would have presented real challenges. It is exactly in the context of the economic hardships brought about by war that we hear of citizen women being forced to work as wet nurses or to open stalls in the Agora, moves that could bring the citizen status of their children into question. Thus even prolonged absence of husband or father, let alone the risk of his death, would mean serious hardships for the women they left at home.

Those women related to the men who would sail, then, had reason to object to the project that had been conceived of and voted upon by others but would have such a disruptive effect on their own lives. And it wasn't only the hoplites and sailors who would leave the city. Merchants were following the fleet to bring it supplies, and bakers, masons, and carpenters were joining the expedition to help with supplying the army and building fortifications. Even those women whose husbands were not preparing for departure that spring had reason to fear. The Spartan threat, much closer than far-off Sicily, was hardly removed. If the city were vulnerable in the absence of such a large fleet, all the women would end up suffering for it, whether slave or free, citizen or metic. They didn't need the evidence of Euripides' tragedy to convince them of this, but it had offered a graphic reminder of what fate awaited the women should Athens be attacked and defeated.

The rewards of bringing Sicily into the Athenian empire, which Thucydides claims had kindled the men's desire for the expedition—the greater honor and prestige accruing to the city as well as wages for the current enterprise and those to come—were unlikely to have seemed as attractive to their wives. To most of them the risks and hardships of war would plausibly loom larger than the rewards of Athenian imperial power. On balance, then, an argument can certainly be made both that women as a group held identifiable interests in common, and that those interests were likely not to have favored the war. The final question I set at the beginning of the chapter is whether they might, therefore, have found a way to voice their opposition. And that brings us back to Aristophanes.

The Adonia

The speech from the *Lysistrata* we began with recalls an occasion in 415 when somebody's wife could be heard yelling "oh Adonis" from her roof. While the official doesn't specify the context of this odd behavior, we know what he's talking about from this detail alone. There was another festival celebrated by women in Athens, called the Adonia. This one fell somewhere in between the publicly financed events like the Thesmophoria and the purely family occasions like a funeral. It seems to have been an Eastern import, and thus the magistrate contemptuously lumps it in with other foreign cults and their accoutrements. The *tympanum*, or drum, was used in the worship of the Phrygian god Sabazios as well as Dionysus and the Great Mother Cybele, and these gods were all associated with wild female behavior. The Adonia recalled Aphrodite's love for the young mortal Adonis, and her grief for him when he died.

Besides the magistrate's speech in the *Lysistrata*, which describes a celebration of the Adonia disrupting a meeting of the assembly in advance of the Sicilian Expedition, Plutarch also reports that this festival was perceived as a bad omen in 415. There are some differences between the comedian and the biographer. Aristophanes describes something noisy happening on rooftops, while Plutarch, writing hundreds of years later, is more focused on what he calls *eidola*, evidently small effigies of (dead) Adonis. Plutarch may be extrapolating from the practice in other times and places. We have no evidence from classical Athens that such figures played a part in the ritual, but a poem set in Alexandrian Egypt, a few centuries later, does make reference to such an effigy. Exactly when the Adonia occurred is also unknown: Plutarch situates it around the time of the departure of the fleet, which happened in the summer, but Aristophanes places it during a meeting of the assembly debating preparations for the expedition, presumably earlier in the spring.

Even with such differences, these texts and other sources allow us to sketch approximately what the festival looked like in the late fifth century, if not precisely when it was celebrated. Before we consider the festival, though, a final word on the nature of the sources is necessary. We have already seen numerous instances of the necessity for caution in reading elite male-authored sources on women's lives. In Xenophon or the legal speeches, women's actions were primarily of interest as either upholding or damaging male reputation, and thus we needed to exercise care in determining exactly how the ideals might reflect women's actual lived experience. When we come to what women do in groups apart from men, however, our sources are not orators or philosophers; they are the comic poets. As was indicated by the chapter opening with Aristophanes' *Lysistrata*, what women did in groups apart from men provided a rich source of comedy (for men). That almost all our classical sources on the Adonia are from comic texts presents a new kind of challenge, which the reader is invited to undertake. The principal textual sources we have for the Adonia, scant as they are, are collected after this chapter. Can details reflecting practice be separated from comic business?

What we know of the festival is this. In preparation, women planted seeds to make "gardens of Adonis" in broken pots. Lettuce or fennel, these seeds sprouted rapidly and rapidly withered, perhaps offering a natural analog for Adonis' quick bloom and early death. It was this feature of the festival occurring against the backdrop of preparations for the expedition that, Plutarch reports, troubled some onlookers. Would the lavish resources on view for the attack on Sicily quickly wither as well?

For the festival itself, women carried these "gardens of Adonis" up to the roofs of houses all over Athens. Rooftops were evidently either flat or very gently pitched, as we hear about many activities happening there that would be impossible on steeply pitched roofs. As houses shared walls, the roof space would also have been contiguous between houses, at least within a single block. The roof thus presents an interesting space between private and public. The voices of women on the rooftops were audible from the street, marketplace, or Pnyx, but the women themselves were not fully visible. They had easy access to near neighbors but not the fuller proximity of a large public area.

On the rooftops, women engaged in ritual lament for Adonis, playing the part of Aphrodite or her fellow mourners. This is what the magistrate in the *Lysistrata* is remembering when he talks about the wife of the speaker at the assembly wailing "aiai (alas) Adonis" or "beat your breast for Adonis." As at the Thesmophoria, and as at real funerals, the lamentation gave way to feasting, drinking (the magistrate claims that the woman was "soused"), and dancing, probably all night. A comedy of Menander includes a young man remembering an Adonia celebration he witnessed and joined. Perhaps this can be taken as evidence that men were not excluded from the ritual, as they were from other all-female festivals like the Thesmophoria. But it is women who are principally associated with it. Lamentation is primarily women's activity, and lamentation over the young lover of the goddess of desire would be more appropriate for women than men.

Since the city neither required nor financed this festival, but neither was it part of family cult, its popularity has been the subject of considerable speculation. Interpretations of its meaning and appeal have varied widely over the past several decades, depending on whether scholars focus on its agricultural elements, sexuality, or death and lamentation. There may have been a special appeal for women whose husbands were so much older than they to fantasize about the gorgeous young lover of Aphrodite, enacting her lamentation over his untimely death. Poets writing in the centuries after the classical era seemed particularly interested in this romanticized aspect of the festival, but it may well have been important in the fifth century as well. If the Thesmophoria offered women an opportunity to mourn necessary separation from their daughters, and then to rejoice in reunion with them, perhaps the Adonia allowed a similar emotional catharsis, as grief over young men lost was followed by celebration of the life that continues.

Women celebrating the Adonia in 415 had husbands, sons, fathers, cousins, uncles, and brothers on the verge of a long and dangerous absence. That their cries of lamentation over Adonis might raise thoughts of other laments to come is psychologically plausible. That some women may have been aware of and pleased by the disruptive effect of their ritual cries on men trying to carry on their normal business is also not out of the question. With a stretch of the imagination we might even speculate that some parties of women may have been intentional in their disruptive noise, hoping that it might make the men less avid to launch the looming expedition.

We have, alas, no evidence as to how the male citizens reacted to the boisterous celebration in the moment. Later, after the Sicilian Expedition had ended in disaster, men looked back on that day and identified its disruptive lamentations as an evil omen of things to come. Had the expedition ended in the quick and total victory of the Athenian fleet, and the subsequent dominance of the Athenian empire over her enemies in the Peloponnese, we would surely never have heard about the festival that year at all. Nobody remembers omens of an evil that fails to materialize. As it turned out, however, those cries of grief were remembered, and noted, and allow us to wonder about what other voices we have lost.

Primary Source Interlude

Textual Sources for the Adonia, excerpts

ARISTOPHANES, *LYSISTRATA* 387–96 (ATHENS, 411 BCE)

An Athenian civic official confronts the women who have occupied the Acropolis.

> What is it this time? Is this some woman thing?
> Is it the thing with the drum-banging and that foreign god
> and the women all having Adoniasms up on the rooftops?
> I remember something like this happening a few years back
> when Demostratus—Mr. Bad Timing himself—had his
> big moment in the assembly. Here he is telling us to sail to Sicily
> while his wife is dancing around, singing, "Oh! Adonis!"
> I mean, here's Demostratus proposing we enlist the Zacinthians,
> and there's Mrs. D., soused, shouting from the rooftops
> "Beat your breasts for Adonis!"

MENANDER, *SAMIA* 39–46 (ATHENS, LATE FOURTH CENTURY BCE)

A young man starts to explain how he got the neighbor's daughter pregnant.

> So, anyway, I hurried home from the farm
> and found them gathered in our house, along with
> some other women, to celebrate the Adonia. As you
> can imagine, the festival was nonstop fun.
> Since I was there, I saw the whole darn thing.
> I couldn't sleep with all the racket they made,
> carrying their potted plants up to the roof, dancing—
> the party didn't break up until morning.

DIPHILUS, *THESEUS*, FRAGMENT 50 (ATHENS, LATE FOURTH CENTURY BCE)

We don't know anything about the context for this comic fragment other than the title of the play it is from; presumably it is some kind of standard joke.

> One Adonia, there were these three Samian girls
> who amused each other with this riddle:
> "What is the strongest thing in the world?"
> "Iron," the first one said, "because it can dig
> and chop, and holds up under constant use."
> "Good answer," said the second, "but the blacksmith
> is stronger than iron, because he works it
> and softens it and shapes it however he pleases."
> But the third said, "The strongest of all is the penis,
> because even the blacksmith groans under its weight."

PLATO, *PHAEDRUS* 276B (ATHENS, C. 370 BCE)

Toward the end of a long dialogue about rhetoric, Socrates makes a critique of writing in comparison to speaking; speaking is the serious art, since a speaker must be able to explain and defend his position to his listeners, while writing is frivolous, as it cannot enter into conversation with others. As a metaphor for this, he contrasts serious farming with the "gardens of Adonis."

So tell me this: the farmer who knows what he's doing, would he take the seeds he cares about and wants to produce fruit, and plant them all seriously in the summer gardens of Adonis, and then get excited watching them get beautiful in eight days? Or would he do that for fun, or for a festival, if he did it at all? And the seeds he was serious about, wouldn't he use all his farmer's knowledge to plant them when it was right, and be happy if they all reached maturity, as many as he'd planted, in the eighth month?

THEOCRITUS, *IDYLL* 15.1–23, 100–149 (ALEXANDRIA, THIRD CENTURY BCE)

The Idylls of Theocritus are an eclectic set of poems. While Theocritus is best known for the bucolic, or pastoral, poems, some of the Idylls have an urban setting. The following are excerpts from one of his poems often associated with the "mime," a genre where actors imitated daily life or mythological scenes with dance and words. This particular poem, then, in which two wives attend the Adonia in

Alexandria, is a close cousin of the comic texts above, as well as evidence that the
lives of Greek women outside of classical Athens could be far less restrictive.

Gorgo:
Is Praxinoa at home?

Praxinoa:
Dear Gorgo! I'm home. But it's been ages!
I'm surprised you came all this way now. Eunoa—
bring a cushion for her chair.

Gorgo:
Really, it's fine.

Praxinoa:
Do sit down.

Gorgo:
I was nearly at my wits' end. I almost didn't make it
through that crowd alive, Praxinoa! And all those chariots!
Boots everywhere, men in cloaks everywhere. And the road—
it goes on forever! You live further away every time.

Praxinoa:
It's that lunatic I'm married to. He moves us out to the ends of the earth,
into this dump—I wouldn't call it a house—just so you and I
can't be neighbors. Pure spite. You see what I have to put up with?

Gorgo:
Hush, dear. You shouldn't talk about your husband Dinon like that
with baby listening. Little pitchers, you know.
It's okay, Zopyrion. Mommy's not talking about daddy.

Praxinoa:
By the Virgin, he understands!

Gorgo:
Good daddy.

Praxinoa:
But just the other day—I'm talking about just the other day—

I say to him, I say, "Papa, just pop out to the shops and bring me
some soda and red dye." And what does he some back with?
Salt! The big fat clod.

Gorgo:
Oh, my Diocleides is the same way. Hopeless when it comes to money.
Yesterday he shelled out seven drachmas for five fleeces
that were more like dog skins or something shaved off a grandmother—
completely disgusting. And it of course means more work for me.
But grab your things! We're heading to Ptolemy's palace
to see the Adonia.

[Praxinoa gets ready to leave the house. She puts on a dress, and hands the baby
to the nurse. After she tells the nurse to call the dog inside and lock the door,
Praxinoa and Gorgo make their way through the crowd to the palace of queen
Arsinoe just in time to hear a famous woman singer sing a lament for Adonis.]

Woman Singer:
Mistress of Golgi, Idalion,
and pinnacled Eryx, golden Aphrodite—
see how the tender Hours, tardiest of gods,
come around to the twelfth month, escorting
Adonis from ever-flowing Acheron.
The dear Hours come, bearing gifts
to satisfy mortal longing.

Cyprian goddess, Dione's daughter,
the stories tell that it was you who gave immortality
to mortal Berenice, anointing
with ambrosial drops, and because of this—
O goddess of many names and many temples—
because of this, beautiful Arsinoe, her daughter,
devotes herself to Adonis.

For him all the fruit of the trees in season,
for him the frail gardens potted in silver,
and the Syrian myrrh in jars of gold,
and the cakes the women knead and shape—
the colorful cakes of finest flour,
the cakes of sweetest honey and richest oil.

Every creature that flies or crawls upon the earth
is with him under green arbors garlanded with dill,
and the Cupids flit overhead like nightingales,
fledglings trying out their wings from branch to branch.

O ebony! O gold! O ivory eagles attending
a boy to pour wine for Zeus, the son of Cronos,
and purple tapestries softer than sleep!
Miletus and the Samian shepherd will say:
"We have spread the couch for beautiful Adonis."
Cypris and pink-armed Adonis lie in mutual embrace.

The bridegroom is eighteen or nineteen years old—
his kiss doesn't scratch, there's still peach-fuzz on his face.
Cypris with her arms still around her man—farewell!
At dew-covered dawn we gather to carry him
down to the echoing waves of the sea,
and unbinding our hair and dropping our robes to our feet,
with bare breasts we will begin our cries of mourning.

O dear Adonis, you alone of all the demigods pass
between this world and the world of Acheron below.
Neither Agamemnon accomplished this, nor Ajax,
weighed down in wrath, nor Hector, eldest of Hecuba's
twenty sons, nor Patroclus, nor Pyrrhus escaped from Troy,
nor the Lapiths of more ancient times, nor the sons of Deucalion,
nor the Pelopidae, nor the Pelasgians who ruled Argos.
O dear Adonis, grace us also next year with your presence.
We rejoice in your coming, both now and when you come again.

Gorgo:
Praxinoa, the woman's a genius!
Such rich knowledge, and an even richer voice!
But we should be going. Diocleides needs his lunch.
The man's vinegar. There's no dealing with him when he's hungry.
Goodbye, Adonis, love. I hope all goes well, for you and me both.

BION, *LAMENT FOR ADONIS* (SMYRNA, C. 100 BCE)

Bion followed Theocritus in composing bucolic poetry; in this ninety-eight-line lament over Adonis the natural world features strongly. This poem focuses not on the ritual of the Adonia, but on the myth informing that ritual; it gives helpful evidence of the rich emotional context in the minds of the celebrants.

I mourn for Adonis, "Lovely Adonis is dead."
"Lovely Adonis is dead," echo the mournful Loves.

Sleep no longer on your purple sheets, Cypris.
Get up, sad goddess, and beat your dark-robed breast,

and say to all: "Lovely Adonis is dead."

I mourn for Adonis; the mournful Loves echo.

Adonis lies in the mountains, a white boar's tusk
wound in his white thigh, and Cypris grieves over him
breathing his last weak breath. Dark drops of blood
stain his snow-white flesh, and his sight grows dim,
and the pink hue leaves his lips, and with it dies his kiss—
Cypris still loves to kiss him, though he is dead
and her kisses are all unfelt and unreturned.

I mourn for Adonis; the mournful Loves echo.
Crueler than cruel the wound in Adonis' thigh,
but greater still the wound Cytherea carries in her heart.
His hounds howl around him, and the nymphs of the mountains
weep. Aphrodite wanders through the brambles
with her hair unbraided and unbound, and the thorns
tear her unsandaled feet, and she leaves a trail of sacred blood.
She shrieks as she passes through the deep gorges,
calling out again and again for her Assyrian spouse.
But the dark blood pooled around his navel, and his once
white chest purpled with the blood that poured from his thigh.

"Oh, oh, for Cytherea," the mournful Loves echo.

She lost her handsome man, and with him her sacred beauty.
Cypris was beautiful when Adonis was alive,

but with Adonis her beauty died. "Oh, oh, for Cypris"
all the mountains say, and the oaks say, "Oh, for Adonis."
The rivers cry for Aphrodite's suffering, and the mountain springs
weep for Adonis, and the flowers turn red with grief, and
up and down every mountain and glade Cytherea sings her grief:

"Oh, for Cytherea! Lovely Adonis is dead."

Echo repeats, "Lovely Adonis is dead!" Who would not
have cried out "Oh!" for Cypris' tragic love?

And when she came upon Adonis and his unbearable wound,
and when she saw the red blood draining from his thigh,
she reached out her arms and cried, "Stay, Adonis!
Stay, poor unfortunate Adonis, and let me hold you in my arms
one last time, and one last time mingle my lips with yours.
Hold on a little longer, Adonis, and give me your last kiss—
put the last ounce of your life into kissing me, breathe your life
into my mouth, and your spirit will suffuse my heart, and I
will hold onto this kiss as if it were Adonis himself, since you
yourself are leaving me, my tragic love. You're going so far,
to Acheron, where the king is gloomy and cruel. But oh!
I am a goddess, and wretched immortality keeps me here
without you. Take my husband, Persephone. You are greater
than I am, and every lovely thing at last belongs to you.
I am the most ill-fated of all, sunk in insatiable grief, I weep
for my Adonis, who is dead, and I dread you, Persephone.
Oh love of my life, you are dying, and my love has flown away
like a dream. Cytherea is widowed, and the Loves have
left her alone. With you my charm has died. Why did you
have to go hunting, my reckless one? You're so fine—
what possessed you to pit your strength against a wild beast?"

So Cypris mourned, and the mournful Loves echoed:
"Oh, oh, for Cytherea! Lovely Adonis is dead."

The tears of the Paphian goddess are as many as the drops
of blood Adonis sheds, and together they turn to flowers:
roses from the drops of blood, anemones from the tears.

I mourn for Adonis, "Lovely Adonis is dead."

No longer mourn your husband among the brambles, Cypris:
a desolate bed of leaves is not fit for Adonis.
Let dead Adonis have your couch, Cytherea.
He is a lovely corpse, an exquisite corpse, as if he's sleeping.
Lay him out on the soft sheets on which he used to
enjoy his nights with you in holy sleep. Lay him out
on your couch of solid gold, poor wreck of Adonis,
and cover him with garlands and flowers. When he died
all the flowers withered and died with him.
Anoint him with Syrian ointments and perfume.
Let all perfumes lose their scent; Adonis has lost his perfume.

Frail Adonis is laid out in purple robes, and around him
the Loves weep and groan, cutting their hair for Adonis.
One lays upon him a feathered arrow, another his quiver.
One has unfastened Adonis' sandal, others bring water
in a golden bowl. One washes his thighs, another stands
behind Adonis and fans him with his wings.
"Oh, oh, for Cytherea!" the mournful Loves echo.

Hymenaeus extinguished all the torches at the doors,
and scattered the wedding garland. No longer did he
sing his own hymn, his "Hymen, Hymen," but groaned:
"Oh! Oh!" and "Oh! Adonis!" louder than "Hymenaee."
The Graces, too, bemoan the son of Cinyras, saying
to each other, "Lovely Adonis is dead," and cry "Oh!"
much louder than the paean. And the Fates summon
Adonis to the Underworld, and sing incantations,
but he does not heed them. It's not that he is unwilling,
but the Maiden Persephone will not let him go.

Leave off your weeping for today, Cytherea. Cease your laments.
In another year you will have to weep and mourn again.

Plutarch refers to the Adonia of 415 twice: note that the accounts do not agree precisely, particularly as to the chronology.

PLUTARCH, *LIFE OF NICIAS* 12.7 (BOEOTIA, FIRST CENTURY CE)

The events of the days surrounding the departure of the expedition were troubling to quite a few Athenians. It was at this time that the women held the Adonia, and little effigies of Adonis were laid out in many places throughout the city, and the women performed burial rites and mourned Adonis with loud cries of lamentation, causing concern among those who found significance in such things, and making them fear that the powerful expeditionary force, which was then so fair and flourishing, soon would wither.

PLUTARCH, *LIFE OF ALCIBIADES* 18.2–3

When the people had voted in the assembly and the preparations were being made to launch the expedition, there was a series of bad omens. First of all, there was the festival of Adonis, in which effigies were carried in burial processions and mourned by the women, who beat their breasts and sang funeral dirges. In addition, there was the mutilation of the herms, most of which were disfigured on a single night, causing concern even among those who usually shrugged off such things.

HESYCHIUS OF ALEXANDRIA, *LEXICON* α1231 (FIFTH–SIXTH CENTURY CE)

We have parts of Hesychius' comprehensive lexicon of all Greek words; he was drawing on a number of earlier works now lost to us. He gives both definitions and explanations of some proverbs.

Adonis, gardens of. In the Adonia, they bring out effigies and gardens in earthenware pots, and all sorts of late summer produce; the gardens for Adonis are planted with plants like fennel and lettuce—because the story goes that Aphrodite laid Adonis out on a bed of lettuce.

PART 3

DESECRATION

The two final chapters confront directly the crimes of impiety that sparked such hysteria in the summer of 415: the mutilation of the herms and desecration of the Mysteries. The discovery of these transgressions just as the Sicilian Expedition was about to launch hurled the city into a panic that had far-reaching consequences. Thucydides, who undoubtedly investigated as thoroughly as he could both while away from Athens and once he returned, claims that no one ever determined the truth of what had happened, but dozens of men would be accused, convicted, exiled, or executed for the crimes.

One of the core challenges in determining what actually happened that summer is the nature of the sources that remain to us. The two fullest contemporary voices are those of Thucydides and Andocides, but a different agenda shapes the account of each. In chapter 5 (Agora) we focus on the historian. Our setting is the city's center for commerce in both goods and information. It was here that the systematic nature of the mutilations must first have become evident, and here that wild theories concerning sabotage or conspiracy circulated. The nature of the herms and of the Eleusinian Mysteries can illuminate how attacks against Hermes and Demeter were perceived. These common perceptions in turn drive Thucydides' narrative and the larger lessons he draws from the episode.

In chapter 6 (Dikastērion) we turn to Andocides, whose defense speech *On the Mysteries* gives us vivid detail, in places contradicting Thucydides' account, about the unfolding crisis. Andocides delivered his speech in a trial that took place some fifteen years after the events in question. We begin the chapter therefore examining the famous Athenian legal system and its implications for the text we have. How might Andocides' history and current situation determine the shape of his account, and what does that tell us about Athenian norms and values? Most intriguingly, Andocides' speech preserves for us the names of some of the people who came forward with information about the religious crimes. These shadowy figures offer a glimpse into the sorts of opportunities the legal system afforded, especially during the hysteria that prevailed during those crucial weeks of 415.

CHAPTER 5

Agora

The Herms and the Mysteries: Hearsay and History

Northwest of the Acropolis stretched the *Agora*, or marketplace: the heart of the city's thriving commercial, administrative, and social life. Around its border stood the public buildings where much of the daily political business of the city happened, but the area is most commonly associated with economic activity. The broad rectangular space, planted in the first half of the fifth century with shady plane trees, filled each morning with stalls selling vegetables, fish, perfumes, wine, clothes, slaves, and all the wares of the craftsmen who flocked to the city. On a low hill on the west side the temple to Hephaestus still overlooks the space; in the fifth century this was surrounded with metalworking shops basking in the support of their divine counterpart. The areas in the market itself were well-known and organized. That great champion of order Ischomachus, whom we met in chapter 4, could tell his young wife that "you may order any sort of servant to buy something in the market and to bring it home, and . . . every one of them is bound to know where he should go to get each article" (*Oeconomicus* 8.22). The bustling and crowded market was occupied not only by those selling and buying, but anyone else looking to run into friends or gather the latest news and gossip. Socrates famously conducted his conversations in the Agora, but evidently everyone else did too: a fourth-century orator can claim: "Each of you is in the habit of paying a call at either a perfumer's or a barber's or a shoemaker's shop, or wherever he may chance to go . . . you are all in the habit of paying a call and passing your time at some shop or other" (Lysias 24.20). In the northwest corner of the Agora, as well as along the south end, were long, open colonnades, providing a shaded space, sometimes elaborately decorated with painting or sculpture, for conversation or business transactions. These are called *stoai*, and from them Stoic philosophy took its name, suggesting that they functioned as public space for discussion and debate of all kinds. In a time before mass media, important news spread by word of mouth, and this central gathering place was where you could find it. The story that was about to erupt in that early summer of 415 would drive this news-gathering and gossip-trading to a fever pitch.

Consider those Athenians on their way to the Agora on that momentous morning. Their first glimpses of broken stone perhaps passed unremarked, but then each subsequent one must have added to the sense that something significant and frightening had happened. By the time the morning crowd had gathered, panic would have set in. In the northwest corner of the Agora stood the stoa of the herms (often referred to simply as "the herms"), where many of the statues were collected. The systematic nature of the damage would be striking here, and would elicit stories from the bystanders about what they had already seen on their journey to the marketplace that morning. For practically every herm in the city had been vandalized, their faces rudely "cut around," presumably smashed on both sides. There in the Agora, where the largest concentration of these statues stood, it was a shocking and sobering sight.

The Herms

The figures that were mutilated that night in 415 are not, perhaps, the type that spring to mind when we think of Greek statues generally. They displayed no lovingly sculpted musculature, no buff torsos or highly articulated abdominals, nor the dynamic body positions suggesting struggle or movement that were the hallmark of classical Greek art. The herms, rather, were simple rectangular pillars of stone, topped with a (usually bearded) head representing the god Hermes. Halfway up the front of the block was an erect phallus, sometimes simply carved in relief, and sometimes projecting more emphatically. Were the phalluses of the herms also smashed, as well as their faces? Thucydides doesn't mention this, although it is implied elsewhere, and they would present a tempting target for vandalism. On either side of the top of the block, where shoulders would have been on a more anthropomorphic form, were short protruding posts; perhaps these were used to drape garments or other offerings on the statues. Their frequent placement at temple entrances may indicate that they were used as intermediaries to ask prayers of other gods, as well as to honor Hermes. To us these herms are very odd-looking, and seem alien to a culture that so highly prized representations of the youthful, male human body. Both Herodotus and Thucydides tell us, though, that this form developed in Athens itself. To the Athenians, herms were part of what made their city unique.

Discussions of the vandalism must have started quickly. Who could have done such a thing, and why? What did it mean? How should the city respond? If we woke one morning to a similar grand act of vandalism, the first reaction would likely be that the culprits were hooligans or gang members, disaffected or disadvantaged youth. This is a mark of how different our society is from ancient Athens, where such an explanation seems never to have occurred to anyone. It's true that some voices at the time, followed by some modern historians, suggested that the incident was the work of rambunctious, aristocratic youths in the later stages of drunkenness: a symposiastic kōmos gone awry. But even this was neither the first or most popular explanation that occurred to the Athenians on that morning when the mutilations were discovered. They instead assumed the act was not only a "bad omen for the expedition," but indicated a "conspiracy aimed at revolution and the destruction of the democracy" (Thucydides 6.27). Athens had a lot of herms. Many were concentrated there in the Agora, but most were widely distributed in sanctuaries and in front of private houses throughout the city. Out of these dozens and dozens of statues, we know of just one herm that was not mutilated. The thorough and systematic nature of the vandalism, then, must have immediately suggested that the attack had been carefully planned, and carried out by more than just one or two people. It is not so outlandish that the first conclusion was that some sort of conspiracy was afoot. But what could its goals be? Why the herms?

To get a sense both of why any group might choose such a target for a spectacular act of vandalism, and to understand the city's response to that act, we have to go back, first to the god Hermes himself, and then to these peculiar figures that represented him. Hermes is a trickster and an inventor. The *Homeric Hymn to Hermes*, a delightful if puzzling archaic poem, describes him as "resourceful, with winning wiles, a thief, a cattle driver, a bringer of dreams, a spy at night, a watcher at the gates" (13–15). The hymn elaborates the story of the day on which Hermes, newly born, invents the lyre and steals Apollo's cattle. When Apollo comes to confront him with his crime, he snuggles under the covers in his cradle and denies everything:

I didn't do it, and besides I care about different things:
sleep, and my mother's milk,
and blankets around me, and warm baths . . .
it's not plausible, what you say!
I was born yesterday, my feet are soft, and the ground beneath is rough.
If you like, I'll swear a great oath on the head of my father.
I promise that neither am I guilty,
nor did I see anyone else stealing your cows,
whatever cows are. I've only heard stories about them. (260–67)

Apollo, unconvinced, picks up Hermes, who sneezes and farts (or as the poet more delicately puts it "sent forth an omen, a wretched servant of the belly, a presumptuous messenger" 294–96). Apollo drops the baby, but he and the troublesome child go to Zeus for arbitration of the quarrel. Hermes finally confesses, and gives Apollo the lyre in compensation for the cattle. The final scene in the poem between Hermes, Apollo, and Zeus indicates the specific areas with which Hermes was to be associated. We learn that Zeus has given Hermes authority over matters of exchange among men; for this reason, Apollo says, he fears that Hermes might steal back the lyre and even Apollo's bow. This is a good indication of how close, in the imagination of the Greeks, trade and exchange were to theft and trickery. In addition, Zeus declares that only Hermes shall be messenger to Hades, an explanation of Hermes' function as the *psychopompos*, the figure who escorts the souls of the dead to the underworld.

Thief, trader, messenger, guide. In all his functions, Hermes operates at and across borders. He oversees the exchange of property (licit and illicit) from one owner to another, he oversees the exchange of information from one realm to another, he escorts the traveler from one world to another. It is this aspect of the god, his affinity with borders and their negotiation, that seems to underlie those peculiar statues, the herms. While the origin of these figures is obscure, we know that they were found primarily at borders, crossroads, and entryways. They marked, for the traveler, the halfway point between the various outlying villages of Attica and the city of Athens. Many, as we have seen, stood at the northwest entrance to the Agora, as seems appropriate given Hermes' association with exchange. They also stood at entrances, both to sanctuaries and houses, marking the border between outside and in, or public and private. Their aggressive phallic display, in fact, has been compared to the way in which male primates, guarding their communities, threaten intruders by signaling their potency.

Unsurprisingly, given this unabashed display of masculine power, the herms were also associated with military victory. In the fourth century, and very likely earlier, generals sacrificed to the herms. In 475 BCE the Athenians won an important military victory in the northeast of Greece at a town called Eion. They voted that a monument should be erected in commemoration. It consisted of three stone herms, bearing inscriptions celebrating not the general's achievements, but those of the hoplite soldiers and, by extension, the Athenian demos. Plutarch asserts that the gesture of dedicating this monument was exceptional; earlier victories had never been so honored. He suggests that Eion was marked out for special recognition because earlier battles had only defended Athens from invaders. This was the first victory to conquer new territory and thus expand the possessions of the city. Eion was an offensive, rather than a defensive, engagement, and it was fought on the margins of Athenian influence.

These odd quadrangular figures, then, had strong ties through the god Hermes to both protecting borders and crossing borders. They defended the entrances to city, marketplace, temple, and home, while also celebrating aggressive attack on and victory over other communities. The mysterious and systematic mutilation of these figures just as the Athenians were preparing a massive military expedition against a distant target was extraordinarily threatening. The anger of Hermes, the very god who ensures safe passage from one place to another, would endanger ships and soldiers, and everyone immediately saw the crime as an ill omen for the expedition. Could it have been intended to disrupt or even prevent it?

The other fear that the mutilation of the herms triggered, that it signaled "a conspiracy aimed at revolution and the destruction of the democracy," seems to us less natural than the first. To understand this fear, we need to look again at the Eion monument. While it no longer exists, a vase-painting of three herms may well represent it. In the painting, the central herm faces forward, while herms on either side face each other. The effect of this grouping is to associate anyone looking at the monument with the herms. You stand and face the central herm, and now you and he are in the same position as the other two herms facing each other. You're all herms together, or, more to the point, you and the herms are all citizens together: remember the inscription on this monument honored not the general, but the army. The democracy liked to emphasize the ways in which all male citizens were essentially interchangeable. Displays of private wealth were discouraged, and the household, where economic differences between citizens would be clearest, was thought of as radically separate from the public affairs of the polis. The very basic, fundamental male form of the herm (bearded head, penis) reflected the essential attributes of the adult male citizen, unencumbered with individual characteristics. The herm that stood outside houses stood in for the male head of that household, just as the herms dedicated after the victory at Eion in the Agora stood in not for the victorious generals but rather for the undifferentiated hoplite soldiers. Any attack against the herms, then, would also be an attack on the democratic ideology that claimed this equivalence between citizens. No wonder people feared conspiracy against the democracy itself.

The Athenians set up a board of inquiry to investigate the matter. They also immediately issued a call for information about the crime, offering substantial rewards and immunity to informers, to encourage even those who may have perpetrated the mutilations to come forward. The affair of the herms is unprecedented in Athenian history of the classical period. At no other point did a single crime cause such a degree of consternation in the city. We have no other incident, then, with which to compare what happened. But two things about the immediate response to the mutilations stand out, both because they seem unusual and because of their far-reaching consequences. First, information was solicited not just about what had happened to the herms, but also (as Thucydides tells us) "about any other sacrilegious act." Would it seem natural, in investigating one offense against the gods, to see if there had been others, just in case? Or was this part of the decree inserted, already in the heat of the first response to the mutilations, for less than purely religious motives, as a convenient way of targeting political enemies? The other notable aspect of the call for information was the width of the net it cast. Immunity was guaranteed to anyone: "citizen, foreigner, or slave," who might offer information to the city. Since information would, in the event, come from slaves testifying against masters and a metic against citizens, it is tempting to wonder if already the authors of the decree were plotting ways in which they might take advantage of the general fear of the people to accomplish ends well beyond the investigation with which they were charged.

The atmosphere in the city was tense even in the immediate aftermath of the discovery, although it would become much worse as time passed. Preparations for the expedition continued, and ships gathered in the harbor of Piraeus, awaiting the launch. At this point, Thucydides tells us:

> There was information from some metics and servants, not concerning the herms, but about earlier vandalism of other statues by young men that had happened in drunken play, and at the same time, claims that the Mysteries had been performed hubristically (*eph'hubrei*) in private houses. They accused Alcibiades as well as others of these things. (6.28)

This brings us to the second religious scandal of 415, uncovered only incidentally through the investigation of the first: the desecration of the Eleusinian Mysteries. It is now clear why the addition of "any other sacrilegious act" to the call for information about the herms was significant. Whether by design or by accident, this wider net caught up a whole new set of suspects, including Alcibiades himself. But what would "performing the Mysteries" in a private house mean, and why did it spark the kind of reaction it did? To understand this, we need to dig deeper into the Eleusinian Mysteries.

The Mysteries

Eleusis, the center of the cult, was a town about fourteen miles northwest of Athens. From Mycenaean times it had been a center for the worship of

Demeter, goddess of agriculture and particularly of grain. Very early on Eleusis had come under the influence of Athens, and by the historical period the celebration of the Eleusinian Mysteries was firmly under Athenian control. Unlike the state-funded festivals of, say, the City Dionysia, or even the more informally organized religious celebrations like the Adonia, the Mysteries were Panhellenic. Anyone who spoke Greek and had not committed murder could participate, and people traveled from all over the Greek world to become initiates in the cult. Notably, slaves and women could participate along with men. The festival was among the most explicitly inclusive of those we know in the ancient world. Yet despite its wide popularity we know very little about the nature of the ceremony. It is called a "mystery" religion because initiates, who have witnessed the ceremonies at the center of the festival, are sworn to secrecy about what they have seen. The secrets of the Eleusinian Mysteries were well kept, and although the festival was celebrated for over a thousand years (well into the Roman period), no accounts of the central ceremony have survived.

We do know the outlines of the festival, which occurred over nine days in the month of Boedromion, in the early fall. Candidates for initiation gathered in Athens, where they participated in preparatory rites like ritual washing in the sea, and the sacrifice of piglets. On the day before the central ceremony, initiates processed from Athens to Eleusis. This fourteen-mile walk, with hundreds, possibly thousands, of participants, took a full day, and finished with torchlight festivities. The following day initiates fasted, in preparation for the revelation of the mysteries they would experience that evening. Their fast was broken with a drink called *kykeōn* ("mixture"). This was likely in imitation of Demeter, who (as we learn from her Homeric Hymn) drinks a mixture of barley, mint, and water as she seeks her daughter. Given the phenomenal popularity of the cult, and the evident strength of the psychological response to initiation, there has been a great deal of discussion about whether any of these ingredients might, on an empty stomach, act as psychotropic drugs. Ergot, a fungus that grows on some grains, is soluble in water and related to LSD. No conclusive arguments have emerged about this however, and it is plausible that the experience alone, with fasting and physical exertion followed by some communal revelation, would be powerful enough to explain people's attachment to the cult.

That evening, in a massive square temple called the Telestērion, the initiates witnessed the Mysteries themselves. These remain unknown to us, other than the vague formulation that they consisted of "things enacted," "things said," and "things shown." It was presumably this highly secret ceremony that Alcibiades and his associates were accused of "doing" at home. These performances criminally revealed the secrets of the mystery cult to any uninitiated guests (or even attendants) present. In addition, those performing the ceremonies appropriated the duties and rights of the official priests who enacted the ritual in the Telestērion at Eleusis. The wrong people engaging in sacred acts in the wrong place profaned the goddess as surely as the revelation of the secrets to the uninitiated. What could motivate such sacrilege? Was it simply the high spirits of privileged men, getting a laugh from mocking a ceremony so many held dear? Or could they have had more serious motives? What might they have to gain from appropriating a ritual as highly emotive and actively inclusive as the Eleusinian Mysteries?

There are two camps on this question: either the enactments were simply party games, performed for their comic value, or some more serious purpose was served. Until quite recently, historians have assumed that Alcibiades and his friends engaged in these performances simply for fun. Analogies are offered of someone imitating a minister, or parodying the communion service. Certainly such behavior wouldn't be out of character for a man of Alcibiades' unconventional beliefs, and it would, the argument goes, have been entertaining. Undoubtedly once again it is the overwhelming respect we have for Thucydides that lends weight to this interpretation. He mentions the accusations in the same sentence as other allegations that some youths vandalized statues "in drunken play." He goes on to say that "the Mysteries were performed *eph'hubrei*," which I translated above as "hubristically," but is regularly rendered "in mockery." Historians commonly use the word "parody" to describe the action. Hubris, as we saw in chapter 2, does imply a sense of superiority; if those who performed the mysteries wanted to signal their superiority to the ritual itself, or to the priests who normally performed them, then mockery is a fair translation. But even so it does not necessarily imply humor as the words "mockery" or "parody" normally do for us.

If we remove the notion of entertainment from the affair we get to the second camp, which sees some deeper purpose in the performances. Here, as with the mutilation of the herms, that purpose would presumably hinge on the perceived sense of what the Eleusinian Mysteries meant to the culture normally. It has been proposed that Eleusis and the priests associated with that cult were strenuously antiwar. Demeter was after all an agricultural goddess, and offerings owed to the cult came from the first fruits of the harvest. Agriculture had suffered a great deal under the ravages of ten years of war with the Spartans, undoubtedly cutting into the revenues of the sanctuary. In addition, the annual procession from Athens to Eleusis had been impossible when the surrounding countryside was occupied by the enemy. Peace was in the interest of the cult, the argument goes, and thus any activity belittling the cult would be characteristic of Alcibiades and those of his comrades who were actively trying to rekindle the war. In this case Thucydides' expression *eph'hubrei* would imply that those appropriating the ritual did it to signal their superiority to the cult and its practitioners themselves. By this interpretation the profanations had serious political purpose, even if they occurred only in private.

Another possibility hinges instead on what we know of the emotional effects of initiation into the mysteries. It is widely agreed that the experience of initiation was highly satisfying; Eleusis remained one of the most popular cults in the ancient world for a thousand years. Perhaps the enactments taking place in private houses were attempts to capture this emotional satisfaction, and the bond among fellow initiates that this seemed to generate. If psychotropic drugs were part of the initiation experience, this also could have contributed to desire for more frequent enactments. The mysteries were celebrated only once a year, and then amid massive and undifferentiated crowds: slaves and foreigners were initiated along with citizens, and women along with men. Perhaps it is not so odd that groups of wealthy men would have wanted to re-create this experience in the privacy of their homes and the absence of the unwashed throng. The sense of superiority in Thucydides' expression *eph'hubrei* was in this case superiority to the rest of the initiates, rather than to the cult.

No matter what the truth is behind Alcibiades' alleged performance of the Mysteries, he responded to the accusations by strenuously denying his guilt and demanding immediate trial. He was eager to be cleared before launching the expedition. This was also a shrewd political calculation. The city was full to bursting with soldiers eager to set out, as well as the allies who had agreed to join mainly at the urging of Alcibiades himself. It seems unlikely under these circumstances that any jury would have convicted him. If the investigation into his activities continued in his absence, however, his risk of conviction could be much higher.

Thucydides, followed by Plutarch, is less concerned with the accusations themselves, and instead emphasizes the way Alcibiades' political rivals took advantage of them when they surfaced to stir up sentiment against him. For these figures a speedy trial would be a waste of a good opportunity. They therefore put forward speakers to argue against delaying the expedition, with the real intention of manufacturing a case against him after his departure. This explanation of the decision to sail may come from the knowledge of what happened later. There were many compelling arguments against delay that had nothing to do with hostility toward Alcibiades. There are economic implications to keeping a large military force idle once it is assembled. Additionally, sentiment among citizens was so strongly in favor of the expedition that it is doubtful whether anyone could have convinced the Athenians to delay at this point. Even in the wake of the mutilations, which were reportedly seen by everyone as a bad omen for the expedition, we have no evidence that anyone seriously proposed pushing back the launch date. Alcibiades, rather, seems to have been a tragic victim of his own rhetorical power. Having whipped the Athenians into a frenzy of desire for conquest in Sicily, he would be constrained to set out before having his innocence decisively proved. The Athenians voted that Alcibiades and the others should face trial on these charges upon their return from Sicily, and the expedition proceeded as planned. Just as Alcibiades anticipated, this was a bad mistake.

It is hard to improve on Thucydides' evocative description of the launch of the expedition in the summer of 415. The day was clearly a memorable one for the entire city, and even more so in retrospect, with knowledge of the disastrous outcome. At dawn the entire force of both Athenians and those of the allies who were there in Athens walked from the city the three miles down to the harbor of Piraeus. Thousands of onlookers lined the road to cheer them on. Wives and young children of the soldiers and sailors, parents, friends, and neighbors shouted farewells to the boys they knew; foreigners gazed in admiration on the spectacular force there assembled.

> They came hoping for profit from the expedition and at the same time lamenting that they might never see these men again, considering the great distance of the journey from their own land. At this moment when they were really on the point of parting from each other with all the risks ahead, the terrors struck them more than they had at the time when they voted for the expedition. All the same they were encouraged by the sight of the assembled force, and the abundance of everything they saw. (6.30–31)

One hundred ships stood in the harbor, each fitted out as gloriously as possible. Five thousand Athenian hoplites filed aboard the transport ships, while sailors and oarsmen filled the triremes. When the ships were manned, a trumpet call commanded silence from the throngs both on shipboard and on shore. A clear-voiced herald directed the prayers for safety. Soldiers and officers poured libations from gold and silver cups. Hymns rang out from shore from those assembled to see the flower of their city off to what they assumed would be the most extraordinary victory Athens had ever known. The prayers over, the force rowed out of the harbor in a column, and then raced each other as far as Aegina, some twelve miles away.

Tyrants and Conspiracies

Investigations continued into both the religious scandals through the summer. Thucydides is scathing about the process. Informers, in his narrative, are *ponēroi* ("wretched") and the accused are *khrēstoi* ("useful"); these are the terms the aristocracy uses to refer to the lower classes and themselves respectively. An explicit class element, then, is evident in Thucydides' account of the episode. The tensions we saw simmering under the surface as stasis erupted in other Greek cities seem to be driving the response to the mutilation of the herms. The connection between the herms and democratic ideology we've looked at explains part of this. Perhaps the symposiastic setting for the illegal performances of the Mysteries, freighted as it was with aristocratic resonance, was also operating. Both religious crimes could plausibly strike the demos as indicative of threats to their primacy. But the way in which the response to the scandals played out takes us beyond hostility between oligarchs and democrats. The whole affair presents an interesting example of the way class tension could function as a tool for other ends.

The investigations would result in the exile of Alcibiades, with far-reaching consequences both to the Sicilian Expedition and the war with Sparta. Thucydides focuses our attention on the reasons Alcibiades might have been a target:

> And those who were most hostile to Alcibiades, because he prevented them from being firmly in control of the demos, seized on this. Thinking that if they drove him out they would be the most powerful, they amplified everything and kept shouting that the desecration of the Mysteries and the mutilation of the herms were both aimed at destroying the democracy, and Alcibiades was involved with all of it; as evidence, they pointed to the rest of his undemocratic conduct and his contempt for norms. (6.28)

Note that what these unnamed enemies are after is "control of the demos," not direct control of the city. They are not seeking oligarchical rule but rather power within the existing democratic system. For this they need the favor of the demos, which Alcibiades currently has. Their path to discrediting Alcibiades was to link the profanation of the Mysteries, of which he had been accused, to the more intuitively antidemocratic attack on the herms, of which he had not. Given the way in which the mutilations were taken to threaten the Sicilian Expedition, while Alcibiades was its most famous proponent, it is implausible that he would have been involved in the mutilations. But his enemies worked to conflate the two scandals, insinuating that both were aimed against the democracy and drawing attention to Alcibiades' "undemocratic conduct and contempt for norms." Remember that when Thucydides first introduced him, before the debate on Sicily, he also drew attention to the fact that these conspicuous traits suggested to everyone that he aimed at tyranny.

We've seen how the threat of tyranny haunted the Athenian imagination, and how institutions like ostracism were designed to protect against it. Actual threats to democratic governments across the Greek world at this time, however, came in the form of oligarchies, rather than tyrannies. The power of playing on anxieties about tyranny, in fact, may have primarily benefited aristocrats seeking influence with the demos. It was a convenient way to produce popular suspicion of a rival more than a true safeguard for democratic power. If the comic poets are any indication, this kind of talk had been common for about a decade already in 415. Aristophanes' plays of the late 420s mock the regularity with which charges of tyranny are produced against almost anyone. To give just two examples: the hip and sophisticated son in the *Wasps* claims:

> Everything with you people is all tyranny and conspiracy,
> Whether the accusation is huge or tiny:
> I hadn't heard the word in fifty years
> But now, it's just like salted fish—
> Tossed about all over the Agora.
> If someone wants to buy anchovies but not sprats,
> The sprat-seller next door says
> "oooh, la-dee-dah, *someone* indulges like a tyrant!"
> And if he wants an onion for sauce on the anchovies,
> The grocer-woman gives him the side-eye and says
> "so you want an onion! Are you after a tyranny,
> or do you think Athens owes you sauces?"
> . . . if now I just want my father to have a nice life
> . . . I get accused of conspiracy and tyrannical thinking. (*Wasps*, 488–507)

Perhaps even more revealingly, in the *Knights*, the Paphlagonian (a thinly veiled caricature of one of the leading politicians of the moment) argues that he should continue as trusted servant of Demos:

> Don't think you'll ever find a better friend than me,
> Who all alone stopped the conspirators, and no
> Plot in the city gets by me, but I blow the whistle! (*Knights* 860–63)

To this his rival the sausage-seller replies:

> You and the eel-fishermen.
> Whenever the lake's calm, they catch nothing:
> But when they stir the muck up and down,
> Success! It's good for you too when you rile up the city. (864–66)

Again, it's worth focusing on the class inflection here. Aristophanes often seems to present a "common man" as his hero, but his satire frequently pillories the gullibility of the demos, rather than the elite. In the example from the *Wasps* the laughter is aimed at the absurdity of common people, the class who would have had market stalls in the Agora, lobbing ridiculous accusations at wealthier ones. All he wants, the young man complains, is to give his father a treat by buying some nice fish and onions. In the *Knights* we explicitly see the effects of this gullibility. Demagogues find power in playing on the common people's fear of tyranny: the claim to stop conspirators or plots is in reality just "stirring up the muck" for personal profit. Thucydides' account of the investigations of the herms and Mysteries fits this pattern precisely. It was to the advantage of those wishing to lead the demos to incite fear of tyranny and conspiracy until the people were suspicious of everyone.

This exploitation of common fear of conspiracy, and the conversations it produced among the stalls and in the stoas of the Agora, may be lurking behind one of the strangest parts of Thucydides' account of this strange affair. While describing the emotional state of the Athenians while the investigations were going on, he tells us that "the people had heard that the tyranny of Peisistratus and his sons had been cruel in the end, and that it had been overthrown not by their own efforts or by Harmodius, but by the Spartans. This made them fearful and suspicious of everything" (6.53). He then inserts a long and unusual digression about a series of events that had happened almost exactly one hundred years before that summer of 415. When he is finished telling his version of the story, he repeats his initial assertion: "All of these stories were in the minds of the Athenians, and reminding themselves of what they knew by hearsay this fed their suspicions, and made them deal harshly with those suspected of involvement in the affairs of the Mysteries. Everything seemed to them to point to an oligarchic and tyrannical conspiracy" (6.60).

This passage in Thucydides has long puzzled classicists. Unlike his predecessor Herodotus, Thucydides is not given to digressions, so the ones that occur attract attention. Why did he feel it important to revisit the story of the tyrannicides? And why might the Athenians, as he claims, have become obsessed with the episode at this particular moment in 415? The answer may well offer a glimpse of the kind of gossip and debate that must have exercised the crowds milling around the Agora that summer. Moments of crisis frequently drive people back to the past, as a way of grappling with or understanding the present. This is, in fact, Thucydides' whole project. His claim at the beginning of his work is that he writes for "those who wish to examine what is clear from the past and the sort of thing that will happen again in the future, given what is human" (1.22). Parallels between past and present must have been much debated in the Agora during the weeks following the launch of the Sicilian Expedition. To get a sense of why, we need to go back to the story Thucydides tells.

Athens, like many other Greek cities, had been ruled by tyrants in the sixth century. The term "tyrant" in this historical context refers to someone who seizes and maintains political power outside of normal constitutional channels. In the mid-sixth century such a man, Peisistratus, held rule in Athens intermittently, and upon his death his sons took control. But after the murder of one son, the rule of the other became more violent until a Spartan force, at the behest of the exiled Alcmaeonid clan, effected regime change in 510. Thucydides starts his account of the end of what we call the Peisistratid tyranny by saying that he will tell the story "to show that the Athenians are not more accurate than the rest of the world in their accounts of their own tyrants and of the facts of their own history." In the popular version of the tale, Hipparchus was the ruling tyrant and his assassination, carried out by two Athenians named Aristogeiton and Harmodius, was key in ending the tyranny. This is the version of the story implied by a drinking song preserved for us in the much later author Athenaeus:

> I will carry my sword in a myrtle bough
> Just like Harmodius and Aristogeiton
> When they killed the tyrant
> And made Athens *isonomos* [a place of equality under the law]. (15.50)

It is also the tradition implied by the privileges that were granted to the men's descendants, and by a famous pair of honorary statues depicting them. We can picture the fevered exchange of versions of these stories, and the lessons that should be drawn from them about the current crisis, as taking place in the shadow of these statues in the Agora.

Thucydides' account, on the other hand, emphasizes the fact that Hipparchus was not tyrant when he was killed, and that the tyrannicides acted out of eros for each other rather than any abstract or patriotic love of freedom. In Thucydides' account, Hipparchus fell in love with Harmodius, but had been spurned by the young man, who was faithful to his middle-class lover Aristogeiton. Hipparchus retaliated by insulting Harmodius' sister. The outraged Harmodius and his jealous lover Aristogeiton plotted to kill both Hipparchus and his brother Hippias, who was at that time the ruling tyrant. At the last minute, wrongly convinced that they had been betrayed to Hippias, they killed only Hipparchus. Hippias became more oppressive in the wake of this close call, and continued to rule for several years until he was expelled by the Spartans and the exiled Alcmaeonids. He eventually obtained sanctuary with the Persians, and accompanied Darius' invasion of Greece in 490.

As investigations into both the mutilations and the desecrations were ongoing, then, those Athenians who hadn't sailed off to Sicily obsessively talked through the mystery of the religious crimes, their motives, and their suspected perpetrators as they awaited news of informants, confessions, or arrests. The story of the end of the Peisistratid tyranny was part of these discussions. Why would Athenians have been discussing this history at this moment? Why would the murder of Hipparchus by Harmodius and Aristogeiton, and the end of Hippias' tyranny, make Athenians "suspicious of the persons charged in the affair of the mysteries," and persuade them that everything had been done "as part of a conspiracy aiming at oligarchy or tyranny"?

There are several intriguing points of contact between the religious scandals then under investigation and the old story of the Peisistratid tyranny. First, as has been mentioned, is the leap from vandalism of the herms to fear of tyranny; perhaps this reminded people of the past tyranny and how oppressive it had been. The fact that not even the traditional local heroes Harmodius and Aristogeiton had been able to bring an end to it when they killed Hipparchus, but that a Spartan invasion had been necessary, could only add to the general fear of conspiracies against the democracy that might lead to one-man rule.

Additionally, though, the herms themselves were associated with Hipparchus. He may well have introduced them to Attica. Many of them, erected to mark the halfway point between outlying demes and the city, were inscribed with his name and some wise words for the traveler ("think just thoughts!"). Perhaps some argued, pushing back on the initial theory, that an attack on the herms was not aimed against the democracy but was rather meant to recall Harmodius and Aristogeiton's attack on the Peisistratid Hipparchus. In that case, the intended message of the mutilations would have been "death to tyrants!" Even so, no one could have been reassured once reminded that Harmodius and Aristogeiton had after all failed to take down the tyranny, and a Spartan invasion had been required.

There is one other possible explanation for the circulation the tyrannicide legend, and that concerns the famous family of Alcibiades, the Alcmaeonid clan. According to the earlier historian Herodotus, the Spartans had made their decision to put down the Peisistratid tyranny after getting insistent oracles from Delphi. No matter what question they put to the priestess, they would receive the same answer: "free the Athenians." The oracle at Delphi acted in this peculiar manner because the Alcmaeonids, who had been exiled from Athens when the Peisistratids rose to power, were bribing the priests. The Alcmaeonids accompanied the Spartan expedition to overthrow the tyrants, and Cleisthenes, an Alcmaeonid, was the man responsible for the institutions of the infant democracy that replaced them. If current gossip maintained that the desecration of the Mysteries of which Alcibiades was accused was connected to an oligarchical or tyrannical conspiracy, the Peisistratid story could have been produced in his defense: Alcibiades would never aim at tyranny! His family has opposed tyrants for generations. Not even the tyrant-slayers rid Athens of the Peisistratids; it was the Alcmaeonids who succeeded in this and the creation of democracy. Yet at the same time, they had done this in collusion with the Spartans, now enemies of the Athenians. And they had done it by subverting Delphi, a center of religious awe, to their own political purposes. Had Alcibiades again engaged in conspiracy with an external foe, in his quest for power within the city? Could the desecration of the Mysteries be another example of the kind of subversion of sacred ceremony the Alcmaeonids had found useful once before? It was no wonder that the Athenians rehashed that old story, and grew increasingly fearful and suspicious.

In addition to giving us a hint of the kinds of debate the Agora must have seen that summer, Thucydides' version of the story offers, in pointed contrast, his own philosophy about the appropriate use of the past. In a famous passage near the beginning of his work, he contrasts his own historiographical process with common attitudes toward history: "For people accept hearsay about the past from each other without testing it, even when it is native to them" (1.22). He himself, on the other hand, has expended enormous care and effort in critical examination of his sources: "I judged it correct to report the actions of the war neither by asking whoever I came across, nor even as I thought they happened, but going through both events for which I was present and those I learned about from others with the greatest degree of accuracy possible. These things required hard work to discover, since eyewitnesses to the events did not agree with each other, but spoke as their partiality or memory held." He goes on to explain that the narrative he has produced with this scrupulous testing will be beneficial to "those who wish to examine what is clear from the past and the sort of thing that will happen again in the future, given what is human" (1.22).

Thucydides' goal, then, is the *saphes*, "what is clear" and this cannot be discovered by those who "accept hearsay without testing it" (as the Athenians, of course, recalled what they knew of the Peisistratids by hearsay). Once you have carefully determined the *saphes*—and his account of the murder of Hipparchus is full of the traces of his care—it is beneficial because it is likely to happen again. Accurate knowledge of the past will be helpful in the present and the future. The Athenians' impulse in reviewing the Peisistratid episode is good. But they are not sufficiently careful about how they do it. The Athenians leap to conclusions about the dangers of tyranny and the way it makes the city vulnerable to the Spartans, and thus panic over conspiracies. Their behavior in this panic is equally destructive, as they receive all informers alike, especially lower-class ones informing on members of the elite, without testing their information. Thucydides' corrected version of the tale of Harmodius and Aristogeiton, in fact, seems to be crafted exactly to foreground the dangers of passion inciting rash action: Aristogeiton was goaded by erotic pain, thinking (wrongly) that Hipparchus might use force against Harmodius, and then, in the event, thinking (wrongly again) that his plan had been betrayed. The result of his rash action and failure to test his assumptions was not only the newly oppressive regime of Hippias, but also Hippias' subsequent flight to the Persian court, and his participation in the Persian invasion of Greece. If the Athenians wanted to use the story as a lesson for their present, they would do better to consider the dangers of leaping to conclusions, and of alienating an otherwise capable leader by making rash and ill-considered attacks against him.

This was not, however, the version of the story circulating in the Agora, and it was not the conclusion the people reached. Instead Alcibiades' enemies succeeded in whipping up passions against him so effectively that the city decided to send the official state ship, the Salaminia, to escort him home from Sicily to face trial for the desecration of the Mysteries. The consequences for the Sicilian Expedition, now in the charge of the man who thought it was a catastrophic mistake, would be disastrous. So too were the consequences to the city itself, which would face both external and internal threats as a result. But we have jumped ahead of ourselves. For before the Athenians recalled Alcibiades to face trial for desecration of the Mysteries, they believed that they had solved the case of the herms. Thucydides gives a very compressed account of this at the end of the excerpt that follows. But we have another source that recounts it, along with subsequent investigations about the Mysteries, in much greater detail. That story is the subject of the final chapter.

Primary Source Interlude

Thucydides, Book 6, Excerpts on the Herms,
Mysteries, and Tyrannicides

THUCYDIDES, BOOK 6.27–29

[27] In the midst of these preparations, all the herms that were in the city—those numerous rectangular pillars of stone that, following Athenian custom, are found in front of both private doorways and temples—all of them in a single night had their faces mutilated. No one knew who did it, but a substantial reward was offered for information, and in addition a decree was passed that if anyone—citizen, foreigner, or slave—knew of any sacrilegious acts, he might give information in exchange for immunity. These events affected the Athenians deeply: they took the mutilations as an omen regarding the fate of the expedition, and saw them as the work of conspirators plotting a revolution against the democracy.

[28] Moreover, certain metics and slaves came forward to give evidence, not about the herms, but about the mutilation of certain other statues at the hands of young men on a drunken spree, and incidentally about the hubristic celebration of the Mysteries in private homes: a profanation of which the informers accused Alcibiades. These accusations were seized upon by men who bore a grudge against Alcibiades for standing in the way of their power over the city, and who calculated that if they could get rid of Alcibiades they would rise to prominence in his place. They proceeded to blow these accusations out of proportion, alleging that the profanation of the Mysteries and the mutilation of the herms were part of a conspiracy to bring down the democracy, and that Alcibiades was behind all of it, citing as proof the undemocratic extravagance of his private life.

[29] Alcibiades immediately denied the allegations, and was prepared to stand trial before the departure of the expedition (which was all equipped and ready to sail), and to accept the punishment if he was found guilty, or to assume his command if he could prove his innocence. He called on the Athenians to ignore any slander circulated against him in his absence, and to execute him immediately if he had done wrong, arguing that it would be more responsible, considering the seriousness of the charges against him, not to dispatch him on such an important mission before a trial had taken place. But his enemies sought a delay, fearing that he would have the army on his side if he were tried at once, and that the people would soften toward him because he was the one who persuaded the Argives and Mantineans to join the expedition. They put pressure on other public figures to say that Alcibiades should sail now and not delay the expedition, and return after a set period to stand trial. Their plan was to turn public opinion against him, which would be easier to do in his absence, and then recall him to stand trial. And so it was decided that Alcibiades would sail.

THUCYDIDES, BOOK 6.53–61

[53] The ship Salaminia came to carry Alcibiades back to Athens to answer charges against him, and with him went a number of other soldiers who had been accused either of profaning the Mysteries, or of the mutilation of the herms. For after the expedition sailed, the Athenians did not let up in their investigation of both these matters. There was no proper vetting of the witnesses, but in a spirit of resentment the Athenians convicted some of their leading citizens on the basis of questionable testimony. They thought it was more advantageous to pursue the investigation than to let off otherwise respectable citizens just because the accusation was brought by someone of questionable character. For the people had heard that the tyranny of Peisistratus and his sons had been cruel in the end, and that it had been overthrown not by their own efforts or by Harmodius, but by the Spartans. This made them fearful and suspicious of everything.

[54] The action of Aristogeiton and Harmodius was the outcome of a love affair. I will recount this story in full in order to demonstrate that no one, not even the Athenians themselves, has given an accurate account of what happened, or of the Peisistratid tyranny in general. When Peisistratus died, an old man still in possession of his tyrannical power, it was not Hipparchus, as most people believe, but his older brother Hippias who took control. Harmodius was then in the full glory of his youth, and Aristogeiton, a middle-class Athenian, became his lover. At some point, Hipparchus, the son of Peisistratus, attempted to

seduce Harmodius, but Harmodius rejected him and told Aristogeiton what had happened. Aristogeiton was tortured by the thought of Hipparchus using his position of power to force himself upon Harmodius, and so far as a man of his means was able, he began to plot the downfall of the tyranny. Meanwhile, having made another unsuccessful attempt at seduction, Hipparchus decided that instead of forcing himself on Harmodius he would find some subtle means of ruining the young man's reputation. It should be noted that the rule of the Peisistratids was not oppressive to most people, and was generally beyond reproach. For the most part the tyrants practiced virtue and good judgment, and though they only exacted from the Athenians a twentieth of what they produced, they were able to beautify the city, win wars, and make sacrifices to the gods. For the most part the city kept all existing laws, except that the Peisistratids made sure that a member of their own family always held public office. Among those who held the eponymous archonship was Peisistratus, the son of the tyrant Hippias and namesake of his grandfather, who during his archonship dedicated the altar of the twelve gods in the Agora and the altar in the sanctuary of Pythian Apollo. The Athenian people later expanded the altar in the Agora, and in the process the inscription was effaced, but the inscription on the Pythian altar can still be made out, though the letters have faded:

> This monument of his archonship Peisistratus, son of Hippias,
> set up in the sacred precinct of Pythian Apollo.

[55] That Hippias was the eldest son of the tyrant Peisistratus, and succeeded his father in ruling Athens, I have on the best authority, and offer the following evidence to support this claim. Based on both the inscription on the Pythian altar and on the stele erected on the Athenian Acropolis to commemorate the crimes of the tyrants, Hippias is the only one of the legitimate sons of Peisistratus whose children are recorded: no children of Thessalus or Hipparchus are mentioned, but the inscription records five children of Hippias and Myrrhine, daughter of Callias, son of Hyperochides. As the eldest, Hippias was most likely the first to marry. Furthermore, on the stele he is the first to be mentioned after his father, from which it is not unreasonable to infer that he was the eldest and heir. If Hipparchus had preceded Hippias as tyrant, and died in that position, it seems unlikely that Hippias could have seized power so easily. In fact, he was already long accustomed to striking fear into the people and commanding the obedience of the mercenaries who secured his regime. This was no inexperienced younger brother coming late to power. It was through an unfortunate circumstance that Hipparchus made a name for himself, and came to have a reputation as a tyrant.

[56] Finding his advances rejected, Hipparchus carried out his plan to insult Harmodius. Harmodius had a sister, a virgin, whom Hipparchus contrived to have invited to serve as a basket bearer in some procession. But when she arrived on the day of the festival, she was turned away on the pretext that she was unfit to take part in the procession. Harmodius took the insult hard, but Aristogeiton was even more outraged on his behalf. All the pieces of the conspiracy were in place: they had only to wait for the day of the Great Panathenaea, the one day on which it would not be suspicious for citizens assembled for the procession to be fully armed. The plan was for Harmodius and Aristogeiton to launch the attack, and for the others to join in and hold off the guards. To avoid detection, the details of the plot had been shared with only a few, but the hope was that the others in the crowd, seeing the first blow struck, would take up their arms and join in the recovery of their freedom.

[57] On the day of the festival, Hippias was out in the Ceramicus with his guards, lining up the procession, and Harmodius and Aristogeiton had their daggers ready to commit the deed. But then they saw one of their coconspirators deep in conversation with Hippias—everyone found Hippias approachable—they were afraid they had been betrayed and were about to be arrested. Their fallback plan was to take revenge on the one directly responsible for their sense of injury, the one who had prompted them to act in the first place. With this in mind, they rushed inside the gates of the city and found Hipparchus near the Leocoreum, where, immediately falling upon him with the combined fury of jealous passion and wounded pride, they struck and killed him. In the confusion of the crowd, Aristogeiton managed to escape the guards for the time being, but he was later apprehended and treated roughly. Harmodius was killed on the spot.

[58] When the news was brought to Hippias in the Ceramicus, he bypassed the scene of the crime and went straight to the hoplites who were lined up for the procession, before the news of what had happened could reach them. Without showing any sign of trouble, he ordered them to leave behind their weapons and assemble in the place he designated. The men filed out, imagining that he would come to them with further instructions. Hippias then told his guards to seize the arms, and named as suspects those who had been found with daggers, since only a shield and a spear were allowed in the procession.

[59] This is how it happened: the plot of Harmodius and Aristogeiton started with sexual jealousy, and ended with a sudden panic and an unplanned assault. After this, the regime became even more oppressive to the Athenians. With increasing paranoia, Hippias murdered scores of citizens, and began to look abroad for possible places of safety in the event of a revolution. Though he was

himself an Athenian, he married off his daughter Archedice to Aiantides, son of Hippocles, the tyrant of Lampsacus, seeing that the Lampsacenes had great influence with King Darius. This is the epitaph on the tomb of Archedice in Lampsacus:

> Of the man who was counted best among his fellow Greeks,
> of Hippias, was this woman the daughter. Archedice is buried here.
> Her father, her husband, her brothers, and her sons were all tyrants,
> but she never had a thought of being more than what she was.

Hippias oppressed the Athenians for three more years, and in the fourth year he was removed by the Spartans and the exiled Alcmaeonids. As condition of his surrender, he went to Sigeum, and then to his son-in-law in Lampsacus, before making his way to the court of King Darius, which is how twenty years later, as an old man, he came to fight on the side of the Persians at Marathon.

[60] All of these stories were in the minds of the Athenians, and reminding themselves of what they knew by hearsay they fed their suspicions, and this made them deal harshly with those suspected of involvement in the affairs of the Mysteries. Everything seemed to them to point to an oligarchic and tyrannical conspiracy. As a result of the anger these suspicions produced, many respectable men were imprisoned, and no end to the trouble appeared in sight, but every day the frenzy increased and more and more suspects were rounded up. At last, one of the prisoners, who seemed to be most responsible in the affair, was persuaded by a fellow prisoner to make a confession. Whether it was true or not, nobody knows. To this day no one can say for sure who committed the crimes. In any case, this man was persuaded, whether or not he was involved, to make a confession and claim a pardon, thereby saving his own life and at the same time putting an end to the prevailing mood of distrust in the city. He was convinced that his chances were better if he confessed and accepted a pardon than if he denied the charges and stood trial. So this man gave evidence against both himself and others in the affair of the herms. The Athenians were relieved. They thought they would never discover who was involved in the plot against the democracy. Now they released the informer and all those who had not been implicated. The ones he had accused were brought to trial, and others were rounded up and executed, and a price was placed on the heads of those who had fled. The guilt of those who were condemned was never established beyond the shadow of a doubt, but the immediate effect on the mood of the city was undeniably beneficial.

[61] It was now that the Athenians seized upon the allegations that the enemies of Alcibiades made against him before the expedition sailed. They thought they had gotten to the bottom of the matter of the herms, and more than ever were convinced that the profanation of the Mysteries, of which he had been accused, was part of a conspiracy against the state. And at about the same time that all of this was coming to a head, a small Spartan force was reported on the Isthmus. The mission of the Spartans had something to do with Boeotia, but the Athenians were convinced that there had been some arrangement made with Alcibiades, and that if it weren't for their swift action in rounding up the alleged conspirators, the city would have been betrayed. For an entire night an armed guard was posted in the Theseum in the event the city was attacked. At the same time, the friends of Alcibiades in Argos were suspected of attempting to overthrow the democracy. . . . There was universal suspicion of Alcibiades. Having reached a decision to pass a sentence of death against him, the Athenians dispatched the Salaminia to Sicily for him and his alleged coconspirators. The Salaminia was under instructions to induce Alcibiades to return and face the charges against him, but not to take him into custody, which might provoke a reaction from their troops in Sicily, or indeed from the enemy, and they were especially concerned not to alienate the Mantineans and Argives whom Alcibiades himself had drawn into the alliance. So he set sail from Sicily in his own ship, along with his codefendants, and accompanied the Salaminia toward Athens. But when they reached Thurii, he and his men slipped away, fearing that in Athens they wouldn't receive a fair trial. The Salaminia searched for them, but with no success, and finally sailed home. Not long afterward, Alcibiades sailed from Thurii to the Peloponnese as a fugitive, and the Athenians sentenced him to death in absentia.

CHAPTER 6

Dikastērion

Informers and Trials

While men traded gossip and theories about the herms and Mysteries at the Agora's fish-stalls and barber-shops that summer, they had a prime view of some other significant structures around the Agora. To their west, below the temple of Hephaistos, stood two crucial political buildings: the *bouleuterion*, where the Council of Five Hundred met, and the circular *tholos*, where whichever of the tribes was presiding at that time posted a delegation always available for emergencies. These buildings would have been the center of the ongoing investigation. The council had been voted extraordinary powers during the crisis, and the board of inquiry created in response to the crimes reported to them. Investigators would have been visible from the Agora escorting informers either to the tholos or the bouleuterion. And at various adjacent locations, some perhaps near the mutilated herms themselves on the north side of the Agora, stood the *dikastēria*, Athens' famous law courts. Accusations, defenses, convictions, and sentences, if not always directly visible or audible to the throngs in the marketplace, would have left plenty of public traces to supply more news and rumor. It is these accusations, the people who made them, and the trials they led to, that will occupy us in this final chapter.

Accusations: The Herms

The narrative we will follow derives from a speech by a man called Andocides. Thucydides does not name him, but refers to him as "one of the prisoners who seemed to be most responsible in the affair" of the herms (6.60). It will be useful to hear some of his story before considering in greater detail how it connects to the legal system of classical Athens. As we learned from Thucydides, Andocides himself was an informer in the case of the herms. His own account also gives us intriguing details about the other informers who came forward about both herms and Mysteries, and the stories they told. One of the challenges of understanding Andocides' account is that rather than proceeding in a strict chronological fashion, he mostly describes the two scandals separately, even though they unfolded at the same time. We will start out in the same way here, but in reverse order, beginning with the herms and continuing with the Mysteries.

After the Sicilian Expedition had departed, the first credible informant about the herms to come forward was a metic (remember Thucydides' phrase "metics and slaves" who had brought information about other episodes in 6.28) called Teucrus. He asked for and was granted immunity, and then named eighteen men who, he claimed, had perpetrated the crime. Some of these fled, others were tried and executed. Instead of allowing Teucrus' information to finish the affair, however, two members of the board of inquiry pressed to continue the investigation: Peisander and Charicles. We know that Peisander had been an enthusiastic investigator from the beginning of the affair, responsible for proposing a second, much higher, reward for information when the first was ineffective. These could well have been the men Thucydides meant by "men who bore a grudge against Alcibiades for standing in the way of their power over the city, and who calculated that if they could get rid of Alcibiades they would rise to the top in his place" (6.28). Four years later both of these men took part in a brief oligarchic coup. Evidently, then, they did not have a strongly held prodemocratic political ideology, but were interested in how best they could maximize their own power.

Andocides tells us that Peisander and Charicles whipped up the emotions of the Athenians in the wake of Teucrus' information about the herms. They argued that such a conspiracy could not have been carried out by only eighteen men, but must rather have involved far more. The remaining conspirators were still at large and potentially still planning to overthrow the democracy, they claimed; the investigation must continue until all were brought to justice. Athens was reduced to a complete hysteria at this point: "The city was in such a state of panic and paranoia that whenever the herald signaled a meeting of the council, people hurried out of the Agora in fear that the council would send someone there to arrest them" (*On the Mysteries* 36). This confirms Thucydides' statement that "every day the frenzy increased and more and more suspects were rounded up" (6.60). The hysteria in the city was exacerbated by what seemed to be growing activity from the Spartans. Could men within the city be colluding with the enemy?

In this panicked atmosphere, a man named Diocleides stepped forward and asked to speak to the council. He had an interesting and detailed story to tell. The night before the herms were mutilated, he claimed, he had needed to make a journey to Laurium, but had mistaken the time and set out while it was still night. By the light of a full moon, he had seen some three hundred men gathered in the theater of Dionysus, standing about in groups of ten or twenty. The detail is significant, because the groups would be about the size of hetaireiai, those associations of wealthy and possibly politically minded men we encountered in chapter 2 when discussing symposia. Such groups were likely automatically suspect to the demos, especially in collaboration with each other. Diocleides claimed that he had recognized many of these men as he crouched in the shadows and observed them. That night he went on to Laurium, but when he heard of the mutilations the following day, he was sure that these men he had seen were responsible.

Rather than coming forward at once with his information, he said, he had instead gone directly to the men he had seen, and asked them for money for his silence. This detail explains the gap between the crime and Diocleides' information about it, but it is hardly the kind of detail calculated to make him more sympathetic to a jury; perhaps he intended to spin his admission of it as a sign of his current honesty. The guilty men, he said, had agreed, and promised to give him the money in the following month, swearing oaths on the Acropolis. However, the time had come and gone that they had promised his payment, so he was now coming forward to the council with his information, and was prepared to name the men he had seen on the night in question. He immediately produced a list of forty-two names. The first two were men called Mantitheus and Apsephion, who were themselves on the council at the time Diocleides delivered his information, and were sitting there in the chamber when he named them along with the others. Peisander at this point made a chilling proposal: that the council should suspend the decree which outlawed the torture of citizens, and that all the men named by Diocleides should be arrested and tortured until every single person involved in the plot was discovered.

Mantitheus and Apsephion immediately sought refuge on the hearth in the council chamber, begging that they be allowed to face trial rather than be tortured. The Greeks had very rigid laws about treatment of suppliants, and once the two had reached the sacred space of the hearth they had official sanctuary. The penalties, not to mention religious consequences, for harming anyone in such a position were extremely severe. The council accordingly agreed to allow them to furnish sureties: the names of people who would guarantee their presence at a trial. The sureties would be liable, in the event that they ran away rather than showing up for trial, to the same punishments they would have had to face had they stayed.

Evidently Mantitheus and Apsephion didn't like their chances even so, and given the atmosphere in the city it's hard to blame them. As soon as they were free of the threat of torture they fled Athens, leaving their sureties vulnerable to the direst of punishments. The council, in the meantime, had rounded up the others on Diocleides' list and imprisoned them all immediately. In fear of the rumored Spartan activity they also called the generals to muster all citizens to arms for the night. The council itself spent the night on the Acropolis, and the prytany remained on emergency duty in the tholos. The city was clearly terrified of betrayal from within and invasion from without.

We do not know the names of all forty men arrested and imprisoned that night on the information of Diocleides, but among them were our speaker Andocides, his father Leagoras, and about nine of their family members. His description of this night is particularly vivid: "And so we were all thrown into prison. And when night fell, and the prison was locked, our families came— mothers and sisters, wives and children—and there was much wailing and weeping over our present misfortunes" (*On the Mysteries* 48). At this moment of crisis, someone in prison (two different names are attached to this figure) persuaded Andocides to ask for immunity and inform upon himself and a few others so as to exonerate the many innocent men currently imprisoned for a crime they had not committed, and to free the city from the panic that had seized it.

Andocides was now in a position reminiscent of tragic figures. Should he protect his friends at the cost of his family's lives? Or should he save his family but betray his friends? Like many aspects of this whole affair, Andocides' dilemma underlined the tension between the private space of the household and the wider concerns of the city. After agonizing over his choice, Andocides at last decided, he claims, that naming the last of those responsible who had not already been arrested would save the city from panic and suspicion, as well as saving the innocent men Diocleides had accused of the crime. Reasoning that the guilty parties were likely, in this atmosphere, to be accused anyway, Andocides came forward to tell his story.

It was Euphiletus, named already by Teucrus, who had proposed the idea of mutilating the herms. It had indeed happened at a symposium, perhaps confirming the suspicions of the people about these elite affairs. Andocides never explicitly says that Euphiletus' suggestion to his hetaireia had to do with an oligarchic plot; he certainly can be forgiven for not emphasizing this rather damaging angle. But the implication lurks behind many elements of his story, and it is likely safe to assume that that was, in fact, the idea. Presumably Andocides' hetaireia wanted to commit some very public and spectacular crime that would effectively bind them together as conspirators. Since all would be equally guilty, none would be tempted to betray the others. As early as 427 we hear of this kind of pledge in the context of the stasis Thucydides described in

Corcyra ("the pledges they made toward each other were strengthened not by sacred law so much as some common crime" 3.82). It is not unreasonable that the hetaireiai might have been thinking along these lines in 415.

At the time, Andocides claimed, he argued against the plan and was successful in dissuading the others in his hetaireia from undertaking it. Later, however, after a fall from his horse he was confined to bed. At this point Euphiletus raised the idea again in his absence, this time telling their companions that Andocides had changed his mind and would go along with the idea. Thus the plan went forward, but the one herm that Euphiletus had promised that Andocides would mutilate, the herm closest to his own house, remained unharmed. The fact that this particular (and quite prominent) herm was found to be untouched on that memorable morning is attested by multiple sources, and evidently for that very reason it became known as "Andocides' herm." While Andocides cites the fact as one proof of his innocence in the affair, Plutarch on the contrary uses it to assert Andocides' guilt, claiming that he had indeed been a part of the conspiracy, but his nerve failed him when it came to mutilating the herm closest to his own house.

When the group became aware that Andocides had not, as promised, taken part in the mutilations, they came to him and threatened retaliation should he betray them. He reiterated his objection to the whole scheme, but he promised to keep silent. Now, however, that the city was in such an uproar, now that so many of his family members were in prison for a crime they had not committed, now that many of those guilty had already been named by Teucrus and had either fled into exile or been executed, now Andocides finally thought that in naming the four remaining conspirators he would be acting for the good of the city rather than in a dishonorable way against his comrades. He therefore added four additional names to those already accused by Teucrus. If we are to believe him, the hetaireia to which he and Euphiletus belonged was entirely responsible for the mutilations. They committed the crime as some sort of pledge among themselves, possibly as a prelude to launching an oligarchic conspiracy, but equally possibly for some other reason we know nothing about. Twenty-two men in total committed the crime, or twenty-three if we include Andocides.

The board of inquiry immediately investigated Andocides' story (in contrast, it should be noted, to Thucydides' contemptuous account of them accepting all accounts without any rigorous testing). Andocides submitted his slaves to torture to confirm his claim that on the night of the mutilations he had been injured and unable to leave his bed. He also identified the house the mutilators had used as a base of operations, and servants in this house evidently confirmed his account. Finally, the commission summoned Diocleides, whose tale of three hundred men was in such complete opposition to Andocides' new information.

But Diocleides caved in immediately. He admitted that his story was entirely false, and begged to be pardoned if he should name the men who put him up to it. These, he claimed, were Alcibiades of Phegous (a cousin of famous Alcibiades) and Amiantus of Aegina. Presumably they had wanted to divert suspicion from Alcibiades by casting it on a different network of aristocrats. The two men Diocleides named as his instigators promptly fled the city, and Diocleides himself was executed for giving false information. Andocides and all the others who had been imprisoned on Diocleides' testimony were released, and the citizens who had been posted at arms all over the city were sent home. This closed the book on the investigation into the mutilation of the herms. The information Andocides had given was full enough that Peisander and Charicles, who had pushed to continue it after Teucrus' information, no longer were able to argue that perpetrators remained at large. The desecration of the Mysteries, on the other hand, was continuing to produce informants.

The Athenian Court System

Before we turn to these, it's worth pausing to consider the legal system in Athens, which had been so efficiently charging and prosecuting men as they were named in this affair. A substantial number of Athenian citizens would have participated as the trials for those accused took place. For the dikastēria, or law courts, were as fundamental a part of the democracy as the assembly of citizens voting on the Pnyx, and the council that prepared their agenda.

Each year, six thousand citizen men over the age of thirty were chosen as *dikastai* to serve on the large panels that heard and judged cases. We often retain the Greek word dikast because "juror," the closest English equivalent, is misleading in many ways: dikasts were as much judge as jury. The courts may have been in session as many as two hundred days in a year, and on each of these an ingenious system of allotment would sort those dikasts who had presented themselves for duty that day into as many panels as were needed for the scheduled trials. The panels were very large. Anywhere from two hundred to several thousand men heard each case, depending on its importance. Each day it is possible that there was need for as many as two thousand out of the full pool of six thousand dikasts. The allotment system ensured that nobody knew who would be judging a case until immediately before it started, making bribery difficult.

The trials consisted of a speech (or speeches; sometimes additional speakers could be recruited in support of either side) from the prosecution, and then from the defense. These speeches were carefully timed with the *klepsydra* or water clock, a device that allowed a set amount of water to flow from one vessel into another. When it ran out your time was up. The clock could be stopped for witness testimony, or for documentary evidence to be read out. The type of case would determine the amount of time granted to prosecution and defense, but the cases never took longer than a single day, and often would have taken less time than that.

Only men could speak in court, although they didn't have to be citizens, since metics also had (albeit limited) rights in Athenian courts. Women's testimony was accepted, but only in the form of written depositions that were read out: no woman could speak in court. The testimony of slaves was accepted only when it had been given under torture. This practice has generated some controversy among classicists, and at first it seems counterintuitive. Surely a slave might say anything under torture. Why should that testimony be more reliable than what he gave freely? But there was a strong sense in the ancient world that a slave could not be sufficiently independent of his master to be trusted to speak the truth, unless some (literal) external pressure were applied.

When prosecution and defense were finished presenting their arguments, the dikasts voted immediately, without instruction from any expert on matters of law or precedent. In the event of a guilty verdict, each side (in at least some types of case) would propose a penalty, and the jury would vote a second time on these. No appeal of the dikasts' decision was possible. The large panels stood in for the city itself, and there was no higher authority to amend their verdict.

The age requirement ensured that dikasts were older, on average, than those who voted on decrees in the assembly. They were likely also poorer. Pay for dikasts had been instituted by Pericles, and while it was raised from the original two obols to three in the 420s, even this much would not have been an incentive for men able to earn twice as much by carving stone on the Acropolis or rowing triremes for the navy. While it may be exaggerated, the picture we get from comedy that juries consisted of cranky old men, intoxicated by their power, likely contained a kernel of truth. All sources agree that the Athenians were notoriously litigious, and prided themselves on their acumen in listening to competing arguments and deciding between them. The assembly did this on the Pnyx (should we go to Sicily?), and a larger audience did the same in the theater (was Helen or Hecuba more responsible for the Trojan War?), just as the dikasts did in the courts. Indeed, the fundamental assumption of the democracy was that large groups of ordinary citizens on balance made good decisions, and that running the city and implementing its laws required no special training or expertise beyond what was available to everyone in their daily lives. The dikastic panels were the natural consequence of this assumption.

While we too choose our juries by lot, we rely on an infrastructure of professionals to guide them: lawyers, judges, police detectives, forensic scientists. The Athenian system, by contrast, ran entirely on self-help. There were three broad categories of court case, depending on the crime involved. In a *dikē* (plural *dikai*), there was a personal victim, as in robbery, assault, failure to fulfill a contract, and so on; a *graphē* (plural *graphai*) was brought when the crime was felt to threaten the city itself, as in treason, shirking military duty, and (notably in this context) impiety. Finally, if a current member of the government was involved, the accusation was brought directly to the council or assembly, in a procedure called *eisangelia*. We conventionally use "lawsuit" to translate dikē, "indictment" for graphē, and "impeachment" for eisangelia, to capture the more public nature of the latter two. The crucial distinction was that in dikai only the victim of the crime could legally prosecute, while anyone could bring a graphē or eisangelia. In a dikē, the victim was responsible for apprehending the alleged criminal, denouncing him before a magistrate, collecting witnesses and documentary evidence, and then arguing the case before the dikasts. The accused in all types of cases had to make his own defense, or *apologia*: the "apology" of Socrates, written by Plato after the actual trial, is our most famous (if probably largely fictional) instance of such a defense speech.

The ability to speak persuasively before a large crowd, then, could be not simply the source of political influence on the Pnyx, but a matter of life or death in the dikastērion. It was legal, if you had the resources, to hire a speechwriter to write your speech, but you had to memorize and deliver it yourself. It is almost certainly the case that full-blown trials generally happened only between fairly well-to-do opponents; less formal remedies, or none, would have sufficed for poorer victims. If the prospect of speaking before the large juries was too daunting, arbitrators (also untrained: all men in their sixtieth year served as arbitrators) could also propose a resolution.

For the wealthier or more ambitious, though, the dikastēria offered appealing opportunities. As mentioned above, the city relied on volunteers (literally "the man who is willing") to prosecute graphai. In some types of case the successful litigant received a portion of any fine imposed on the defendant. There was some ambivalence about the kind of man who would prosecute such a case: the word *sykophantēs*, while etymologically obscure (the sense that the English "sycophant" has of "flatterer" developed later), was a negative name for a man who brought wealthy men to court in hopes of profit. Yet if a defendant was unpopular, prosecution could be appealing. The trials that resulted from the investigations of the religious scandals of the summer of 415 must have offered some brilliant opportunities for political hopefuls to show off concern for the civic good before large and emotional crowds, in cases that practically couldn't be lost. Note Thucydides' offhand "bringing the accused to trial executed as many as were apprehended" at 6.60. Even for those who fled before facing trial, like many named by Teucrus, the dikasts must have assembled, listened to the prosecutors' speeches, and cast their votes to convict.

Accusations: The Mysteries

Let's return, then, to the summer of 415. The case of the herms has been solved, and the perpetrators have either fled into self-imposed exile or been arrested, charged, tried, and executed. If ambitious politicians (perhaps the Peisander and Charicles who agitated to continue the investigation of the herms even after Teucrus had given his information) were gaining popularity from pursuing these indictments before large and angry juries, they might have been less relieved than the city generally when the prosecutions were finished. But the desecration of the Mysteries presented a very different kind of crime, and the opportunities there were far less limited. Because the criminal activities happened in the private setting of the andrōn, information had to come either from the participants themselves or from other members of the household where they had taken place. Thus this affair, even more than the mutilation of the herms, offers an intriguing case study into the intersection of oikos and polis, private and public, personal and political.

Thucydides had told us only that, in response to the call for information on the herms, "metics and slaves" had come forward with information on the illegal enactment of the Mysteries in private houses. Andocides gives us much greater detail on these informants. In the sensational opening to the story we hear that it was Alcibiades' own slave, a man called Andromachus, who first named Alcibiades in conjunction with the desecrations. A citizen named Pythonicus dramatically offered to produce him during a meeting of the assembly, just as the Sicilian Expedition was getting ready to launch. Once the assembly had been cleared of men who had not been initiated into the Mysteries and thus were forbidden from hearing the details of the ceremony, Andromachus, himself a noninitiate, was granted immunity, and described what he had seen. He gave the names of ten free men in all, as well as the owner of the house: three of these, including Alcibiades, had enacted the ceremonies, and the rest had watched. In addition, he named four slaves, including himself, who had been present to witness the performance. Some ten men, then, had been involved in that first enactment to be revealed.

As we learned in the last chapter, the decision was made to delay the trial of these men so that the Sicilian Expedition could sail. Only after its departure did the metic Teucrus come forward. He gave information on most of those guilty of mutilating the herms, but he also asked for immunity because he himself had participated in an illegal performance of the Mysteries. He named eleven other men who had also been present for that occasion. The two groups named by Andromachus and Teucrus had no overlap with each other. They were again of just the right size to be identified as hetaireiai, and a hetaireia had already proved to be responsible for the mutilation of the herms. That such groups might intend harm to the democracy was, as we've seen, plausible and unsettling to the demos. Now there was evidence that two of them separately had engaged in sacrilegious activities. Could this, also, have constituted some sort of pledge aimed at political revolution?

All the men Teucrus named along with himself as desecrators of the Mysteries fled Athens before they could be apprehended. Word must have gotten around the Agora that he had asked for immunity, and his friends saw what was coming, or it is possible that he had himself warned them of his intentions. In prosecution speeches, a defendant's flight is generally used to indicate guilt, but we've seen the panic that was roiling Athens during these weeks, as well as the results of the trials in the case of the herms. It may well have seemed safer to many simply to leave the city until things had calmed down.

While Andocides' speech makes it difficult to reconstruct chronology very exactly, we know that at least three more informers emerged after Andromachus and Teucrus with stories about enactments of the Mysteries. Andocides gives us some detail on two of these. One, a woman called Agariste, claimed that Alcibiades and two others had performed the Mysteries on an occasion different from the one Andromachus had revealed. Unlike Andromachus she did not name those who watched. The other, a slave named Lydus, claimed that the Mysteries had been performed in the house of his master. We do not know how many participated in or witnessed this enactment; Andocides mentions "others" but gives only three names from this accusation. One of these was his father, Leagoras. Lydus had identified him as being present, but said that he had been asleep during the proceedings, with his head wrapped in a cloak. We'll return to the legal consequences of this accusation. The two other men Lydus named fled before they could be tried.

We know about one further accusation of desecration of the Mysteries. Andocides does not mention it, but Plutarch preserves it in the text of the charge that was brought against Alcibiades: "Thessalus, son of Cimon, of the deme Laciadae, impeaches Alcibiades, son of Cleinias, of the deme Scambonidae, for committing a crime against the goddesses of Eleusis, Demeter and Korē, by mimicking the mysteries and showing them forth to his companions in his own house, wearing a robe such as the High Priest wears when he shows forth the sacred secrets to the initiates, and calling himself the High Priest, Poulytion the Torch-bearer, and Theodorus, of the deme Phegaea, the Herald, and hailing the rest of his companions as Mystae and Epoptae, contrary to the laws and institutions of the Eumolpidae, Heralds, and Priests of Eleusis."

As these accusations mounted, consider the perspective of the demos. Whatever had happened was much more extensive than a single symposium for a limited set of friends. On five separate occasions a total of thirty to forty men were accused of enacting the Mysteries in private homes: almost double the twenty-two who were convicted of mutilating the herms. We saw in the last chapter how Alcibiades' enemies had worked to conflate the two crimes, to associate the more obviously antidemocratic attack on the herms with the desecration of the Mysteries. If they really were all part of some larger oligarchic conspiracy, then the number of elite men involved would have been understandably frightening. How plausible was it that the crimes were connected in any way?

There was certainly some overlap between those convicted. Some five or six men who were judged guilty of the mutilations also profaned the Mysteries (although it remains very difficult to be sure in each case that it was really the same man, and not a different man with the same name). In addition to the names preserved in Andocides' speech and Thessalus' indictment, we have a fragmentary set of inscriptions known as the Attic Stelae. These stones record lists of possessions confiscated from those convicted, along with the prices they sold for, because a portion of the proceeds from these sales went to the goddess Demeter as reparation for the crime. Fifteen names appear on the Attic Stelae, all of which are included in the lists Andocides gives in his speech. A few of these carry the designation "concerning both" and we assume this means the men were convicted of both religious transgressions.

In other cases, we have good reason to believe that there were ties of family or friendship between the men accused of the different crimes. A single example: in Plato's *Symposium*, which we encountered in chapter 2, two of the guests are Phaedrus and Erixymachus. Plato's account of the party, which supposedly took place just the year before these scandals broke, implies that these two are a lover-beloved pair. Teucrus named Phaedrus as participant in the enactment of the Mysteries, and Eryximachus as a mutilator of the herms. Additionally, Lydus named Eryximachus' father as having desecrated the Mysteries. It seems then that the same kin and friendship circles overlapped at least somewhat in the two crimes. It must have been easy for the Athenians to believe that both were symptomatic of the same arrogance characteristic of the elite. It would not be hard to persuade the suspicious demos that all such activity was antidemocratic by its nature, and to conflate the two different ways of attacking the traditional Athenian gods.

But were the two crimes actually connected? The two acts feel very different. The sort of pledge the mutilations purportedly constituted must necessarily be a very public crime. The profanations, on the other hand, occurred safely in private. If it hadn't been for the investigation of the more spectacular mutilations, they would likely never have been discovered. The very privacy of the enactments of the Mysteries makes it much harder to know whether the informers were telling the truth in their accusations. Only Andromachus and Teucrus give much confidence in their stories: Andromachus because, as a noninitiate, he had knowledge of the Mysteries, and Teucrus because he confessed his own participation. The cases of other informers seem much flimsier.

As we have seen, four of the five accusations came from two slaves, one metic, and one citizen woman. While Thucydides' phrase "slaves and metics" is not precisely accurate as a description, it does convey what both he and Plutarch evidently found important about the informers: most were not citizen men. This is a really astonishing feature of the whole affair. Athens was catapulted into a state of panic, and in the end convicted its most popular politician, throwing a newly launched military expedition, and then the larger war against Sparta, into a tailspin from which it never really recovered, on the information of one woman and three men who lacked the full legal standing of Athenians. Yet we know even less about the truth behind these accusations than we do in the case of the herms.

Prosecutors and Informers

Thucydides, as we saw, is not kind to the informers. He claims that the Athenians arrested and imprisoned "the best" citizens upon the evidence of scoundrels. There seems to have been more general animus especially against those who obtained immunity for themselves by giving information against others. Andocides himself, of course, falls into this category, as does Teucrus. Fairly soon after the trials were finished, the Athenians passed a decree making it illegal for anyone who had confessed impiety to enter any of the temples or the Agora at Athens. This would make life difficult for anyone with commercial or political interests, and Andocides left the city for an extended self-imposed exile in the years after. Teucrus as well must have been a target of this legislation. That he also was unpopular even after having given good information is shown by a fragment from the comic poet Phrynichus, in which a statue of Hermes says that he will be careful not to fall down and damage himself, as he doesn't want to provide any rewards to Teucrus, that guilty foreigner (Plutarch, *Alcibiades* 20). The word used for "guilty" specifically means bloodguilt; Teucrus was evidently held responsible for the deaths of those he informed against. We'll consider below the potential motivations of the informers we know about. Yet it must have been those who prosecuted the cases who reaped the real advantage from the situation.

Plutarch claims that informers were "produced" by a man called Androcles, a popular leader who was a rival of Alcibiades. Andocides' account on the other hand has Pythonicus introduce Andromachus, the slave who first accused Alcibiades. He tells us that later there was a dispute about whether

Andromachus or Pythonicus should receive the reward that had been offered for information. Presumably both Androcles and Pythonicus were seeking the political advantage that would come from prosecuting such high-profile cases, not to mention the chance to eliminate political rivals or enemies. They certainly succeeded in ridding themselves of Alcibiades.

That prosecutors faced some risk as well as reward, though, is evident from the story of Andocides' father, Leagoras. He had, remember, been accused by the slave Lydus of being present at one of the enactments, but asleep with his cloak over his head. As the trials triggered by the many accusations played out, this is the only case in which we know there was no conviction. Leagoras lodged a countersuit against the councilor who prosecuted his case. While the underlying details are obscure, the jury sided overwhelmingly with Leagoras in deciding that the case against him had been illegal. Public opinion could not be counted on, therefore, to convict in every case where there was an accusation; the Athenians did not consistently believe either the informers or the prosecutors. In cases where a minimum number of guilty votes was not attained, the prosecutor himself could be liable to severe penalties for frivolous claims. There were limits, then, on who could be accused and what sort of evidence it would take to get a conviction.

While the risks and rewards for those who prosecuted the cases are straightforward and political, it is also intriguing to consider the motivations of those who came forward with accusations. Why would they have spoken out? What did they have to gain from the stories they told? If the religious scandals of 415 offer us a case study in the intersection of polis and oikos, these accusers take us back from the former into the latter. What did that panicked summer feel like to those who informed, rather than the men they informed upon or their prosecutors?

The first informer to come forward, remember, was Andromachus, one of Alcibiades' slaves. The inducement for any slave to offer information was presumably the reward money available, which Andromachus did in the end receive. This case, then, seems to be one of a slave choosing to inform on his master for financial gain. Because a slave could buy his freedom in Athens, he likely also ended up free as well as comfortably off. Freedom may even have been part of the package involved in the immunity he received for giving information. Even so, the decision could not have been an easy one for him. Andromachus' brother was also a slave in Alcibiades' household, and had also been present on the night in question. The fact that Andromachus needed immunity before he could testify to the assembly indicates that everyone present for the enactment of the Mysteries was guilty of some sort of crime. If so, this means that his testimony would have convicted his own brother as well as Alcibiades and the other aristocrats at the symposium. This is exactly the kind of story lurking beneath the surface of ancient accounts which remains frustratingly hidden to us. The affair of the Mysteries involved slaves as much as the elite, yet we catch only the barest glimpses of what happened to them. If Andromachus' brother was found guilty along with the others present he would have been condemned to death. If he was not prosecuted for the crime, he was certainly sold along with Alcibiades' other slaves when the property was confiscated; the very fragmentary Attic Stelae still preserve the records of dozens of slaves among the properties of those convicted of the crimes, and the prices for which they were sold. Perhaps Andromachus used some of his reward money to buy his brother.

The other slave informant, Lydus, was also in an interesting position. Assuming we are right about the relative chronology, then when he gave his testimony about the Mysteries, his master Pherecles had already been named as one of the mutilators of the herms by Teucrus. When Lydus came forward, Pherecles had either fled Athens (leaving his household in someone else's hands, perhaps), was in prison awaiting trial, or had already been executed for his guilt in the other affair. In this latter case, Lydus would have been among the property confiscated and awaiting sale. The implicit betrayal in his choice to give information against his master must have seemed of little importance to him, given that Teucrus had already named Pherecles. That initial accusation had already altered Lydus' own situation. Perhaps it was this alteration that brought him forward, to avoid being sold into a strange household with the rest of Pherecles' confiscated property, or to avoid being tortured to testify against his master in the case of the herms. There is also the possibility that under these circumstances Lydus was conveniently available, held in the prison near the Agora, to the investigators. Anyone who had reason to wish for further accusations to be brought could have persuaded Lydus to bring them.

While Diocleides was the only informer who admitted to having given false information, it would seem that the successful case of Leagoras mentioned above might have cast some doubt on Lydus' testimony as well. Evidently this was not the case, though. Andocides names two men who went into exile on the strength of his accusations, and we know from the Attic Stelae that Pherecles was convicted of both mutilating the herms and profaning the Mysteries, so Lydus' information against his master led to a conviction in his case. Perhaps the argument was made that he misidentified Leagoras because his head was hidden in his cloak as he slept. But the fact that Lydus named at least one man who claimed not to have been there, indicates that at least some of his testimony was deemed false by a jury. Was he one of the "slaves and metics" Plutarch claims was "produced" by Androcles? Or had he, on his own initiative, shrewdly chosen an opportune moment to improve his own situation?

Given the nature of the crime, the fact that information about it came from slaves is not in itself surprising. Activities at a symposium would be known only to participants and members of the household who had access to the dining room; these would be the only possible informers. Slaves would have the inducement of the financial rewards promised for information, so they would have ample motivation to come forward if they knew of any criminal activity. They would also, however, have been convenient resources for citizens who wanted to use the opportunity the crisis afforded to have their enemies accused. They would, one assumes, have been particularly susceptible to bribes to give false information. It is likely this last fact that drove the practice of not admitting in court any slave testimony unless it had been obtained under torture. This may well also be why Thucydides and Plutarch seem to dismiss their accusations as unreliable, and likely to be the product of political machinations or personal ambition.

But both historians group metics along with slaves in this class of putatively unreliable witness. Both mention "metics" in the plural, as if there were many such informers. But Teucrus is the only metic we know of who gave information. His case is also tantalizing. If we can believe Andocides, the men Teucrus informed against in the case of the herms were in fact guilty, yet Teucrus did not implicate himself in this affair. How did he know the names of eighteen guilty men (but not the full twenty-two who ultimately were convicted)? And why did he decide to come forward not only to inform in the matter of the herms, of which he was innocent, but also that of the Mysteries, in which he admitted guilt?

One of the particularly interesting things about Teucrus is that he did not name Alcibiades in either of his lists. When Plutarch mentions slaves and metics being "produced" he clearly means that witnesses of dubious value were suborned for political purposes by unscrupulous politicians. The three separate accusations against Alcibiades presumably were what he had in mind. But what political purposes, if any, were served by the information Teucrus gave? One intriguing possibility lies in the fact that he accused a man named Diognetus, a brother of Nicias. This connection may suggest that Teucrus' accusation, too, was part of the larger political strategy and counterstrategy focused on the expedition: if the accusations began as a way of neutralizing Alcibiades' power, perhaps implicating Nicias' brother was a shot across the bow at his rival.

It seems equally likely, however, that Teucrus made the decision to come forward on his own. Again, the financial reward may well have been a real inducement for him. Perhaps there was a nonfinancial inducement, though: awards of citizenship were made, occasionally, to metics who had been of real benefit to the city. If citizenship was a possible reward for information, metics might have had an even greater motivation than citizens to come forward with what they knew of the crimes, just as freedom could be an inducement for slaves' information. Whatever the reason, Teucrus must have felt urgently compelled to offer his information rather than simply waiting out the crisis in safety. Perhaps he was a victim of the classic "prisoner's dilemma." For Diognetus, the brother of Nicias he named as having participated in the desecrations of the Mysteries along with himself, may also have been one of the investigators. If a fellow desecrator was on the board of inquiry, Teucrus could plausibly have assumed that it was only a matter of time before his part in the Mysteries would come out. He would be better off himself being the informer and obtaining immunity than he would be if he were denounced by Diognetus first. Wherever his information about the herms came from, it put him in an even better position to mitigate his guilt in the Mysteries.

Of the "slaves and metics" we have detailed knowledge of, then, only Andromachus seems plausibly to have been "produced" by one of Alcibiades' enemies, as Plutarch claimed: Teucrus and Lydus both had plenty of their own motivation to give information. The one confirmed case of a suborned witness was Diocleides, and he was both citizen and the agent of Alcibiades' friends, rather than his enemies.

The last of the informants recounted by Andocides, though, is the most remarkable of the lot: Agariste. Her name is associated with the Alcmaeonid clan; Pericles' mother had had the same name. Andocides tells us that Agariste was married twice. Her first husband was the musician Damon, an intellectual closely associated with Pericles. Next she married a man called Alcmaeonides, presumably from her own extended family. When (or why, for that matter) one marriage ended and the next began we do not know.

Agariste testified that Alcibiades, along with his uncle and a friend, had enacted the Mysteries in the house of someone called Charmides. Everything about this accusation is tantalizing. How did Agariste get her information? She named neither her first nor her second husband as having been present on the occasion she described. But even if one of them had been, we have seen that Athenian women did not accompany their husbands to social events. An elite woman would certainly not have attended any standard symposium. She could, presumably, be reporting information she had heard from someone else, but it is difficult in this case to reconstruct why her name would attach to the information rather than the name of the eyewitness. It is much more likely that she herself was for some reason present on the occasion. But why?

A frustrating consequence of the convention of suppressing the names of Athenian women is that when we reconstruct family trees we only rarely can include females at all. For this reason, tracing relationships among women at best tricky, and often impossible. But even in the absence of anything like evidence on this point, various ways of relating Agariste to members of the party through female relatives have been suggested. Alcibiades and his uncle would have had mutual connections to Pericles and other Alcmaeonids. Even if she were related to the guests in the house, though, a respectable Athenian woman would not have been part of such a dinner party either as a relative of a guest or as his wife. The more likely explanation for Agariste's presence in Charmides' house thus was that she was herself related to the host Charmides or perhaps to his wife. This would put her not dining with the men, but visiting, or even living, in the women's quarters. There would be nothing scandalous about her presence in the house under these circumstances. Remember, though, that our discussion of house structure in chapter 4 indicated a careful separation between the dining rooms where symposia would have taken place and the rest of the house. There were no sight lines possible from where women may have seen into the andrōn. This is why it is so suggestive that Agariste named only the three men who actually enacted the Mysteries, and none of those who were present to watch. Perhaps her identification of the men rested purely on their voices. She may have heard, rather than seen, the desecrations that she reported.

As in the cases of Andromachus, Lydus, and Teucrus, there is also the question of why Agariste would have come forward, and whether she might have acted at the behest of others for political reasons. As with Andromachus, this is a case that does, indeed, look like it could have been concocted by the enemies of Alcibiades. Agariste names not only the general but two men who are associated closely with him through much of his career. If she was already married to Alcmaeonides, she might have been acting on her husband's urging, giving us a glimpse of a fissure within the clan over the controversial Alcibiades. If she was still married to Damon, she might have been acting for a birth family she ended up returning to on his death.

The informers, the slaves as well as Agariste, had one final and perhaps decisive motivation to come forward, though. The accusations may simply have been true. The Eleusinian Mysteries, as we noted in the last chapter, were unusually and explicitly inclusive: almost anyone who spoke the Greek language could be initiated. The experience was evidently highly emotionally satisfying, and the promise of a pleasant afterlife may have appealed most strongly to those whose lives were least happy. Slaves and women, then, could plausibly have felt an especially intense attachment to these rites, and could have been particularly outraged by seeing or hearing elite men appropriate and thus desecrate them. As one informer after the next came forward, others may have felt empowered to review their own memories, and add their own voices in accusation.

When the Salaminia returned without Alcibiades and the others who had been recalled to face trial, the Athenian dikastēria condemned all of them to death by default. Their property was confiscated and sold, along with that of all others who had been convicted of either or both crimes, and the sale of each item was carefully recorded and carved on a series of stones set up in the Eleusinion near the Agora. The priests and priestesses of Athens publicly cursed their names, facing west and shaking out purple robes. The council voted to award ten thousand drachmas to Andromachus for his information, and one thousand to Teucrus; the awards were made at the Panathenaic festival at the end of that summer. So ended the religious crisis precipitated by the discovery that fateful morning of the mutilation of the herms.

Primary Source Interlude

Andocides, On the Mysteries, excerpts

[11] The generals who would lead the expedition to Sicily—Nicias, Lamachus, and Alcibiades—called an assembly at the last minute, when the lead trireme, under the command of Lamachus, was already on the point of departure. At this assembly, Pythonicus stood up and said, "Athenians, you are about to send this great expeditionary force on a hazardous mission. I will prove to you that one of the commanders you've chosen, Alcibiades, has celebrated the Mysteries with others in a private home. If you grant immunity to the individual I name, a servant of one of the men here, he will describe those celebrations to you, although he himself has not been initiated in the Mysteries. If I am not telling the truth, deal with me as you see fit."

[12] Alcibiades immediately denied everything, and the prytanies decided to dismiss all the uninitiated from the assembly and to go themselves for the boy named by Pythonicus. Accordingly, they went and came back with a servant of Alcibiades himself, whose name was Andromachus. They granted him immunity, and he told them that the Mysteries had taken place in the house of Poulytion. He testified that Alcibiades, Nicides, and Meletus were the actual celebrants, and that others were there and saw what happened: in addition to himself, there was his brother, Hicesius the flute player, and a slave of Meletus.

[15] There was a second piece of information. Teucrus was a metic in Athens, who slipped away to Megara, and from there sent word to the council that if he was granted immunity, he would testify that he took part in the Mysteries, and would name the others who participated with him, and would tell them what he knew about the defacement of the herms. The council voted to use their authority to grant immunity in this instance, and members of the council were dispatched to Megara. When Teucrus arrived in Athens, under a grant

of immunity he informed on those who were with him. Those men fled from Athens. Here are the names of the accused.

NAMES. Phaedrus, Gniphonides, Isonomus, Hephaestodorus, Cephisodorus, Teucrus (the informer), Diognetus, Smindurides, Philocrates, Antiphon, Teisarchus, Pantacles. Take note, men of the jury, that there is additional confirmation of everything I have said.

[16] A third informant came forward: the wife of Alcmaeonides and ex-wife of Damon, a woman named Agariste, testified that Alcibiades, Axiochus, and Adeimantus celebrated the Mysteries in the home of Charmides near the Olympeum. These men also fled as a result of her testimony.

[17] There was still one more piece of information. Lydus, the slave of Pherecles of Thermacus, testified that the Mysteries were celebrated in the home of his master Pherecles in Thermacus. He also named others, and said that my father was present, but with his cloak over his head, taking a nap. Speusippus, a member of the council, proposed bringing them to trial. But my father posted bail and brought a suit against Speusippus, charging that his proposal was illegal. He argued his case in front of six thousand Athenians, and not even two hundred of them sided with Speusippus. My relatives and, above all, I myself convinced my father to remain in Athens.

[34] As promised, I will start from the beginning and review the complete testimony that was given concerning the desecration of the herms. When Teucrus returned from Megara under a grant of immunity, he testified about both the Mysteries and the desecration of the herms, and named eighteen men in connection with the latter. Some of these men fled, and others were apprehended and put to death on the testimony of Teucrus. Read the list of their names.

[35] NAMES. In the matter of the herms, Teucrus named Euctemon, Glaucippus, Eurymachus, Polyeuctus, Plato, Antidorus, Charippus, Theodorus, Alcisthenes, Menestratus, Eryximachus, Euphiletus, Eurydamas, Pherecles, Meletus, Timanthes, Archidamus, Telenicus.

Some of these men subsequently returned to Athens, and are present here, as are many of the relatives of those who were executed. If any of you wish to make a statement, and explain how I am responsible for the exile or execution of any of these men, I will yield a portion of my time to you.

[36] Moving along to what happened next, Peisander and Charicles, members of the board investigating the charges and at the time the most fervent democrats, said that this wasn't the work of a few isolated individuals, but an organized plot against the democracy, and that it was crucial not to put a premature end to the investigation. The city was in such a state of panic and paranoia that whenever the herald signaled a meeting of the council, people hurried out of the Agora in fear that the council would send someone there to arrest them.

[37] Prompted by the hardships the city was facing, Diocleides came forward and told the council that he knew who had mutilated the herms, and that there were about three hundred people involved. In addition, he explained how he had happened to be a witness of the desecration. Members of the council, you can testify to the truth of my statements. Diocleides reported to you. You were present when he gave his testimony.

[38] Diocleides said that he needed to go to Laurium to pick up the wages of one of his slaves who was working in the mines. He got up early, thinking it was later than it was, and set out under a full moon. As he was passing the gate of the theater of Dionysus, he saw a crowd of men coming down from the Odeum to the orchestra. He was afraid of being seen, so he slipped into the shadows between the pillar and the bronze statue of a general. He counted three hundred men standing around in groups of fifteen or twenty. The light of the full moon made it possible for him to recognize the faces of most of the men.

[39] Think about his story for a moment. He could claim that anyone was there. What's to stop him? But to resume. He says he saw these things, and then continued on his way to Laurium. The next day, he heard that the herms had been mutilated, and knew right away that this is what those men had been planning to do.

[40] When he returned to the city, he found that investigators had been appointed and a reward of a hundred minas had been posted. Seeing Euphemus (brother of Telocles, son of Callias) sitting in his blacksmith shop, he led him to the temple of Hephaestus and told him what I have told you, namely, the story of seeing us that night. He would rather take hush money from us than the reward the city offered. He said he wanted to keep things friendly between us. Euphemus said that Diocleides had done the right thing in coming to him, and asked him to come along to the house of Leagoras "to consult with Andocides and the others."

[41] He said he came the next day and knocked on the door. He said that my father happened to be going out, and stopped to ask him, "Are you the one they're expecting? We can't turn away friends like you, can we?" This was an attempt to implicate my father and have him condemned to death. Diocleides went on to allege that we offered him two silver talents—twenty minae more than the reward the city was offering—and told him that if we achieved our aims, he would be one of us. All we needed was an exchange of guarantees. He said he would think about it.

[42] He goes on to allege that we told him to come with us to the house of Callias, son of Telocles, so that he could also be present. Again, this was an attempt to implicate and condemn my brother-in-law. He alleges that he came to the house of Callias, and went with us to the Acropolis to provide assurances, and that we promised to pay him the agreed upon amount the following month. It was when we failed to deliver on our promise, or so he claims, that he had no choice but to turn state's evidence.

[43] These were the allegations brought by Diocleides. He provided a list of the men he claimed he recognized, forty-two of them, starting with Mantitheus and Apsephion, who were sitting members of the council. Peisander stood up in the council and called for suspending the decree of Scamandrius against the torture of citizens, and bringing forward the accused to be examined under torture. In that way, he said, the names of every man involved would be known before nightfall. The council shouted their approval.

[44] When they heard this, Mantitheus and Apsephion sought sanctuary at the shrine of Zeus, begging to be allowed to provide sureties and await trial rather than being tortured. The request had scarcely been granted, and the guarantees made, when they mounted their horses and defected to the enemy, leaving their guarantors liable for whatever punishment they themselves would have received.

[45] The council went into closed session, where it was decided to arrest us and place us in the stocks. Then they called in the generals and had them issue the following orders: the Athenians in the city were to arm themselves and assemble in the Agora, those on the Long Walls were to assemble in the Theseum, and those in Piraeus were to assemble in the Hippodamean agora. A trumpet call would signal the knights to assemble after dark in the Temple of the Dioscuri. Finally, the council was to go up to the Acropolis for the night, and the prytanies were to spend the night in the tholos. At the news of the state of affairs in Athens, the Boeotians massed on the border, spoiling for a

fight. Meanwhile, the man responsible for all of this trouble, Diocleides, was acclaimed as the savior of the city, awarded a crown, and carried by a pair of steeds to the Prytaneon, where he feasted.

[46] First of all, I ask those of you who were present at the time to review these facts and confirm their truth for those who were not. Then I call as witnesses Philocrates and the others who were members of the prytanies at that time.

[WITNESSES]

[47] Now I will read to you the names of the accused, from which you will see how many of my own relatives this man implicated . . .

[48] And so we were all thrown into prison. And when night fell, and the prison was locked, our families came—mothers and sisters, wives and children—and there was much wailing and weeping over our present misfortunes. While this was going on, Charmides, a cousin my age who grew up with me in the same house, said to me:

[49] "Andocides, you can see the gravity of the situation we find ourselves in. You know it has never been my intention to say anything that would cause you pain, but these dire circumstances force me to speak. You have friends and associates outside of the family who have faced the same charges we now face, some of whom have been executed, and some of whom have confessed their guilt by fleeing.

[50] If you know anything about what happened, say so. Save yourself. Save your father, who surely has a special claim on your affections. Save your brother-in-law, the husband of your only sister. Save your relatives and their families. Save me. Never in my life have I sought to be a burden to you, and I have always been at your side when something needed to be done."

[51] The others imprisoned with us echoed the pleas Charmides had made. I thought to myself: "Has anyone ever had to cope with such a disaster? Am I to stand here and do nothing while my guiltless relatives are condemned to death, their assets are seized, and their innocent names are enrolled in lists of those who have sinned against the gods? Am I to allow three hundred Athenians to go to their deaths, and the city to be destroyed by the worst kind of in-fighting? Or should I expose the actions of Euphiletus?"

[52] As I was thinking about these things, and reviewing in my mind the names of the guilty parties, it occurred to me that, accounting for those who had been condemned on Teucrus' testimony and those who had fled and been convicted in absentia, only four remained whom Teucrus had not exposed to prosecution: Panaitius, Chairedemus, Diacritus, and Lysistratus.

[53] It seemed more than likely that they were among those denounced by Diocleides, since they were in fact friends of the condemned. Their fate was far from certain, but there was no doubt that members of my family would be put to death if I didn't come forward and tell the Athenians what I knew. It seemed better to me to be responsible for the exile of men who deserved it—men who survived and have subsequently returned to reclaim their property—than to stand by while innocent men went to their deaths.

[54] If there is anyone, men of the jury, who is of the opinion that I informed against my associates to save myself at the price of their deaths—something which my enemies slander me with—I ask you to examine the facts of the matter.

[55] It is necessary for me to give a truthful account of what happened, since there are those present at these proceedings who were judged guilty of these crimes and went into exile, and they know better than anyone if I am perjuring myself or telling the truth. I will yield a portion of my time to any one of them who objects to anything I have to say.

[56] At the same time, you must judge me fairly. My greatest concern is to dispel the notion that I committed a wrong in order to save myself. I want it to be clear to everyone that I did not act out of villainy or cowardice, but that I disclosed my conversations with Euphiletus out of concern for my family and out of concern for the entire city. My intentions were not malicious, but honorable. This is what I believe. If this is found to be the case, I deserve to be acquitted, and not to be treated as a criminal.

[57] I ask you to put yourselves in my position. What would you have done? Had I been given the choice between an honorable death or living in disgrace, one might say that I had done wrong—although many might have made the same choice, considering it far better to live than to die with honor.

[58] But my situation was exactly the opposite. If I said nothing, I would die for a crime I didn't commit. My father, my brother-in-law, my cousins—my relatives would all die if I didn't come forward and name those who bore

the real responsibility for the crimes of which they were accused. The lies of Diocleides had led to their imprisonment, and the only way of saving them was to let the Athenians know the truth. I would be their murderer if I said nothing. The lives of three hundred Athenians were at stake. And, meanwhile, the city was growing desperate.

[59] This is what would have happened had I not come forward. As it was, I gave my evidence, and saved not only myself, but my father and the other members of my family, and released the city from the grip of fear and brought an end to the state of emergency. My testimony sent four men into exile, but they were guilty. The others had been denounced by Teucrus, and not one of them died or went into exile on my account.

[60] Considering my options, men of the jury, I chose the lesser of two evils: as quickly as possible I reported what had happened and exposed the lies of Diocleides, and brought to justice a man who caused innocent men to be condemned and defrauded the city by making himself out to be a great benefactor and accepting a reward for his supposed services.

[61] And so I told the council that I knew those who had committed the crime, and showed them what had happened: Euphiletus had laid out the plan at a drinking party, but I spoke against it and temporarily prevented it from being carried out. But later I was thrown from my horse in Cynosarges and broke my collarbone and suffered a concussion, and had to be carried home on a stretcher.

[62] Seeing the condition that I was in, Euphiletus told the conspirators that I had been persuaded to join them and take part in the mutilations by attacking the herm near the shrine of Phorbas. He said this to trick them. This is why the herm which you have all seen, the one that Aigeis set up near my family home, was the only one in the city left undamaged. Because Euphiletus told the others that I would take care of it.

[63] The conspirators were outraged when they found out the truth. Now they had to deal with someone who knew their plan without having taken part in it. The next day, Meletus and Euphiletus came to me and said, "What's done is done, Andocides. If you keep your mouth shut about it, we'll continue to get along just fine. But if you go telling others, I think you'll find you've made more enemies than you have friends."

[64] I told Euphiletus exactly what I thought of him, but promised not to make any trouble for them. They'd made enough trouble for themselves.

To prove that I had spoken the truth, I handed over my slave to be interrogated under torture, and he confirmed that I was completely bedridden. In addition, the prytanies arrested the women who were attending the conspirators when they made their plans.

[65] The council and the investigators confirmed my account of the events. Then they called Diocleides. There was no need for a lengthy cross-examination. He instantly confessed that he had lied and sought a pardon if he informed on those who had convinced him to lie. They were Alcibiades of Phegous and Amiantus of Aegina.

[66] Those men fled the country in fear, and you remanded Diocleides to the court and had him executed, and through my actions you released all of my family members who were in custody awaiting their death sentences, and received back those who had gone into exile. The state of emergency was cancelled.

Epilogue

Aftermath

The mutilation of the herms will remain an unsolved mystery, but its timing and target surely imply that the perpetrators hoped it would delay or deter the fleet's departure for Sicily. The fact that Nicias was well known for his piety (or superstition) may have played into this expectation. Yet while the populace was agitated by the event, we have no indication that they ever reconsidered the Sicilian adventure. The revelation of repeated desecrations of the Mysteries during the investigations into the mutilations, though, would fundamentally alter the course of the expedition. Regardless of the true impetus for these private performances, or even the motivations of the informers, politics surely drove the wave of prosecutions against those named. These certainly provided a convenient opportunity for Alcibiades' rivals, who were able to use them, along with Alcibiades' flamboyant personal habits, to incite the demos against their favorite.

Alcibiades was sufficiently familiar with swings in Athenian mood to be unwilling to risk a trial while the city remained so exercised. In Italy, he slipped away from the Salaminia. Plutarch records a couple of one-liners attributed to Alcibiades at this juncture; while he may not have actually said them, they give a good idea of his image in the public imagination. "When someone recognized him and asked, 'Don't you trust your fatherland?' Alcibiades replied 'Completely: but when it comes to my life I don't even trust my mother, in case she casts the guilty ballot instead of the innocent by mistake.' Later, when he heard that the city had condemned him to death, he said 'I'll show them that I'm alive!'" (*Alcibiades* 22). He had indeed already started down that road before he jumped ship. He managed to interfere in a plan to bring the Sicilian city of Messina over to the Athenian side, ensuring the victory of the pro-Syracusan faction within that city.

Alcibiades went on to make good on his threat to let the Athenians know he was alive. He ended up in Sparta, promising to be as good a friend to them as he had been an enemy before. The first of his achievements there was to persuade the Spartans to send a force to Sicily in support of the Syracusans. The Spartan general Gylippus arrived in Sicily with a small fleet in time to stymie the Athenian siege of Syracuse. Thucydides' caustic assessment ("the danger to Syracuse had indeed been great" 7.2) implies that had Nicias and Lamachus been just slightly more energetic about the war, and had the Spartans not been persuaded to send Gylippus, the Athenians could have quickly prevailed that first summer.

Instead, the Syracusans were encouraged to fight on by both Spartan and Corinthian aid. Syracuse was the first large democracy Athens had faced, and proved to be a formidable enemy, as bold and adaptable as Athens itself. Their forces were led by a brilliant general named Hermocrates. Nicias, now ill with a kidney disease, sent to Athens a detailed account of the Athenian situation, requesting either a withdrawal or substantial reinforcements, and asking to be relieved of command. The Athenians agreed only to the first request. A new force almost as big as the first was sent the following spring, but Nicias continued in office. Even in Alcibiades' absence, the demos was evidently still enthusiastic about conquest in Sicily, and confident that they could prevail.

Intermittent fighting continued for another year. The Athenians had some victories, but, as Nicias had predicted, keeping the force supplied was difficult, and desertion, especially from the slaves and allies rowing the triremes, was high. Normal maintenance of the boats required regularly drying them out, but this was impossible under the circumstances, as was continued training of the oarsmen, so the Athenian ships and crew degraded as Syracuse's grew stronger. Even under these trying conditions the Sicilians arrayed against Athens under Hermocrates could not achieve a definitive victory. But it became ever clearer that the Athenians couldn't either. In the summer of 413, losses in a naval battle determined the Athenian generals finally that retreat was their best and only option. Just at this crucial moment there was a lunar eclipse, and the pious Nicias refused to make any decision without consulting the priests. They told him to do nothing for thirty days. As one set of impieties in 415 had removed the commander who might have won the war, this balancing act of piety ensured that the failure of the expedition would mean total devastation.

Defeated at sea, the Athenians were forced to retreat over land, where thousands were killed before Nicias finally surrendered. He had reason to think his Spartan counterpart Gylippus would spare him, but the Syracusans and Corinthians were afraid that his wealth would exempt him from penalty, and that his survival might expose collusion on their side. Both Nicias and the other Athenian general still in office were therefore executed. The thousands of Athenian prisoners were held under brutal conditions in quarries, and almost all of these died from hunger, thirst, and exposure to the elements. Hermocrates ("strength of Hermes"), a later historian noted, had inflicted fitting vengeance for the mutilation of the herms. There were a few Athenian captives to survive; these, Plutarch tells us, won their freedom in exchange for teaching their captors odes from Euripides' tragedies. It is tempting to imagine that some of these were from the *Trojan Women*.

The defeat in Sicily, devastating as it was, was not the end of the damage Athens would suffer at the hands of Alcibiades. The other suggestion he made to the Spartans was that they fortify a place in Attica called Decelea, some fourteen miles north of the city. This they did in the spring of 413. In the first part of the Peloponnesian War, Pericles had urged those Athenians living in the countryside to seek shelter in the walled city and allow the Spartans to ravage their farms, vineyards, and olive groves. But the Spartans only made their invasions for a few weeks each summer. Now they had a permanent fortification, and could inflict much greater and more sustained damage. Some twenty thousand slaves from the countryside and the silver mines at Laurium eventually deserted to the Spartans at Decelea, depriving the Athenians of the fruits of their labor as well.

Combined with the catastrophe in Sicily, Spartan action in Attica, taken on the advice of Alcibiades, left the Athenians with frighteningly depleted resources. The tributary allies were poised to take advantage of their weakness to rebel, depriving them of imperial revenues. It is astonishing that the Athenians pushed on. They effected a general reorganization of finances, and suspended allied payments of tribute in favor of a harbor tax. They melted down emergency stores of precious metals in the temples on the Acropolis for cash. They rebuilt the hundreds of ships lost in Sicily, and trained new crews.

Alcibiades, meanwhile, had run into the same kind of trouble among the Spartans as he had in Athens. He was enormously popular, but for that reason also generated envy and malice. The wife of one of Sparta's two kings fell in love with him and bore his child; in private she called the baby Alcibiades. He had seduced her, the story went, not out of passion but in order to see one of his own children rule over the Spartans. This obviously caused tension with the Spartan king Agis, and as a result Alcibiades fled to the Persian satrap, or governor, Tissaphernes, who had been supplying the Spartans with aid in the war against Athens.

Once again, the Persian was utterly charmed by Alcibiades. Plutarch sums up his amazing abilities to adapt himself to any situation: "in Sparta he was athletic, frugal, grave, in Ionia luxurious, pleasure-seeking, indolent, in Thrace hard-drinking, in Thessaly hard-riding, and while associating with Tissaphernes the satrap he surpassed even Persian opulence with the enormity of his extravagance . . . everyone, no matter what kind of personality or nature, was captured by the charm of spending time with him. Even those who hated and feared him felt pleasure and affection in his company" (Alcibiades 23–24).

The full tale of Alcibiades' machinations in exile is an exciting one, and interested readers should consult the final books of Thucydides and especially Plutarch's biography for details. Regarding the lingering consequences of 415's events, we note simply that his efforts to be restored to Athens, along with the pressure on resources caused by the defeat in Sicily, arguably set in motion a brief oligarchic coup in 411; but this was soon followed by the restoration of the democracy and Alcibiades' recall and election as general. He returned in triumph to his city, after several spectacular naval victories, in 408. That summer he led a cavalry force to escort the year's initiates to the Eleusinian Mysteries as they walked the fourteen miles from Athens to Eleusis; the full celebration of the festival had been impossible since the Spartans had fortified Decelea, at Alcibiades' suggestion, in 413. He was hailed, Plutarch tells us, as High Priest. This was precisely the same title he had originally been convicted of assuming in the desecration of the Mysteries in 415.

Alcibiades' moment of success, and Athens', didn't last. Alcibiades was voted out as general after a few reverses. Even after some substantial victories, Athens suffered a devastating naval defeat at Aegospotami in 405. Besieged by Sparta, Athens capitulated in the following year. But that defeat and its aftermath are a different story.

It is sometimes argued that the events of 415 were a crucial turning point in Athens' history. The decision to send forces to Sicily proved enormously costly in both men and resources. The expedition failed at least partially because the investigations into the mutilation of the herms exposed Alcibiades' own impiety, and gave his rivals the opening they needed to expel him from the city. The social rifts exposed by those investigations would rupture more seriously under the economic pressure the defeat in Sicily created, and oligarchy would briefly prevail over democracy. Ultimately the city would fall to the superior naval strategy of the new Spartan commander Lysander, with the aid of Persian money, and only Sparta's moderation kept the more vengeful Thebans and Corinthians from utterly destroying Athens and enslaving its inhabitants when it fell in 404. Without the social tensions and loss of resources engendered by the decisions of 415, the argument goes, Athens might have prevailed over Sparta and retained its naval empire into the next century.

There is no doubt that the losses Athens incurred in Sicily weakened the city. The tension evident in 415 between mass and elite, as well as between ambitious rivals for power over the demos, drove, at least in part, the continuing push toward oligarchy. But if these factors had been decisive, Athens would have lost the war in those years immediately after 413, while still reeling from the defeat in the west, under pressure from Spartan attack at home, and suffering repeated rebellion of the tributary allies in the east. Instead, the Athenian demos just kept fighting. They also continued making the same mistakes. The assembly habitually turned on their generals, as Nicias had feared they would if he returned unsuccessful. In a breathtakingly self-destructive move late in the war, the assembly voted to condemn to death six of the eight commanders in the naval battle of Arginusae. These men had defeated the Spartan fleet, but had failed to pick up their own shipwrecked men because of a storm at sea. This decimation of experienced leaders contributed much more directly to the Athenian defeat in 404 than anything that had happened back in 415. That the Athenians rebuilt their navy as quickly and successfully as they did after the Sicilian disaster, and that they came through the eight months of an oligarchic regime without the harrowing bloodshed that followed stasis in other Greek cities of the time, show us that the democracy was remarkably resilient.

The dramatic events of 415 were not the principal cause of Athenian defeat in 404, then. They can, however, give us some insight into the qualities that allowed the city to survive through the grueling war and political upheavals to the end of the century and beyond. The demos could be impulsive and vindictive, to be sure: that is evident from the hysteria over the religious scandals, which led to the execution and exile of dozens of men and drove Alcibiades into the arms of Sparta. This characteristic anger undoubtedly factored into Nicias' risk aversion. He knew what faced him back in Athens if he should suffer reverses, and so doubled down on the venture for far too long. The tendency of the demos to exact penalties from individuals, even those trying to help it, is one of the charges laid against the radical democracy by many of its elite critics both at the time and subsequently. The trial and execution of Socrates, which occurred just months after the trial and acquittal of Andocides, became the prototypical emblem of this sort of destructive action.

Yet there is another side to popular sovereignty on view in those crisis months of 415. In spite of the complaints of the wealthy, the men who voted on decrees in the assembly were fully capable of placing the interests of the city as a whole above their own private advantage. The wide participation in the mechanics of the democracy gave many of them some level of experience with civic affairs. Most had likely served at some point or other on the council, or in the dikastēria, or as one of the magistrates at the deme or city level. The decisions they made, both on the Pnyx and in the courts, were informed by their experience of governing. That those men who happened to have been chosen by lot to serve on the council during those weeks in the summer of 415 were able to shepherd the city through the crisis, and bring the entire episode to a close expeditiously even in the fevered atmosphere that prevailed, is evidence of the strength and flexibility of the system.

The voices that remain from the period are, as we've seen, almost exclusively from the elite, and they were mostly resentful at the control the demos had over them. But the balance of power between the wealthy few and poorer majority proved remarkably durable over the long run. This balance kept the democracy functional despite the devastation occasioned by losing the Peloponnesian War and the empire at a stroke. The two brief episodes of oligarchy, in 411 and 404/3, both ended with the restoration of the democracy. Competition for influence over the demos, along with enduring anxieties about tyranny, kept individuals within the elite from accruing excessive power. We see this vividly in the messy aftermath of the mutilation of the herms, where the opportunity to reduce Alcibiades' supremacy proved irresistible. Since the suspicion generated by this competition militated against enduring power blocs, elite individuals had more to gain by courting the demos than by plotting with each other. Forensic oratory offers an instructive view of this dynamic in the way, for instance, Andocides argues that his own decision to inform on his hetaireia was made for the good of the city.

While the wealthy in Athens may have resented the share of their private fortunes they had to contribute to the public coffers, they also reaped power and prestige from their liturgies, which were so much more visible and personal than anonymous tax payments. Both Alcibiades and Nicias were shrewd exploiters of this system. And despite complaints about the greed of the people, we know that the empire worked to the profit of the elite as well as the poor. Thucydides remarks that the allies saw no advantage to themselves in a change to oligarchy at Athens ("the allies thought that the so-called elite would offer them no less trouble than the demos, as they were the ones who authored and supplied to the demos the harsh policies from which they for the most part benefited" Thucydides 8.48). The benefit all classes saw from the Athenian empire drove the eros for expansion to Sicily incited by Alcibiades in 415. Having both groups on the same side of major policy decisions must have reduced the potential for tension between them. As long as the elite were willing to achieve power through the demos rather than in opposition to it, they had a handy cudgel with which to reduce their rivals, and the demos was happy to reward their favorites, confident in their own supremacy. While the fear of conspiracy on display in 415 certainly indicated the tensions inherent in the system, the investigations and trials that followed showed the system effectively working to contain threats. Stability may have come, in this instance, at the price of justice for some individuals (Thucydides certainly implies this in his assessment). But even twenty-five hundred years later, it's hard to argue that we have achieved both stability and justice for all.

Clearly even at its most radical, the democracy excluded the majority of people living in the region from its broad allocation of political power. We should in no way idealize the system, or close our eyes to those cut off from the privileges of citizenship. But the dominance of religious observance within the civic calendar made available a mode of participation in the life of the city that was much more inclusive, and signaled the value to the polis also of those who could not vote on the Pnyx. Lacking direct voices, we cannot know how much discontent women or metics or slaves regularly felt with the constraints on their lives. But the events of 415 allow us some indication that the city recognized the need for their participation at crucial moments. In retrospect, the lamentations of women celebrating the Adonia were seen as truly prophetic of the disaster in Sicily. Large financial prizes were awarded to a metic and a slave at the end of the summer for their service to the city.

The intriguing story of 415 offers a window on a society that feels both familiar and alien. It is tempting to draw lessons from it for our own time, about the dangers of distant military entanglements, for instance, or the consequences of fanning the flames of populist desires, or the destructive suspicion that can arise as factions polarize. The ancient world is full of wisdom, even if each generation hears something slightly different from the last. But it is also a fascinating and worthwhile exercise to try to read the ancient sources as much as possible on their own terms, to use them to reconstruct a flawed but remarkable polis that would capture our imaginations for millennia after its demise.

Primary Source Interlude

Thucydides 7.84–87

[84] At daybreak, Nicias led his army onto the field. The Syracusans and their allies had them surrounded, and nearly pinned down under a barrage of javelins. Under constant attack from the enemy, suffering from exhaustion and dying of thirst, the Athenians pressed on to the River Assinarus, hoping to cross the river and gain a moment to rest and regroup. But as soon as they reached the Assinarus, the Athenians broke ranks and rushed headlong into the river, falling over each other, tripped up by their own spears, dragged under by their heavy packs. From the bluff above the river, the Syracusans rained down spears upon the Athenians as they stood desperately attempting to quench their thirst in the river. Then the Peloponnesians attacked and butchered the floundering Athenians. The melée stirred up the silt and the river ran red with blood, but still the Athenians desperately slaked their thirst.

[85] The river was choked with bodies. The Athenian retreat had collapsed: those who had escaped being slaughtered in the river had been rounded up and taken prisoner. Finally, Nicias surrendered to Gylippus, the Spartan commander, because he trusted him more than he trusted the Syracusans. He put himself at the mercy of the Spartans, but begged them to spare his men. Gylippus agreed to these terms, and took the survivors as prisoners. Three hundred who had managed to evade the guard under cover of darkness were pursued and rounded up. All together there were not many prisoners: Sicily was full of Athenians who had been taken and enslaved, and many more had been killed. The slaughter at the river had been as great as any during the Sicilian campaign. A large number had been killed during the Athenian retreat, but many others made it to safety in Catana, some at the time, and some after escaping slavery.

[86] Now the Syracusans and their allies assembled, gathered up the spoils, and marched their prisoners back to the city. The rest of the Athenians and their allies were sent to work in the quarries. As for Nicias and Demosthenes, over the objections of Gylippus they were put to death. Gylippus had wanted to parade them through the streets of Sparta. One of the Athenian commanders, Demosthenes, was the greatest enemy of the Spartans because of their defeat at his hands at Pylos and Sphacteria. On the other hand, Nicias was one of their greatest friends. It was Nicias who negotiated the release of the Spartan prisoners from Pylos and Sphacteria, and who persuaded the Athenians to make peace with the Spartans. The Spartans had reasons for feeling generous toward Nicias, and Nicias had counted on those feelings when he surrendered to Gylippus. But there were Spartans who had been colluding with him who were afraid he would be tortured and reveal things that would cause them trouble. And there were others, especially the Corinthians, who were afraid that, because of his wealth, he would ransom himself and come back to haunt them. In the end, these people succeeded in having Nicias put to death. This was the end of a man who, of all the Greeks in my lifetime, least deserved such a fate, a man whose entire life had been devoted to virtue.

[87] In the first days of their captivity, the prisoners in the quarries were treated harshly. They were all crowded into a small space, with no shelter from the heat of sun during the day or the frost at night, and the constant change of temperature made the prisoners more susceptible to illness. The bodies of those who died, either of wounds or from the cold, were left to decompose in that same cramped space, and there was no escaping the stench. Hunger and thirst were constant: for eight months, the daily ration was half a pint of water and a pint of grain. Anything that someone who has fallen into such a place might suffer, the prisoners suffered. For seventy days they were kept in captivity, after which all of them, except the Athenians and their Sicilian allies, were sold. It would be difficult to put an accurate figure to the prisoners taken during the campaign, but it was not less than seven thousand.

This was the single greatest episode in the Peloponnesian War. As far as I know, it was the greatest episode in the history of relations between the Hellenes, both in terms of glorious nature of the victory and the calamitous nature of the defeat. The Athenian defeat was total. The suffering of the Athenians was incalculable. Their fleet and their ground troops were annihilated. Few who left their homes in Athens ever returned. This is what happened in Sicily.

Map of Athens

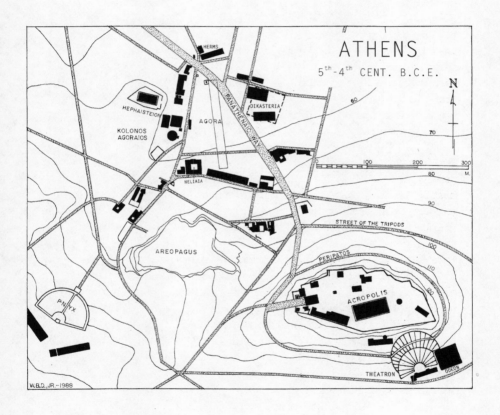

Glossary of Greek Terms

andrōn	Name used for the room in which symposia were held; literally "men's."
apragmōn, apragmosynē	Adjective and noun for word meaning "lacking busy-ness," "quietude"—used positively by aristocrats to designate lack of activity in the law courts; used negatively by popular politicians to condemn lack of participation in democracy.
archon	Literally "ruling man"; term given to magistrates in Athens.
khorēgos	Literally "chorus-leader"; the man who undertook the liturgy of funding a dramatic performance.
khrēstos (pl. khrēstoi)	Literally "useful"; the term the elite use to refer to themselves in contrast to the poor.
demos	The people; also used to designate the poorer as opposed to the elite classes.
dikast	A juror.
dikastērion (pl. dikastēria)	Court.
dikē (pl. dikai)	A lawsuit that can only be prosecuted by the victim; the word also means "justice."
geras	Prize of honor for Homeric heroes; political power in early Athenian democracy.
gynaikonitis	Women's quarters within the house.
hetaira	Literally "female companion"; highest class of prostitute.
hetaireia	Association of men, often of about the same age, who attended symposia together; some had political agendas.
hetairos	Literally "male companion"; friend or fellow member of hetaireia.

hoplite	The type of soldier who carried a massive shield, shoulder-to-shoulder with fellow hoplites in phalanx.
hubris	Generally "arrogance" but technically a crime involving a victim, in which the perpetrator shames the victim for no reason other than his own satisfaction.
isēgoria	The right to open public speech in the assembly; a hallmark of political equality.
kōmos	The informal procession of drunken symposiasts after a party; also informal small parades after the main *pompē* at a festival.
kratēr	The large vessel in which wine was mixed with water at a symposium.
kratos	"power."
leitourgia	Literally "works for the people"; the obligation to fund religious festivals required of the wealthy.
Melos	an island off the southern coast of the Peloponnese conquered by the Athenians in 416; the Greek word *mēlon* also means "apple."
oikos	House or household.
polis	City or city-state.
polypragmosynē	"Busy-body-ness"; negative term used by the elite to characterize popular figures who were active in the law courts or advocated for expansionist imperial policy.
pompē	The large procession in a religious festival.
ponēros (pl. ponēroi)	Literally "wretched"; term used by the elite to refer to the poorer classes.
proagōn	The event at which each tragic poet, together with his chorus, gave a preview of his plays for the Dionysia.
prytany	This word refers both to the fifty-man contingent chosen by lot from each of Athens' ten tribes to serve in the *boulē* each year and the period of one tenth of the year they would have charge of the city.
stasis	Civil discord. The word is derived from the verb meaning "to stand" and thus includes both the more common meaning of inactivity or equilibrium ("standing") and this specialized sense

of factional strife. Presumably the latter derives from the notion that people "standing" together constitute a faction.

symposion (pl. symposia)   Literally "drinking together"; a party focused on regulated consumption of wine and entertainment.

timē   Honor; also used to designate civic rights and offices in the democracy.

trireme   The principal warship of the Athenian navy; one hundred and eighty men on three levels rowed these narrow, fast vessels.

Timeline of Important Events (all dates BCE)

546–510	Tyranny of Peisistratus and his sons
508/7	Reforms of Cleisthenes
490	Battle of Marathon
480	Battle of Thermopylae |
	Battle of Salamis | Persian Wars
	Battle of Plataea |
431	The Peloponnesian War
427	Stasis in Corcyra
	Athenians send aid to Leontini in Sicily
424	Athenians leave Sicily
421	Peace of Nicias
416	Dramatic date of Plato's *Symposium*
	Egesta and Leontini request aid from Athens; embassy sent to investigate funds
	Athenians send force to Melos; conquer island
415	(early spring): embassy returns from Sicily
	two assembly debates on Sicilian Expedition
	Euripides' *Trojan Women* performed at City Dionysia
	(early summer): celebration of Adonia
	mutilation of herms
	Andromachus accuses Alcibiades of desecration of Mysteries
	Sicilian Expedition launched
	(midsummer): investigations into religious crimes
	Alcibiades convicted and sentenced to death; escapes to Sparta
	rewards to Andromachus and Teucrus for information
413	Destruction of Athenian forces in Sicily; death of Nicias
411	Alcibiades recalled and elected general
408	Alcibiades returns in triumph to Athens

406   Alcibiades removed from generalship; goes into self-imposed exile
404   Alcibiades murdered in Phrygia
404   Athens defeated by Sparta; end of Peloponnesian War

Suggestions for Further Reading by Chapter

CHAPTER 1. PNYX: DEMOCRACY, EMPIRE, AND SICILY

On the Pnyx, its area and the history of its layout see Goette (2010). Low (2008) and Ma, Parker, and Papazarkadas (2009) both provide a good sense of the genesis of the Athenian empire, its operation, and current debates; Low prints the classic and influential essays by Geoffrey de Ste. Croix and (contra) Jacqueline de Romilly on whether social class determined views of the empire. Malcolm McGregor (1993) is very accessible and still worth reading. Hansen (1999) and Cartledge (2016) are both excellent sources on the Athenian democracy. Ober (1989) is persuasive on class relations in Athens. Kagan (2003) is a comprehensive history of the Peloponnesian War; more recent and very readable is Roberts (2017).

CHAPTER 2. SYMPOSION: ALCIBIADES, NICIAS, AND EROS

A very good collection of recent work on the symposium is Murray (1990b). Athenian male sexuality is comprehensively covered by Ormand (2009); slightly different in perspective is Skinner (2013). Rhodes (2011) gives a straightforward biography of Alcibiades; Gribble (1999) focuses more on myths and attitudes surrounding him; narrower in focus is the very suggestive Wohl (1999). Influential studies of hubris, honor, and shame are Fisher (1992) and Cairns (1996 and 2011). Rhodes (1994) is the most comprehensive study of the ostracism of Hyperbolus. The possible role of hetaireiai in that ostracism is discussed in Connor (1992) (for an opposing view see Hansen 2014), who is generally useful on the politicians of this period; generally Calhoun (1970) is still interesting on the hetaireias. Adkins (1976) is very interesting on the term *polypragmosunē*.

CHAPTER 3. THEATRON: THE CITY DIONYSIA AND EURIPIDES'
TROJAN WOMEN

Hall (2010), particularly the first half, is an excellent introduction to Athenian tragedy and its contexts. Dodds (1951) is still a good starting point on Dionysus; more recent is Csapo (1997). Pickard-Cambridge, Gould, and Lewis (1968) remains the most comprehensive source on the dramatic festivals. My estimate on meat consumption at the festival is from Rhodes and Osborne (2004); figures of total cost are from Wilson (2008). Goldhill (1987) was groundbreaking on the relationship between tragedy and the Dionysia; different views are found in Griffin (1998) and Rhodes (2003). On the *Trojan Women* and Euripides as criticizing and instructing Athens, Croally (1994) and Gregory (1997) are both very good; I have been more influenced by the contrarian ideas of Green (1999) and Koniaris (1973). On the *Trojan Women* as an antiwar play in modern times see Slater (2015).

CHAPTER 4. OIKOS: ATHENIAN WOMEN IN AND OUT OF THE
HOUSEHOLD

A good recent resource for study of women in the ancient world, with a focus on sources and methodology, is James and Dillon (2012). Murnaghan (1988) and Gini (1993) both offer interesting and accessible readings of Xenophon's *Oeconomicus*. The oikos-polis opposition has been interrogated since Foley (1982); Roy (1999) provides a general introduction, particularly on polis legislation affecting the oikos. Golden and Toohey (2003) collect several pieces on the issue of women's separation or seclusion and the ancient and modern ideologies operating in this context; Nevett (1994) and Walter Graham (1974) are helpful on the material evidence for domestic space. Kamen (2013c) gives an admirably full and clear account of citizen women's legal status. Dillon (2002) and Parker (2005) are particularly helpful on women's religious practice and experience. An examination of women's relation to warfare is found in both Loman (2004) and Georgoudi (2015). Reitzammer (2016), with her full and recent bibliography, is a good starting point for study of the Adonia; Lyons (2007) is compelling in her analysis of the challenges presented by our sources for women's religious practice.

CHAPTER 5. AGORA: THE HERMS AND THE MYSTERIES: HEARSAY
AND HISTORY

Wycherly (1978a) remains an excellent introduction to the material remains of Athens generally and the Agora in particular. Hamel (2012) is a fun and informal account of the episode of the herms and Mysteries; it provides an excellent bibliography for those interested in digging deeper into both religious scandals; Furley (1996) is the only other full monograph devoted to the subject. Evans (2010) gives a clear narrative of both within a larger look at the intersection of religion and politics in classical Athens. Osborne's (1985b) analysis of the significance of the herms is still the most persuasive. An intriguing (although necessarily speculative) theory on the scandals and their relation to the ostracism of Hyperbolus is constructed by Munn (2002). Meyer (2008) and now Tamiolaki (2015) give readings of Thucydides' digression on the tyrannicides, with earlier bibliography; Gomme, Andrewes, and Dover (1970) is still the best starting point for thoughtful historical analysis of the historian.

CHAPTER 6. DIKASTĒRION: INFORMERS AND TRIALS

Garner (1987) and, for greater detail MacDowell (1993) are good general introductions to Athenian law and the courts; a focused look at the theatrical aspects of legal practice can be found in Riess (2014). Andocides (1989 [MacDowell's edition]) provides the most comprehensive examination of Andocides' *On the Mysteries* and the informers and criminals named there; also very helpful on (many of) the names is Nails (2002). The possible role of hetaireiai in the desecrations of the Mysteries is addressed by McGlew (1999) and Todd (2004); an interesting look at particularly the slave testimony can be found in Osborne (2010). To date the most comprehensive inquiry into Agariste is Wallace (1992).

Bibliography

Adkins, A. W. H. 1976. "*Polu Pragmosune* and 'Minding One's Own Business': A Study in Greek Social and Political Values." *Classical Philology* 71 (4): 301–27.

Alexiou, Margaret Roilos. 2002. *The Ritual Lament in Greek Tradition*. Lanham, MD: Rowman and Littlefield.

Andocides. 1989. *Andokides:* On the Mysteries. Edited with introduction and commentary by Douglas M. MacDowell. Oxford: Clarendon Press.

Aurenche, Olivier. 1974. *Les groupes d'Alcibiade, de Léogoras, et de Teucros: Remarques sur la vie politique athénienne en 415 avant J.C.* Collection d'Études Anciennes. Paris: Belles Lettres.

Bagby, Laurie M. Johnson. 2009. "Democracy and Empire: The Case of Athens." In *Enduring Empire: Ancient Lessons for Global Politics*, edited by David Tabachnick and Toivo Koivukoski, 20–40. Toronto: University of Toronto Press.

Bassi, Karen. 1998. "The Theater of Dionysus." Chap. 5 in *Acting Like Men: Gender, Drama, and Nostalgia in Ancient Greece*, 192–244. Ann Arbor: University of Michigan Press.

Blamire, Alec. 2001. "Athenian Finance, 454–404 B.C." *Hesperia: Journal of the American School of Classical Studies at Athens* 70 (1): 99–126.

Boegehold, Alan L. 1990. "Andokides and the Decree of Patrokleides." *Historia: Zeitschrift für Alte Geschichte* 39 (2): 149–62.

Boegehold, Alan L. 2002. *Athenian Identity and Civic Ideology*. Baltimore: Johns Hopkins University Press.

Boegehold, Alan L., John McK. Camp II, Margaret Crosby, Mabel Lang, David R. Jordan, and Rhys F. Townsend. 1995. "The Lawcourts at Athens: Sites, Buildings, Equipment, Procedure, and Testimonia." In *The Athenian Agora*. Vol.28, iii–256. Princeton, NJ: American School of Classical Studies.

Bosworth, A. B. 1993. "The Humanitarian Aspect of the Melian Dialogue." *Journal of Hellenic Studies* 113: 30–44.

Bowie, A. M. 1997. "Thinking with Drinking: Wine and the Symposium in Aristophanes." *Journal of Hellenic Studies* 117: 1–21.

Bradeen, Donald W. 1960. "The Popularity of the Athenian Empire." *Historia: Zeitschrift für Alte Geschichte* 9 (3): 257–69.

Brock, Roger. 2009. "Did the Athenian Empire Promote Democracy?" In Ma, Parker, and Papazarkadas, *Interpreting the Athenian Empire*, 149–66. London: Duckworth.

Burkert, Walter. 1979. *Structure and History in Greek Mythology and Ritual*. Sather Classical Lectures 47. Berkeley: University of California Press.

Burnett, Anne. 2012. "Brothels, Boys, and the Athenian Adonia." *Arethusa* 45 (2): 177–94.

Burton, Joan. 1998. "Women's Commensality in the Ancient Greek World." *Greece & Rome* 45 (2): 143–65.

Cairns, Douglas L. 1996. "Hybris, Dishonour, and Thinking Big." *Journal of Hellenic Studies* 116: 1–32.

Cairns, Douglas L. 2011. *Aidōs: The Psychology and Ethics of Honour and Shame in Ancient Greek Literature*. Oxford: Clarendon Press.

Cairns, Douglas L., Ronald A. Knox, Douglas M. MacDowell, and I. Arnaoutoglou, eds. 2004. *Law, Rhetoric and Comedy in Classical Athens: Essays in Honour of Douglas M. MacDowell*. Swansea: Classical Press of Wales.

Calhoun, George Miller. 1970. *Athenian Clubs in Politics and Litigation*. New York: Franklin.

Camp, John M. 2001. "Classical Athens." Chap. 4 in *The Archaeology of Athens*, 59–160. New Haven, CT: Yale University Press.

Cartledge, Paul. 2016. *Democracy: A Life*. New York: Oxford University Press.

Chambers, Mortimer, Ralph Gallucci, and Pantelis Spanos. 1990. "Athens' Alliance with Egesta in the Year of Antiphon." *Zeitschrift für Papyrologie und Epigraphik* 83: 38–63.

Cole, Susan Guettel. 1984. "Greek Sanctions against Sexual Assault." *Classical Philology* 79 (2): 97–113.

Connor, Walter Robert. 1992. *The New Politicians of Fifth-Century Athens*. Indianapolis, IN: Hackett.

Cox, Cheryl Anne. 1989. "Incest, Inheritance and the Political Forum in Fifth-Century Athens." *Classical Journal* 85 (1): 34–46.

Cox, Cheryl Anne. 1998. *Household Interests: Property, Marriage Strategies, and Family Dynamics in Ancient Athens*. Princeton, NJ: Princeton University Press.

Croally, N. T. 1994. *Euripidean Polemic: The* Trojan Women *and the Function of Tragedy*. Cambridge: Cambridge University Press.

Csapo, Eric. 1997. "Riding the Phallus for Dionysus: Iconology, Ritual, and Gender-Role De/Construction." *Phoenix* 51 (3/4): 253–95.

De Romilly, Jaqueline. 1964. *Thucydides and Athenian Imperialism*. New York: Barnes and Noble.

De Romilly, Jaqueline. 2008. "Thucydides and the Cities of the Athenian Empire." In Low, *The Athenian Empire*, 277–93. Edinburgh: Edinburgh University Press.

De Ste. Croix, Geoffrey. 2008. "The Character of the Athenian Empire." In Low, *The Athenian Empire*, 232–76. Edinburgh: Edinburgh University Press.

Dillon, Matthew. 2002. *Girls and Women in Classical Greek Religion*. London: Routledge.

Dillon, Matthew. 2003. "'Woe for Adonis': But in Spring Not Summer." *Hermes* 131 (1): 1–16.

Dodds, E. R. 1951. *The Greeks and the Irrational*. Berkeley: University of California Press.

Dyson, M., and K. H. Lee. 2000. "The Funeral of Astyanax in Euripides' *Troades*." *Journal of Hellenic Studies* 120: 17–33.

Edwards, Charles M. 1984. "Aphrodite on a Ladder." *Hesperia: Journal of the American School of Classical Studies at Athens* 53 (1): 59–72.

Evans, Nancy. 2010. *Civic Rites: Democracy and Religion in Ancient Athens*. Berkeley: University of California Press.

Faraone, Christopher A., and Laura McClure, eds. 2006. *Prostitutes and Courtesans in the Ancient World*. Wisconsin Studies in Classics. Madison: University of Wisconsin Press.

Fisher, N. R. E. 1976. "'Hybris' and Dishonour: I." *Greece & Rome* 23 (2): 177–93.

Fisher, N. R. E. 1979. "'Hybris' and Dishonour: II." *Greece & Rome* 26 (1): 32–47.

Fisher, N. R. E. 1992. *Hybris: A Study in the Values of Honour and Shame in Ancient Greece*. Warminster: Aris and Phillips.

Foley, Helene P. "The 'Female Intruder' Reconsidered: Women in Aristophanes' Lysistrata and Ecclesiazusae." *Classical Philology*, vol. 77, no. 1, 1982, pp. 1–21.

Fornara, Charles W. 1968. "The 'Tradition' about the Murder of Hipparchus." *Historia: Zeitschrift für Alte Geschichte* 17 (4): 400–424.

Fredal, James. 2002. "Herm Choppers, the Adonia, and Rhetorical Action in Ancient Greece." *College English* 64 (5): 590–612.

Furley, William D. 1996. "Andokides and the Herms: A Study of Crisis in Fifth-Century Athenian Religion." *Bulletin of the Institute of Classical Studies*, Supplement 65, iii–162.

Gagarin, Michael. 1996. "The Torture of Slaves in Athenian Law." *Classical Philology* 91 (1): 1–18.

Gagné, Renaud. 2009. "Mystery Inquisitors: Performance, Authority, and Sacrilege at Eleusis." *Classical Antiquity* 28 (2): 211–47.

Galpin, Timothy J. 1983. "The Democratic Roots of Athenian Imperialism in the Fifth Century B.C." *Classical Journal* 79 (2): 100–109.

Georgoudi, Stella. 2015. "To Act, Not Submit: Women's Attitudes in Situations of War in Ancient Greece." In *Women and War in Antiquity*, edited by Jacqueline Fabre-Serris and Alison Keith, 200–213. Baltimore: Johns Hopkins University Press.

Gilhuly, Kate. 2008. *The Feminine Matrix of Sex and Gender in Classical Athens*. Leiden: Cambridge University Press.

Gini, A. 1993. "The Manly Intellect of His Wife: Xenophon 'Oeconomicus' Ch. 7." *Classical World* 86 (6): 483–86.

Goette, Hans Rupprecht. 2010. *Athens, Attica and the Megarid: An Archaeological Guide*. London: Routledge.

Goff, Barbara E. 2004. *Citizen Bacchae: Women's Ritual Practice in Ancient Greece*. Berkeley: University of California Press.

Golden, Mark, and Peter Toohey, eds. 2003. *Sex and Difference in Ancient Greece and Rome*. Edinburgh: Edinburgh University Press.

Goldhill, Simon. 1987. "The Great Dionysia and Civic Ideology." *Journal of Hellenic Studies* 107: 58–76.

Goldman, Hetty. 1942. "The Origin of the Greek Herm." *American Journal of Archaeology* 46 (1): 58–68.

Gomme, Arnold Wycombe, Antony Andrewes, and K. J. Dover. 1970. *A Historical Commentary on Thucydides*. Vol. 4. Oxford: Clarendon Press.

Graf, F. 1984. "Women, War, and Warlike Divinities." *Zeitschrift für Papyrologie und Epigraphik* 55: 245–54.

Graham, A. J. 1998. "The Woman at the Window: Observations on the 'Stele from the Harbour' of Thasos." *Journal of Hellenic Studies* 118: 22–40.

Graham, J. Walter. 1974. "Houses of Classical Athens." *Phoenix* 28 (1): 45–54.

Green, Peter. 1999. "War and Morality in Fifth-Century Athens: The Case of Euripides' *Trojan Women*." *Ancient History Bulletin* 13 (3): 97–110.

Gregory, Justina. 1997. *Euripides and the Instruction of the Athenians*. Ann Arbor: University of Michigan Press.

Gribble, David. 1999. *Alcibiades and Athens: A Study in Literary Presentation*. Oxford Classical Monographs. New York: Clarendon Press.

Griffin, Jasper. 1998. "The Social Function of Attic Tragedy." *Classical Quarterly* 48 (1): 39–61.

Hall, Edith. 2010. *Greek Tragedy: Suffering under the Sun*. Oxford: Oxford University Press.

Hamel, Debra. 2012. *The Mutilation of the Herms: Unpacking an Ancient Mystery*. Lexington, KY: Self-published, CreateSpace Independent Publishing Platform.

Hansen, Mogens Herman. 1979. "The Duration of a Meeting of the Athenian Ecclesia." *Classical Philology* 74 (1): 43–49.

Hansen, Mogens Herman. 1993. *The Athenian Democracy in the Age of Demosthenes: Structure, Principles, and Ideology*. Oxford: Blackwell.

Hansen, Mogens Herman. 1999. *The Athenian Democracy in the Age of Demosthenes: Structure, Principles, and Ideology*. 2nd rev. ed. Norman: University of Oklahoma Press.

Hansen, Mogens Herman. 2010. "The Concepts of *Demos, Ekklesia*, and *Dikasterion* in Classical Athens." *Greek, Roman, and Byzantine Studies* 50 (4): 499–536.

Hansen, Mogens Herman. 2014. "Political Parties in Democratic Athens?" *Greek, Roman, and Byzantine Studies* 54 (3): 379–403.

Hanson, Victor Davis. 2005. *A War Like No Other: How the Athenians and Spartans Fought the Peloponnesian War*. New York: Random House.

Holst-Warhaft, Gail. 1992. *Dangerous Voices: Women's Laments and Greek Literature.* London: Routledge.

Humphreys, Sarah C. 1977. "Public and Private Interests in Classical Athens." *Classical Journal* 73 (2): 97–104.

Humphreys, Sarah C. 1988. "The Discourse of Law in Archaic and Classical Greece." *Law and History Review* 6 (2): 465–93.

Humphreys, Sarah C. 2007. "Social Relations on Stage: Witnesses in Classical Athens." In *Oxford Readings in the Attic Orators*, edited by Edwin Carawan, 140–213. Oxford: Oxford University Press.

Hunt, Peter. 2016. "Violence against Slaves in Classical Greece." In *The Topography of Violence in the Greco-Roman World*, edited by Werner Riess and Garrett G. Fagan, 136–61. Ann Arbor: University of Michigan Press.

Hunter, Virginia. 1990. "Gossip and the Politics of Reputation in Classical Athens." *Phoenix* 44 (4): 299–325.

Hunter, Virginia. 1994. *Policing Athens: Social Control in the Attic Lawsuits, 420–320 B.C.* Princeton, NJ: Princeton University Press.

James, Sharon, and Sheila Dillon, eds. 2012. *A Companion to Women in the Ancient World.* Blackwell Companions to the Ancient World. Malden, MA: Wiley Blackwell.

Kagan, Donald. 1981. *The Peace of Nicias and the Sicilian Expedition.* Ithaca, NY: Cornell University Press.

Kagan, Donald. 2003. *The Peloponnesian War.* New York: Viking.

Kagan, Donald. 2013. *A New History of the Peloponnesian War.* Ithaca, NY: Cornell University Press.

Kallet, Lisa. 2002. *Money and the Corrosion of Power in Thucydides: The Sicilian Expedition and Its Aftermath.* Berkeley: University of California Press.

Kamen, Deborah. 2013a. "Metics (Metoikoi)." In *Status in Classical Athens*, 43–54. Princeton, NJ: Princeton University Press.

Kamen, Deborah. 2013b. "Privileged Metics." in *Status in Classical Athens*, 55–61. Princeton, NJ: Princeton University Press.

Kamen, Deborah. 2013c. *Status in Classical Athens.* Princeton, NJ: Princeton University Press.

Koniaris, George Leonidas. 1973. "*Alexander, Palamedes, Troades, Sisyphus*: A Connected Tetralogy? A Connected Trilogy?" *Harvard Studies in Classical Philology* 77: 85–124.

Konstan, David. 2003. "Shame in Ancient Greece." *Social Research* 70 (4): 1031–60.

Kousser, Rachel. 2015. "The Mutilation of the Herms: Violence toward Images in the Late 5th Century BC." In Miles, *Autopsy in Athens: Recent Archaeological Research on Athens and Attica*, 76–84.

Kovacs, David. 1983. "Euripides, *Troades* 95–7: Is Sacking Cities Really Foolish?" *Classical Quarterly* 33 (2): 334–38.

Lang, Mabel. 1955. "The Murder of Hipparchus." *Historia: Zeitschrift für Alte Geschichte* 3 (4): 395–407.

Lardinois, A. P. M. H, and Laura McClure. 2001. *Making Silence Speak: Women's Voices in Greek Literature and Society*. Princeton, NJ: Princeton University Press.

Liebeschuetz, W. 1968. "The Structure and Function of the Melian Dialogue." *Journal of Hellenic Studies* 88: 73–77.

Lloyd, Michael. 1984. "The Helen Scene in Euripides' *Troades*." *Classical Quarterly* 34 (2): 303–13.

Loman, Pasi. 2004. "No Woman No War: Women's Participation in Ancient Greek Warfare." *Greece & Rome* 51 (1): 34–54.

Low, Polly, ed. 2008. *The Athenian Empire*. Edinburgh: Edinburgh University Press.

Luschnig, C. A. E. 1971. "Euripides' 'Trojan Women': All Is Vanity." *Classical World* 65 (1): 8–12.

Lyons, Deborah. 2007. "The Scandal of Women's Ritual." In Parca and Tzanetou, *Finding Persephone*, 29–54.

Ma, John, Robert Parker, and Nikolaos Papazarkadas, eds. 2009. *Interpreting the Athenian Empire*. London: Duckworth.

MacDowell, Douglas Maurice. 1993. *The Law in Classical Athens*. Ithaca, NY: Cornell University Press.

Marr, J. L. 1971. "Andocides' Part in the Mysteries and Hermae Affairs 415 B. C." *Classical Quarterly* 21 (2): 326–38.

McGlew, James F. 1999. "Politics on the Margins: The Athenian 'Hetaereiai' in 415 B.C." *Historia: Zeitschrift für Alte Geschichte* 48 (1): 1–22.

McGregor, James H. S. 2014. "The Athenian Agora." Chap. 3 in *Athens*, 78–100. Cambridge, MA: Harvard University Press.

McGregor, Malcolm Francis. 1993. *The Athenians and Their Empire*. Vancouver: University of British Columbia Press.

Meyer, Elizabeth A. 2008. "Thucydides on Harmodius and Aristogeiton, Tyranny, and History." *Classical Quarterly* 58 (1): 13–34.

Miles, Margaret M. 2015. *Autopsy in Athens: Recent Archaeological Research on Athens and Attica*. Havertown, PA: Oxbow Books.

Mirhady, David C. 1996. "Torture and Rhetoric in Athens." *Journal of Hellenic Studies* 116: 119–31.

Mitchell, Lynette G., and P. J. Rhodes. 1996. "Friends and Enemies in Athenian Politics." *Greece & Rome* 43 (1): 11–30.

Morrison, James V. 2000. "Historical Lessons in the Melian Episode." *Transactions of the American Philological Association* 130: 119–48.

Munn, Mark Henderson. 2002. *The School of History: Athens in the Age of Socrates*. Berkeley: University of California Press.

Murnaghan, S. 1988. "How Can a Woman Be More Like a Man: The Dialogue between Ischomachus and His Wife in Xenophon's *Oeconomicus*." *Helios* 15 (1): 9–22.

Murray, Oswyn. 1990a. "The Affair of the Mysteries: Democracy and the Drinking Group." In *Sympotica: A Symposium on the Symposion*, 149–61.

Murray, Oswyn, ed. 1990b. *Sympotica: A Symposium on the Symposion*. Oxford: Clarendon Press.

Murray, Oswyn. 2016. "Violence at the Symposion." In *The Topography of Violence in the Greco-Roman World*, edited by Werner Riess and Garrett G. Fagan, 195–206. Ann Arbor: University of Michigan Press.

Nails, Debra. 2002. *The People of Plato: A Prosopography of Plato and Other Socratics*. Indianapolis, IN: Hackett.

Nevett, Lisa. 1994. "Separation or Seclusion? Towards an Archaeological Approach to Investigating Women in the Greek Household in the Fifth to Third Centuries BC." In *Architecture and Order: Approaches to Social Space*, edited by Michael Parker Pearson and Colin Richards, 98–112. London: Routledge.

Ober, Josiah. 1989. *Mass and Elite in Democratic Athens: Rhetoric, Ideology, and the Power of the People*. Princeton, NJ: Princeton University Press.

Ober, Josiah. 2005. *Athenian Legacies: Essays on the Politics of Going on Together*. Princeton, NJ: Princeton University Press.

O'Higgins, Laurie. 2003. *Women and Humor in Classical Greece*. Cambridge: Cambridge University Press.

Ormand, Kirk. 2009. *Controlling Desires: Sexuality in Ancient Greece and Rome*. Westport, CT: Praeger.

Osborne, Robin. 1985a. *Demos: The Discovery of Classical Attika*. Cambridge: Cambridge University Press.

Osborne, Robin. 1985b. "The Erection and Mutilation of the Hermai." *Proceedings of the Cambridge Philological Society* 31: 47–73.

Osborne, Robin. 2000. *Classical Greece, 500–323 BC*. The Short Oxford History of Europe. Oxford: Oxford University Press.

Osborne, Robin. 2010. *Athens and Athenian Democracy*. Cambridge: Cambridge University Press.

Osborne, Robin, and Simon Hornblower, eds. 1994. *Ritual, Finance, Politics: Athenian Democratic Accounts Presented to David Lewis*. Oxford: Clarendon Press.

Ostwald, Martin. 1987. *From Popular Sovereignty to the Sovereignty of Law: Law, Society, and Politics in Fifth-Century Athens*. Berkeley: University of California Press.

Palmer, Michael. 1982. "Alcibiades and the Question of Tyranny in Thucydides." *Canadian Journal of Political Science / Revue Canadienne de Science Politique* 15 (1): 103–24.

Parca, Maryline G., and Angeliki Tzanetou. 2007. *Finding Persephone: Women's Rituals in the Ancient Mediterranean*. Bloomington: Indiana University Press.

Parker, Robert. 2005. *Polytheism and Society at Athens*. Oxford: Oxford University Press.

Päs, Heinrich. 2014. "Eleusis, Plato, Magic Mushrooms." Chap. 2 in *The Perfect Wave*, 7–16. Cambridge, MA: Harvard University Press.

Pickard-Cambridge, Arthur Wallace, John Gould, and David M. Lewis. 1968. *The Dramatic Festivals of Athens*. 2nd ed. Oxford: Clarendon Press.

Powell, C. A. 1979. "Religion and the Sicilian Expedition." *Historia: Zeitschrift für Alte Geschichte* 28 (1): 15–31.

Quinn, Josephine Crawley. 2007. "Herms, Kouroi and the Political Anatomy of Athens." *Greece & Rome* 54 (1): 82–105.

Raaflaub, Kurt A., Josiah Ober, and Robert W. Wallace. 2007. *Origins of Democracy in Ancient Greece*. With chapters by Paul Cartledge and Cynthia Farrar. Berkeley: University of California Press.

Rawlings, Hunter R. 1981. "Books I and VI as Introductions." Chap. 2 in *The Structure of Thucydides' History*, 58–125. Princeton, NJ: Princeton University Press.

Rawlings, Hunter R. 2016. "Ktema Te Es Aiei. . . . Akouein." *Classical Philology* 111 (2): 107–16.

Reed, Joseph D. 1995. "The Sexuality of Adonis." *Classical Antiquity* 14 (2): 317–47.

Reitzammer, L. 2008. "Aristophanes' *Adôniazousai*." *Classical Antiquity* 27 (2): 282–333.

Reitzammer, L. 2016. *The Athenian Adonia in Context: The Adonis Festival as Cultural Practice*. Wisconsin Studies in Classics. Madison: University of Wisconsin Press.

Rhodes, P. J. 1994. "The Ostracism of Hyperbolus." In Osborne and Hornblower, *Ritual, Finance, Politics: Athenian Democratic Accounts Presented to David Lewis*, 85–98.

Rhodes, P. J. 2003. "Nothing to Do with Democracy: Athenian Drama and the Polis." *Journal of Hellenic Studies* 123: 104–19.

Rhodes, P. J. 2011. *Alcibiades: Athenian Playboy, General and Traitor*. Barnsley: Pen and Sword.

Rhodes, P. J., and Robin Osborne. 2004. *Greek Historical Inscriptions, 404–323 BC*. Oxford: Oxford University Press.

Riess, Werner. 2014. "The Athenian Legal System and Its Public Aspects." In *Symposion 2013: Vorträge zur griechischen und hellenistischen Rechtsgeschichte (Cambridge MA, 26–29 August 2013)*. Akten der Gesellschaft für griechische und hellenistische Rechtsgeschichte 24,153–72. Vienna: Austrian Academy of Sciences Press.

Roberts, Jennifer Tolbert. 2017. *The Plague of War: Athens, Sparta, and the Struggle for Ancient Greece*. Ancient Warfare and Civilization. New York: Oxford University Press.

Roisman, J. 1997. "Contemporary Allusions in Euripides' *Troades*." *Studi Italiani di Filologia Classica* 15: 38–47.

Rosenbloom, David. 2004a. "Ponêroi vs. Chrêstoi: The Ostracism of Hyperbolos and the Struggle for Hegemony in Athens after the Death of Perikles, Part I." *Transactions of the American Philological Association* 134 (1): 55–105.

Rosenbloom, David. 2004b. "Ponêroi vs. Chrêstoi: The Ostracism of Hyperbolos and the Struggle for Hegemony in Athens after the Death of Perikles, Part II." *Transactions of the American Philological Association* 134 (2): 323–58.

Rosenbloom, David. 2006. "Empire and Its Discontents: *Trojan Women, Birds,* and the Symbolic Economy of Athenian Imperialism." *Bulletin of the Institute of Classical Studies,* Supplement 87, 245–71.

Rosivach, Vincent. 2011. "State Pay as War Relief in Peloponnesian War Athens." *Greece & Rome* 58 (2): 176–83.

Roy, J. 1997. "An Alternative Sexual Morality for Classical Athenians." *Greece & Rome* 44 (1): 11–22.

Roy, J. 1999. "'Polis' and 'Oikos' in Classical Athens." *Greece & Rome* 46 (1): 1–18.

Schaps, David. 1982. "The Women of Greece in Wartime." *Classical Philology* 77 (3): 193–213.

Schaps, David. 1998. "What Was Free about a Free Athenian Woman?" *Transactions of the American Philological Association* 128: 161–88.

Scodel, Ruth. 1980. *The Trojan Trilogy of Euripides.* Göttingen: Vandenhoeck und Ruprecht.

Scodel, Ruth. 1998. "The Captive's Dilemma: Sexual Acquiescence in Euripides *Hecuba* and *Troades.*" *Harvard Studies in Classical Philology* 98: 137–54.

Seaford, Richard. 2007. *Dionysos.* London: Routledge.

Seaford, Richard. 2010. *Reciprocity and Ritual: Homer and Tragedy in the Developing City-State.* Oxford: Clarendon Press.

Seaman, Michael G. 1997. "The Athenian Expedition to Melos in 416 B.C." *Historia: Zeitschrift für Alte Geschichte* 46 (4): 385–418.

Simms, Ronda R. 1997. "Mourning and Community at the Athenian Adonia." *Classical Journal* 93 (2): 121–41.

Skinner, Marilyn B. 2013. *Sexuality in Greek and Roman Culture.* Malden, MA: Wiley Blackwell.

Slater, Niall W. 2015. "'The Greatest Anti-War Poem Imaginable': Granville Barker's *Trojan Women* in America." *Illinois Classical Studies* 40 (2): 347–71.

Starr, Chester G. 1987. "Athens and Its Empire." *Classical Journal* 83 (2): 114–23.

Stears, Karen. 2008. "Death Becomes Her: Gender and Athenian Death Ritual." In Suter, *Lament: Studies in the Ancient Mediterranean and Beyond,* 139–55.

Sternberg, Rachel Hall. 2006. "The Judicial Torture of Slaves." Chap. 5 in *Tragedy Offstage,* 146–73. Austin: University of Texas Press.

Stevens, P. T. 1956. "Euripides and the Athenians." *Journal of Hellenic Studies* 76: 87–94.

Strauss, Barry Stuart. 1986. *Athens after the Peloponnesian War: Class, Faction and Policy 403–386 BC.* London: Croom Helm.

Suter, Ann. 2008. *Lament: Studies in the Ancient Mediterranean and Beyond.* New York: Oxford University Press.

Tamiolaki, Melina. 2015. "Rewriting the History of the Tyrannicides: Thucydides versus Herodotus?" *Synthesis (La Plata)* 22: 57–71.

Taylor-Perry, Rosemarie. 2003. *The God Who Comes: Dionysian Mysteries Revisited*. New York: Algora Publishing.

Todd, S. C. 2004. "Revisiting the Herms and the Mysteries." In Cairns, Knox, MacDowell, and Arnaoutoglou, *Law, Rhetoric, and Comedy in Classical Athens: Essays in Honour of Douglas M. MacDowell*, 87–102.

Vernant, Jean Pierre, and Pierre Vidal-Naquet. 1996. *Myth and Tragedy in Ancient Greece*. New York: Zone Books.

Wagner-Hasel, B., and Reyes Bertolín-Cebrián. 2003. "Women's Life in Oriental Seclusion? On the History and Use of a Topos." In Golden and Toohey, *Sex and Difference in Ancient Greece and Rome*, 241–52.

Wallace, Robert W. 1992. "Charmides, Agariste and Damon: Andokides 1.16." *Classical Quarterly* 42 (2): 328–35.

Wasson, R. Gordon, Stella Kramrisch, Jonathan Ott, and Carl A. P. Ruck. 1986. "Mushrooms and Philosophers." Chap. 6 in *Persephone's Quest*, 151–78. New Haven, CT: Yale University Press.

Webster, T. B. L. 1965. "The Order of Tragedies at the Great Dionysia." *Hermathena* 100: 21–28.

Westlake, H. D. 1969. *Essays on the Greek Historians and Greek History*. Manchester: Manchester University Press.

Wilson, Peter. 2000. *The Athenian Institution of the Khoregia: The Chorus, the City, and the Stage*. Cambridge: Cambridge University Press.

Wilson, Peter. 2008. "Costing the Dionysia." In *Performance, Iconography, Reception: Studies in Honour of Oliver Taplin*, edited by Martin Revermann and Peter Wilson, 88–127. Oxford: Oxford University Press.

Winkler, John J. 1985. "The Ephebes' Song: *Tragôidia* and *Polis*." *Representations* 11: 26–62.

Wohl, Victoria. 1999. "The Eros of Alcibiades." *Classical Antiquity* 18 (2): 349–85.

Wycherley, R. E. 1978a. "The Agora: Political and Religious Center." Chap. 2 in *The Stones of Athens*, 27–90. Princeton, NJ: Princeton University Press.

Wycherley, R. E. 1978b. "The Market." Chap. 3 in *The Stones of Athens*, 91–103. Princeton, NJ: Princeton University Press.

Zeitlin, Froma I. 1985. "Playing the Other: Theater, Theatricality, and the Feminine in Greek Drama." *Representations* 11: 63–94.

Index